The #1 Personal Development & Activity Training Resource & PLAYbook for Young Athletes

Barb V

Host of the #1 Internationally Rated Podcast
The KID FACTOR

© 2025 Barb V   All Rights Reserved.

The information provided in this material is for educational and informational purposes only. The Author and Publisher are not dispensing medical advice or prescribing the use of any technique as a form of treatment for physical, emotional, or medical problems without the advice of a physician, either directly or indirectly.

The intent of this program/book is only to offer information of a general nature to help you in your quest for well-being. In the event you use any of the information in this program/book for yourself, the Author and Publisher assume no responsibility for your actions or the consequences thereof.

The use of this material by minors should be monitored by a parent, guardian, or with appropriate adult supervision.

The Author and Publisher accept no responsibility for any liability, loss, or risk, personal or otherwise, that is incurred as a direct or indirect consequence of the use and application of any of the contents of this material.

Results may vary from person to person. The experiences, results, and testimonials described in this material should not be interpreted as promises or guarantees of specific outcomes.

Any names, characters, places, events, organizations, or incidents described in this material are either products of the author's imagination or are used fictitiously. Any resemblance to actual persons, living or dead, events, or locales is entirely coincidental.

The information contained in this material was current and accurate at the time of publication. However, knowledge and best practices evolve over time, and the content may not reflect the most current information available

This material is not intended to be a substitute for professional advice, including but not limited to legal, financial, medical, psychological, or other professional services. Always seek the advice of qualified professionals in the relevant field regarding specific questions or concerns.

If you have medical, physical, or psychological concerns, please consult with the appropriate healthcare professional before implementing any of the ideas or suggestions contained herein.

No part of this book may be reproduced or transmitted in any form or by any means without written permission from the publisher.

ISBN: 979-8-89300-061-0

© 2025 Barb V All Rights Reserved

For inquiries about this material and bulk orders, please contact:

Website:
https://TheKidFactor.Fun

140 W. 29th Street #325
Pueblo, Colorado, 81008

Dear Parents,

Thank you for investing in your child's development by choosing this material. Your decision speaks volumes about your commitment to nurturing their potential and providing them with the tools they need to grow, both in sports and in life.

In today's fast-paced and ever-changing world, young athletes face challenges we may not have encountered in our own youth. By seeking out resources like this one, you are taking a proactive step to equip your child with skills that will serve them far beyond the game. Your involvement, encouragement, and belief in their journey are invaluable. I have included a weekly opportunity for you to write something to your Superstar In Training on the My Habits & Goals Tracker page. I encourage you to supportively share with your athlete here with wisdom and encouragement as they will always be their own hardest critique of themselves as their performances and outcomes will often reflect areas where they need to focus more of their attention.

This material was created with the understanding that every child is unique, with their own learning style, pace, and interests. As you work through this material, I encourage you to observe what resonates most with your child, read their entries, ask growth questions and allow them to turn inward for their own answers. Your ability to provide a supportive environment—one that fosters exploration, resilience, and self-motivation—will enhance their experience and long-term growth.

The time you invest in engaging with your athlete through these activities is perhaps the most powerful investment you can make. These moments of connection will create lasting memories and also strengthen your bond, reinforcing the lessons learned through sports and training. Yes, this is a tool that I wish I had had along my athletic journey. It is also something that I wish my parents, coaches and trainers could have had to instill their love, knowledge and wisdom on me when I went through the various stages of knowing "everything" to knowing nothing. You know what I'm talking about! Taking the time to sit down, write, and reflect is a powerful tool that took me decades to learn, understand, and then implement with my athletes.

Remember, growth isn't always linear. There will be moments of triumph and moments of frustration. Your student-athlete will experience setbacks, losses, and failures — each of which presents an opportunity to develop resilience and mental toughness. When these challenges arise, remember that your most important role is not as a fixer, critic, accountant, or coach, but as a source of unconditional support and encouragement. The greatest gift you can give your child in these moments is a listening ear, a steady presence, and unwavering belief in their ability to navigate their own journey.

It's also important to recognize the distinct roles in your child's development. You have entrusted your young athlete to a coach or trainer—allow them to fulfill their role in guiding technical skills, strategy, and performance feedback. Your role, as a parent, is irreplaceable: to be their greatest source of love, encouragement, and emotional support. This separation of roles creates an environment where your child can thrive both emotionally and athletically, free from the pressure of being over-managed.

As an elite athlete, coach, mentor and teacher who has worked with more than 30,000 youth and their parents, coaches, teachers, and medical professionals, I appreciate the profound responsibility we feel to guide our youth well. Please know that by choosing to be present and actively involved in your child's development, you're already succeeding at one of life's most important tasks. I know how deeply we want to set our children up for success. Please know that by simply being present, by believing in them, and by allowing them the space to grow into their own greatness, you are already providing exactly what they need.

I know this material serves as a valuable resource for both you and your Superstar In Training, leading to meaningful conversations, shared discoveries, and a lifelong love of learning and growth in both sports and life.

With sincere appreciation for all that you do,
Barb V

YOU ARE A... Superstar In Training

How to BEST Use This Book

Welcome to **SUPERSTAR In Training: The #1 Personal Development & Activity Training Manual for Young Athletes**! This book was created to help you train like the best, think like the best, and **become the best version of yourself**—both in and out of your athletic environment.

FOR YOUNG ATHLETES:

This book is designed to be your **personal training companion** for the next 90 days. Each day, you'll complete:

- ☑ **Training and mindset activities** to build mental toughness, confidence, and focus while working on your goals.

- ☑ **A daily reflection** to track your progress, nutrition, feelings, habits, challenges, and personal gratitude.

- ☑ **An educational or personal development exercise** to help you sharpen your focus, improve your routines, and develop the same habits that elite athletes utilize but often didn't learn until late in their athletic journey.

💡 How to Get the Most Out of This Book:

- Be consistent! Set aside time every day to complete your page.
- Be honest with yourself—track your habits and progress accurately. Skipping information only hurt your game.
- Take action! Apply what you learn to your training and daily life.
- **Push yourself to improve, but don't be afraid to learn from setbacks.**

This is your journey. The more effort you put in, the greater the results you'll see. You're #1 **COMPETITOR** is **YOU!**

FOR PARENTS:

This book is a **powerful tool** to support your Superstar In Training in both athletics and life. It encourages independence, self-discipline, resilience, coachability, decision making, intrinsic motivation, accountability, along with leadership and teamwork—key traits of **high achievers** in every field.

◆ How You Can Support Your Athlete:

- ❖ Encourage consistency but allow them to take ownership of their progress.
- ❖ Ask open-ended questions instead of critiquing their answers.
- ❖ Focus on effort and growth rather than just results.
- ❖ Let the **coaches coach**—your role is to be a supportive and loving presence.

This book is designed to help your student-athlete **develop elite-level habits while building confidence, resilience, and personal discipline**. Your encouragement and trust in their journey make all the difference!

FOR COACHES:

This book is a **game-changer** for helping young athletes develop the mental skills that separate the good from the great, and the great from the exceptional. It provides **a structured system** for tracking training, mindset development, nutrition, sleep, goal setting, and daily habits—all crucial components of high-performance athletes.

🏆 Ways to Use This Book in Your Training Program:

- ☐ Assign daily exercises to reinforce mental training and personal responsibility.
- ☐ Use reflection and "Brain Dump" pages to facilitate team discussions on growth and resilience.
- ☐ Encourage athletes to track their goals and habits for accountability.
- ☐ Create a team-wide 30-Day Challenge – you know they're competitive... make good habits a competition.
- ☐ Reinforce **the importance of sleep, recovery, and focus—just like elite professionals do.**
- ☐ **Build Visualization & Mindset** teamwide. Become a F.I.X.ed Athlete's Team.

The lessons inside this book will help shape **disciplined, driven, and self-motivated athletes** who are prepared to reach their full potential.

THIS BOOK BELONGS TO...

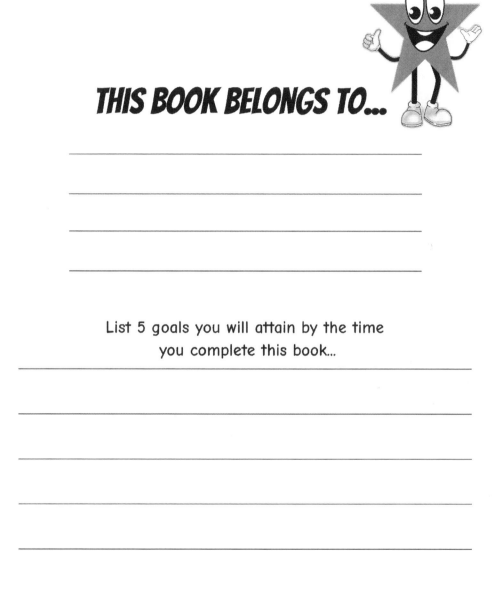

_____

_____

_____

_____

List 5 goals you will attain by the time
you complete this book...

_____

_____

_____

_____

_____

NOTE:

Go to pages 22, 23, and 24 to learn about setting SMART Goals, and then to pages 64-69 to work on your habits and 5 most important goals that you want to attain as you complete this section of your athletic journey...

More Books By BARB V

More on the way...

Follow Barb as an Amazon Author

Scan this QR Code or go to **BOOKS** on Amazon and type in "**Barb V**" and click the **Follow** button

Hey SUPERSTAR...
Meet Your Coach, Author, & Master Champion-Maker

Barb V is a leading expert in youth sports psychology and mental performance training, specializing in developing champions of all ages. As a professional master educator, curriculum specialist, and behavioral expert, Coach V, as her athletes refer to her, brings a unique blend of educational methodology and athletic development to the critical challenge of building mental toughness in young athletes. The rare combination of her classroom expertise and elite competitive athletic experience provides a comprehensive understanding of how young minds develop both on and off the field.

Recognizing the increasing impact of screen time on youth development, Coach V has pioneered innovative screen-free training techniques that build the same mental and athletic skills used by elite Olympic and professional athletes, adapted specifically for children's developmental needs. These methods have helped thousands of athletes overcome performance anxiety, build unwavering confidence, and develop laser-sharp focus.

Coach V is passionate about translating complex sports psychology concepts into practical, accessible strategies that coaches, parents, and professionals can immediately implement with their young athletes. Through workshops, clinics, consultations, speaking engagements, and her writings, Coach V has become a trusted advisor to youth sports organizations globally.

What distinguishes Coach V's approach is the unique integration of cutting-edge neuroscience with time-tested mental training techniques used by the GOATs (Greatest Of All Time) across various sports. This methodology addresses both conscious mindset development and the subconscious patterns that often undermine an athletes' performance.

As an advocate for balanced development, Coach V is dedicated to helping athletes build mental resilience that extends beyond sports into academics and life. When not writing, coaching or training for her next competition, Coach V can be found mentoring youth sports programs and speaking at conferences about the transformative power of mental skills and mental health training for athletes, or pouring into her exclusive - The F.I.X.ed Athlete program - community.

To invite her to your next event or join The F.I.X.ed Athlete program community, reach out to Barb or her team through the website: https://SuperstarInTraining.com

Foreword

What separates a **good athlete** from a **great one**, and a **great one** from an **elite one**? Is it talent? Strength? Speed? While all those things matter, the real difference often comes down to **mindset**. The best athletes in the world don't just train their bodies — they train their **minds**. Elite athletes train their minds and "clear-the-clutter" by letting go of all the negative thoughts and feelings.

One of the most powerful tools for developing a strong mindset is **journaling** and keeping a **training log**. Writing things down may seem simple, but it can **transform your performances, sharpen your focus, and build mental toughness**. It's not just about keeping track of workouts — it's about understanding yourself as an athlete and learning how to **think like a champion**.

The world's greatest athletes rely on journaling and training logs to gain an edge:

- **Michael Phelps**, the most decorated Olympian in history, tracked every swim, meal, and recovery session. Journaling helped him manage his mental health and stay focused through the highs and lows of his career.
- **LeBron James** records every detail of his training, diet, and even his sleep habits, ensuring he stays at peak performance year after year.
- **Simone Biles**, the most decorated gymnast of all time, writes down her goals, past achievements, and reflections to stay motivated and confident.
- **Katie Ledecky** began keeping a journal at 14, documenting her training leading up to the 2012 Olympics and her journey of winning seven Olympic gold medals.
- **Suni Lee**, preparing for Paris 2024, journals to handle pressure, track progress, and keep her mind strong under intense competition.
- **Zharnel Hughes**, a British sprinter, predicts race times in his journal—turning goals into reality!
- **Matt Myers**, a former WSL surfer and U.S. Surf Team coach, tells his athletes: *"When you're putting pen to paper, it sinks in a bit more."*
- **Kobe Bryant**, meticulously tracked his workouts and skill development.
- **Tom Brady**, kept detailed records of his nutrition, training, and mindset to sustain his legendary NFL career.
- **Usain Bolt**, used training logs to monitor his progress and identify areas for improvement.
- **Novak Djokovic**, keeps a journal to track his training, diet, and personal growth.

Keeping track of your journey on a consistent basis is like having a **personal coach in your pocket**. It helps you:

- ☑ **Track progress** – See how far you've come and **what's working** in your training, **and what's not**.
- ☑ **Stay focused** – **Clears out distractions** and keep your goals front and center. Allows you to think clearly.
- ☑ **Build confidence** – Remind yourself of your strengths and past successes. It helps you **repeat what works**.
- ☑ **Solve problems** – Break down challenges and find ways to improve. It's like **keeping your own scoreboard.**
- ☑ **Manage pressure** – Handle nerves, setbacks, and emotions with a clear head. Your **battle-tested mental armour**.

This journal is your **training manual for success**. It's where you'll set goals, reflect on your progress, and strengthen the **mental side of your game**. Use it daily, and you'll see results — not just in how you play, but in how you think, react, and grow as an athlete.

Great Athletes Train Their Bodies. **Elite Athletes Train Their Minds!**

Now it's your turn. **Let's get started!**

Top 10 Reasons to Reduce Screen Time

Extended screen time for athletes and students can pose several risks
Overview & Potential dangers

1. **Eye strain and vision problems:**
   - Digital eye strain or Computer Vision Syndrome
   - Increased risk of myopia (nearsightedness), especially in developing eyes
   - Dry eye syndrome from reduced blinking
2. **Physical health issues:**
   - Poor posture leading to neck, shoulder, and back pain
   - Increased risk of obesity due to sedentary behavior
   - Reduced physical activity and overall fitness levels
3. **Sleep disruption:**
   - Exposure to blue light can interfere with melatonin production
   - Difficulty falling asleep or poor sleep quality
   - Altered sleep-wake cycles
4. **Cognitive and academic impacts:**
   - Reduced attention span and concentration
   - Decreased academic performance
   - Impaired critical thinking and problem-solving skills
5. **Mental health concerns:**
   - Increased risk of anxiety and depression
   - Social isolation and reduced face-to-face interactions
   - Potential for internet or gaming addiction
6. **Reduced athletic performance:**
   - Decreased reaction time and hand-eye coordination
   - Lowered overall physical conditioning
   - Less time for sport-specific training and practice
7. **Developmental issues:**
   - Delayed language development in younger children
   - Reduced emotional intelligence and social skills
   - Impaired ability to read non-verbal cues
8. **Cybersecurity and online safety risks:**
   - Exposure to inappropriate content
   - Vulnerability to cyberbullying or online predators
   - Privacy concerns and potential for data breaches
9. **Repetitive stress injuries:**
   - Carpal tunnel syndrome
   - Tendonitis in fingers, wrists, or elbows
10. **Reduced creativity and imagination:**
    - Over-reliance on digital stimulation
    - Less time for free play and creative activities

It's important to note that while these risks exist, they can be mitigated through responsible use of technology, regular breaks, maintaining a balanced lifestyle, and setting appropriate limits on screen time. The key is to find a healthy balance between the benefits of digital tools and the need for diverse, real-world experiences and physical activity.

Benefits of Strategic, Competitive, & Cognitive Training & Activities for Athletes

Cognitive brain training, as well as strategic competition training, offers numerous benefits for athletes. These approaches can enhance various aspects of athletic performance and overall well-being for both the individual athlete as well as for entire teams.

Strategic and Competition Training Benefits:

- **Tactical Awareness:** Improves understanding of game strategies and the ability to adapt to opponents' tactics.

- **Emotional Regulation:** Enhances control over emotions during high-pressure competitive situations.

- **Team Cohesion:** For team sports, it can improve communication and coordination among team members.

- **Mental Rehearsal:** Allows athletes to practice and perfect techniques mentally, complementing physical training.

- **Goal Setting and Achievement:** Improves the ability to set realistic, achievable goals and work systematically towards them.

- **Resilience:** Builds mental toughness and the ability to bounce back from setbacks.

- **Performance Analysis:** Enhances the ability to critically analyze one's own performance and identify areas for improvement.

You can find further information along with research and studies in Barb's books **DOMINATE YOUR ATHLETIC JOURNEY** and **DOMINATE YOUR MINDSET**.

Benefits of Cognitive, Brain, and Strategic Training & Activities for Athletes

Many studies provide strong evidence for the efficacy of cognitive and strategic training in enhancing athletic performance across various sports and skill levels. They highlight the importance of integrating these approaches into comprehensive athletic training programs. Research also suggests that incorporating cognitive and strategic training into athletic programs can provide a competitive edge, particularly valuable for sports that require quick decision-making under pressure.

Cognitive and Brain Training Benefits:

- **Improved Decision-Making:** Enhances the ability to make quick, accurate decisions under pressure.

- **Enhanced Focus and Concentration:** Increases the capacity to maintain attention on relevant cues and ignore distractions.

- **Better Memory:** Improves both short-term and long-term memory, aiding in strategy recall and learning from past performances.

- **Faster Processing Speed:** Allows athletes to react more quickly to changing situations in their sport.

- **Increased Mental Stamina:** Helps athletes maintain high cognitive performance throughout long competitions or training sessions.

- **Stress Management:** Improves the ability to handle pressure and perform well in high-stress situations.

- **Enhanced Visual-Spatial Skills:** Particularly beneficial for sports requiring strong spatial awareness and hand-eye coordination.

MINDSET MATTERS...
🏃 ✨ Breaking Barriers: The Power of Belief ✨ 🏃

Hey Athletes! Let's talk about something epic—something that's not just about running, but about mindset, heart, and doing what others say is *impossible*.

🌟 The Legend of the 4-Minute Mile

Have you ever seen the movie or read the book *Unbroken*? 🎬📖 It's the story of **Louis Zamperini**, a high school track star from Southern California 🌴 who made it all the way to the **1936 Olympics** in Berlin. His best mile time was 4:21— super fast for the time. But back then, people believed something wild: that it was **physically impossible** for a human to run a mile in under 4 minutes.

Doctors even claimed that if someone did it, their **heart would explode** ❤️ ✨. Seriously.

But on **May 6, 1954**, a guy named **Roger Bannister** changed everything. He crossed the finish line in **3:57** ⏱️ ⚡
— and in the next **46 days**, 22 more runners did the same. **Why?**

Because belief is powerful. Once people *saw* it was possible, they believed *they* could do it too. 💭 👣

🔘 Young Runners Making History

Today, running a mile in under 4 minutes is still a massive achievement. But guess what? A few young athletes have done it **before turning 18!**

✅ **Sam Ruthe (New Zealand)**: Youngest ever at 15 years and 11 months! Time: 3:58.35 *(March 19, 2025)*

✅ **Jakob Ingebrigtsen (Norway)**: 16 years old – 3:58.07 🏃

✅ **Cam Myers (Australia)**: Ran 3:55.44 at just 16 years old!

✅ **25 U.S. high schoolers** have run sub-4 since Jim Ryun first did it in 1964

💬 These athletes didn't just train hard — they believed hard.

🔥 What About the Girls?

As of now, **no female athlete—of any age—has officially run a mile in under 4 minutes**.

The current women's world record is **4:07.64**, set by **Faith Kipyegon** of Kenya in 2023 🌍 👟. But scientists believe it's only a matter of time.

The gap is closing. The dream is alive. And *you* could be the one who breaks it. 💫

💬 Final Thought: What Are You Telling Yourself?

"Whether you think you can or you think you can't—you're right." – Henry Ford

Your mind is your biggest muscle.

Whether it's on the track, in the classroom, in your relationships, or chasing any big goal—**belief is the difference**.

👉 So ask yourself today: WHAT DO YOU BELIEVE YOU CAN DO? ✨

TABLE OF CONTENTS

MEET THE AUTHOR 9

SECTION #1 17
ATHLETIC SECRETS "THEY" DON'T TEACH UNTIL COLLEGE & WHY YOUR YOUNG ATHLETES SHOULD KNOW IT NOW!!!

SECTION #2 65
MONTHLY PLANNING, WEEKLY PLANNING & 30-DAY CHALLENGES

SECTION #3 103
PERSONAL DEVELOPMENT ACTIVITIES & ATHLETE'S PLAYbook

SECTION #4 300
ANSWER KEYS

SECTION #5 310
BRAIN DUMPS

SECTION #6 315
MY COMPETITIONS

SECTION #7 319
RESOURCES

I use to be a "no-body" until I realized how unique and different we all are because of the choices and decisions we get to make.

Thank for opening this book. I look forward to being able to share with you all about becoming the best version of yourself as you go through what we call the Personal Development activities on the next pages. My friend, Coach, and Mentor, Barb V, has so much to teach us about what it takes to be an elite athlete... I'll tell you more about her on the next pages. Until then, know that Coach V doesn't do anything unless she's tried or done it herself first - then it must be **FUN** and if we **HAVE to do it**, she **finds a way to MAKE IT FUN!**

Throughout this book I will ask you things about yourself and you will write them here in your Superstar's journey book of records, statistics, and training tips. Coach V says that she would pay thousands of dollars to have the information you are about to create about her own athletic journey from when she was your age. The more information you put in your book, even though it might sound strange today, will be more valuable as your athletic journey continues.

Section # 1
ATHLETIC SECRETS "THEY" DON'T TEACH UNTIL COLLEGE & WHY YOUR YOUNG ATHLETES SHOULD KNOW IT NOW !

PATTERN RECOGNITION

MEMORY RECALL

VISUAL TRACKING

HAND-EYE COORDINATION

MINDSET

EMOTIONAL REGULATION

FOCUS

MINDFULNESS

ANTICIPATION

SITUATIONAL AWARENESS

The F.I.X.ed ATHLETE

CONCENTRATION

STRATEGIC THINKING

About Me

my name is

my big dreams

things I can do...

Sit Ups in 1 minute

Push Ups in 1 minute

Jump rope in 1 minute

Vertical Jump

Standing Broad Jump

Distance throw a baseball/softball

Speed throw a baseball/softball

Run a 20 or 40 yard dash

Run 1 mile

Today's Date

I like

I don't like

3 words that describe me...

my favorite:

food

snack

drink

color

sport

team

book

movie

My Athletic Skills Tracker

Sports I Play:
date

What I love about my athletic abilities...

_____

_____

_____

Basic Athletic Skills

- Balance
- Stability
- Agility
- Mobility
- Power
- Speed
- Endurance
- Stamina
- Strength
- Body Control
- Reaction Time
- Body Awareness
- Spatial Awareness
- Hand-Eye Coordination
- Foot-Eye Coordination
- Acceleration & Deceleration

Skills I'm Good At

* _____
* _____
* _____
* _____
* _____
* _____
* _____

Skills I'm Working To Improve

* _____
* _____
* _____
* _____
* _____
* _____
* _____

My Athletic Journey Timeline

Dates	Team, Sport	What I learned, skills I gained.	Dates	Team, Sport	What I learned, skills I gained.

USE THIS PAGE TO REMIND YOU HOW TO WRITE YOUR GOALS...

TODAY'S DATE: _____ **MY GOAL DATE:** _____

MY SMART GOALS PLANNER

Identify a goal that is specific, measurable, achievable, relevant, and timed (SMART). Break it into actionable steps, each with its own deadline.

EXAMPLE: I will reduce my running speed from home plate through first base by 0.25 seconds on or before the Allstar game this season by gaining 50% more strength in my squats and doing **Coach V's treadmill-sprinting** workout up to three times a week starting today.

S — Specific
What exactly do you want to achieve?

EXAMPLE: "I will reduce my running speed from home plate through first base"

M — Measurable
How will you measure your progress?

EXAMPLE: "reduce by 0.25 seconds" "gaining 50% more strength in my squats" "doing **Coach V's treadmill-sprinting** workout up to three times a week"

A — Attainable
Is your goal attainable?

EXAMPLE: "by gaining 50% more strength" "doing **Coach V's workout** up to three times a week"

R — Relevant
How does it fit into your journey?

EXAMPLE: "I will reduce my running speed from home plate through first base"

T — Timed
What is your deadline?

EXAMPLE: "on or before the Allstar game this season" "up to three times a week"

©2025 Barb V All Rights Reserved
The Silent Assassins
HABITS & GOALS
The F.I.X.ed Athlete's Program
The Kid Factor, LLC

THE POWER OF SMART GOALS & HABITS

What if I told you that **your success in sports and life isn't about talent alone**? The best athletes in the world don't just wake up great—they create a plan, take action, and develop the right habits to reach their dreams.

Elite and professional athletes use goals to turn their dreams into reality by setting both long-term and short-term targets. Long-term goals, like winning a championship or making the Olympic team, give them a big vision to chase, while short-term goals, like improving their speed or mastering a skill, help them stay focused and motivated every day. By setting, tracking, and adjusting their goals, they create a step-by-step path to success—one practice, one game, and one season at a time.

That's where **SMART goals** and daily habits come in.

What Are SMART Goals?

A **SMART goal** is a goal that is:

- ☑ Specific – You know exactly what you want to achieve.
- ☑ Measurable – You can track your progress.
- ☑ Attainable – It's challenging but possible.
- ☑ Relevant – It helps you become a better athlete.
- ☑ Time-bound – You set a deadline to achieve it.

Example of a Vague Goal: "I want to get better at soccer."

SMART Goal Version:

"I will improve my passing accuracy from 70% to 85% in the next 6 weeks by practicing 30 minutes daily and reviewing my progress with my coach every Friday."

Why SMART Goals Work

> - **They keep you focused.** You'll know exactly what you're working toward instead of just "hoping" to improve.
> - **They give you a plan.** Once you write a SMART goal, you'll see what steps you need to take.
> - **They help you build confidence.** Every small win along the way will push you forward.

Using *My SMART Goals Planner* (on the page on the left)

Over the next 90 days, as you focus on everything you do to become a better athlete, you will use "My SMART Goals Planner" pages to set your personal and athletic goals. We have provided seven pages for you to set two long-term goals and two medium-term goals, and three short-term goals. Consider the medium-term goals you want to attain in the next three months as you work your way through this training manual.

Create three short-term goals as the goals you want to achieve during your 30-day challenges or within each month during the next 90 days.

Talk with your coach, parents, and teammates and discuss what you think are the most important goals you should work towards. Remember – these are your goals and you should make the final choices to which ones you will focus on. These are your goals, and this is your athletic journey, and only you will decide whether or not you these goals really mean enough to you to attain them.

Nobody will do your push-ups for you, so these must be what you want and not what others want for you!

This is the GOALs & HABIT Tracker that you will use on a weekly basis as you work on your SMART GOALs & HABITS

Parents & Coaches - this is where you have the opportunity to provide positive feedback and encouragement in writing.

The F.I.X. Code

Unlock your full potential with **The F.I.X. Code**, a Non-Invasive Guided Quantum Visualization technique - a groundbreaking approach in athletics and personal growth rooted and backed by neuroscience.

This method works by leveraging the brain's neuroplasticity - its ability to form new neural connections throughout life. Here's how it can benefit you:

- **Rewire your brain:** Science shows that repeated thoughts and experiences strengthen neural pathways. This technique helps weaken negative pathways while reinforcing positive ones.
- **Harness your subconscious:** Research indicates that up to 95% of our brain activity occurs at the subconscious level. By addressing subconscious blocks, this method can create profound change.
- **Align your conscious and unconscious mind:** Studies reveal that conflicting beliefs between our conscious and unconscious minds can hinder progress. This technique helps bring these into harmony.

The F.I.X. Code allows you to:

- Disconnect negative emotions from past memories
- Reduce and potentially eliminate future anxieties, worries, and fears
- Cultivate a more positive outlook

By addressing emotional experiences stored in your subconscious and unconscious mind, you can overcome barriers holding you back from attaining joy, success, and fulfillment.

Whether you're a driven athlete, coach, personal trainer, a business professional, a dedicated parent, or an ambitious youth, this science-based method offers a path to living 'on-point' - fully present and engaged in every moment.

Ready to reshape your neural pathways and unlock your full and true potential?

Experience the transformative power of **The F.I.X. Code** and embark on a journey to a more empowered, vibrant you by booking your 15-minute introductory session now. No strings attached, no sales pitch, just you harnessing the full power and benefit of **The F.I.X. Code** with one of our Internationally Certified F.I.X. Code practitioners/Coaches.

Become A F.I.X.ed Athlete™

Elevate your athletic performance with **The F.I.X. Code,** a non-Invasive quantum guided visualization - a cutting-edge mental training method for athletes at every level.

This scientifically-grounded approach taps into the power of your mind to enhance your physical performance. Here's how it can transform your performances:

- **Mental resilience:** Strengthen neural pathways associated with focus, determination, and grit. Whether you're a weekend warrior or a pro athlete, this technique helps you push through mental barriers.
- **Overcome performance anxiety:** By addressing subconscious fears and past setbacks, you can compete with newfound confidence. Visualize success and disconnect from negative emotions that may be holding you back. Ending slumps quickly and effortlessly.
- **Faster recovery:** Harness the mind-body connection to potentially speed up healing and reduce recovery time. Studies show that positive visualization can influence physical healing processes.

The F.I.X. Code allows athletes to:

- Let go of past failures or injuries that may be impacting current performance
- Reduce pre-game jitters and performance anxiety
- Eliminate negative self-talk
- Generate athletic and personal gains in and out of competitions
- Cultivate a champion's mindset for peak performance

By aligning your conscious goals with your subconscious mind, you will unlock your full athletic potential. This technique addresses the emotional experiences and future worries that might be blocking your path to athletic excellence.

Whether you're a young athlete dreaming of going pro, a college player aiming for the big leagues, or a seasoned professional looking to stay at the top of your game, this method offers a way to compete at your absolute best.

Ready to take your mental game to the next level? Experience the game-changing effects of The F.I.X. Code and unleash the champion within. It's time to perform on-point, every time you step onto the field, court, or track!

© 2024 Barb V   All Rights Reserved

HEY SUPERSTAR,

Let's Talk About the Voices in Your Head *(Yep, We All Have 'Em!)*

Okay Superstar—real talk…

Have you ever heard a little voice in your head say something like:

"I'm not good enough…"

"What if I mess up?"

"I'm so stupid."

"I'd don't want to get hit by that pitcher, again."

"Everyone's better than me…"

"I hate this sport, why can't I do……. instead?"

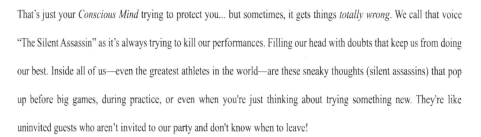

Guess what? **That voice isn't YOU.**

That's just your *Conscious Mind* trying to protect you… but sometimes, it gets things *totally wrong*. We call that voice "The Silent Assassin" as it's always trying to kill our performances. Filling our head with doubts that keep us from doing our best. Inside all of us—even the greatest athletes in the world—are these sneaky thoughts (silent assassins) that pop up before big games, during practice, or even when you're just thinking about trying something new. They're like uninvited guests who aren't invited to our party and don't know when to leave!

But here's the secret: **you don't have to believe what they say** – and more importantly *How They Make You Feel*!

In fact, you're about to become the kind of athlete who hears those voices… and then *flips the script.*

You're not alone. Your F.I.X. Code Coach (that's me!) and the entire F.I.X.ed Athlete Program are here to help you *spot those negative voices* and then *kick 'em to the curb.* 🗙 Totally get rid of them!

So, look at the silhouette on the next page. Have you ever felt like that? Surrounded by those silent assassins?

All around it are empty speech bubbles—waiting for you to fill in those thoughts and phrases you hear most often.

Be Brave!   **Be Honest!**   **Be Real!**   …No judgements!

This is your moment to call them out so we can get rid of them. As a SUPERSTAR In Training, you've got this! Let's make you a F.I.X.ed Athlete - and unleash your inner **GOAT**. 🐐✨

Barb V

HABIT TRACKER

	1	2	3	4	5	6	7	8	9	10	11	12
1												
2												
3												
4												
5												
6												
7												
8												
9												
10												
11												
12												
13												
14												
15												
16												
17												
18												
19												
20												
21												
22												
23												
24												
25												
26												
27												
28												
29												
30												
31												

1
2
3
4
5
6
7
8
9
10
11
12

Assign name and color to a specific habit and color the squares for each day

My Reading List

SUMMARY

Done	Tittle	Author	Start	Finished	Thoughts
♥	Dominate Your Athletic Journey PLAYbook		02/02/2025	03/02/2025	Awesome, Loved the games
♥	The Silent Assassins	by Barb V	04/21/2025	05/22/2025	I want to join the F.I.X.ed Athlete's Program
☐					
☐					
☐					
☐					
☐					
☐					
☐					
☐					
☐					
☐					

NOTES

----------------.
----------------.
----------------.

MOVIES I WANT TO WATCH

✓	MOVIE	A – F RATING	WHAT I LEARNED

The Magic of Movies: Inspiring Young Athletes

Movies can help athletes like you dream big about sports! When you watch a good sports movie, it can help make you feel strong and brave.

Sports movies show us cool things. They teach us that winning isn't just about being the fastest or the best kid. It's also about working with friends and giving it your best.

In these movies, kids just like you learn new skills. Sometimes they face tough teams or difficult things. But they get back up and keep trying! This shows that it's okay to make mistakes as you grow.

The best part? These movies show that sports and life are fun! Yes, trophies are nice, but making friends and feeling good about yourself matters too. Sports can make you happy for your entire life.

When you watch these movies with your parents, coaches, or teams, you can talk about being kind and never giving up. These movies can help you remember to be brave when things get hard in your own competitions.

These movies show that if you practice and keep a smile on your face, you can do amazing things! Not just in sports, but in everything you attempt on and off the field, the court, in the pool, on the track, in the ring, wherever you are.

NOTE TO COACHES & PARENTS:

Parents and coaches, you can use these films as conversation starters to discuss important values like respect, determination, and fair play. The colorful characters and exciting stories create memorable reference points that children can recall during their own moments of challenge on the field, court, in the pool, or at school or in the community.

By watching these inspiring stories with your young people, young athletes learn that they are part of a long tradition of dreamers and doers. They begin to see that with practice, perseverance, and a positive attitude, they too can achieve and even overcome amazing things—not just in sports, but in everything they set their minds to accomplish.

As a coach, I often select a certain movie (with my team) at the beginning of each season and make it our theme movie for the season. As a team we pull out certain lines from the movie and repeat them during practices and games when an athlete needs a pick-me-up or reminder. It's a perfect team bonding activity that only our team members understand. The power in this is that years later, when my athletes return for visits, they will often share some of those motivational and inspirational words of wisdom their team selected. One such slogan is, **"Don't Look Back – Leave It ALL On The Track!"** *from the movie Racing Stripes that many of my middle school track teams loved. We would also get together prior to a big game or championship competition and have a team movie event with healthy snacks or a team meal as or after the last practice before the big competition. This type of activity created some of the strongest team bonds that our coaching team couldn't create in any other way.*

TOP 51 SPORTS & MOTIVATIONAL MOVIES FOR YOUNG ATHLETES

Sorted by Rating (G, PG)

This list features inspiring sports and motivational movies that showcase perseverance, teamwork, resilience, and the power of mindset and believing in yourself, your goals and your dreams. Each movie includes key takeaways that athletes and teams can apply to their own athletic journey.

G-Rated Movies

- **The Rookie (2002)** – Baseball (G)
    - Key Takeaway: It's never too late to chase your dreams.

PG-Rated Movies

- **Miracle (2004)** – Ice Hockey (PG)
    - Key Takeaway: Teamwork and belief in the impossible can lead to legendary victories. How sports can unite a country.
- **Racing Stripes (2005)** - Horse Racing (PG)
    - **Key Takeaway:** Don't let others define your limitations; with determination and heart, you can compete in races you were never "supposed" to run.
- **Remember the Titans (2000)** – Football (PG)
    - Key Takeaway: Leadership, unity, and overcoming adversity make champions.
- **The Karate Kid (1984 & 2010)** – Martial Arts (PG)
    - Key Takeaway: Hard work, patience, and learning from setbacks build success. Find and work with a mentor.
- **Woodlawn (2015)** - Football (PG)
    - Key Takeaway: Faith and unity can overcome racial tensions and create a winning team culture.
- **Cool Runnings (1993)** – Bobsledding (PG)
    - Key Takeaway: Believe in yourself, no matter what others say about your potential.
- **Hoosiers (1986)** – Basketball (PG)
    - Key Takeaway: Discipline, teamwork, and smart strategy lead to big wins.
- **McFarland, USA (2015)** – Cross Country (PG)
    - Key Takeaway: Perseverance and teamwork can overcome any obstacle.

- **Rudy (1993)** – Football (PG)
    - Key Takeaway: Never give up on your dreams, no matter how many times you're told you can't.
- **A League of Their Own (1992)** – Baseball (PG)
    - Key Takeaway: Women can break barriers and achieve greatness in sports.
- **The Sandlot (1993)** – Baseball (PG)
    - Key Takeaway: Friendship and passion for the game are just as important as winning.
- **The Mighty Ducks (1992)** – Ice Hockey (PG)
    - Key Takeaway: Never underestimate the power of teamwork and believing in yourself.
- **Secretariat (2010)** – Horse Racing (PG)
    - Key Takeaway: Dedication and faith in your dreams can defy all odds.
- **Invincible (2006)** – Football (PG)
    - Key Takeaway: Keep working hard, even when no one believes in you.
- **Chariots of Fire (1981)** – Track & Field (PG)
    - Key Takeaway: Passion and faith can fuel extraordinary achievements.
- **Facing the Giants (2006)** – Football (PG)
    - Key Takeaway: Overcoming fear and doubt through faith and determination.
- **The Greatest Showman (2017)** – Musical/Inspirational (PG)
    - Key Takeaway: Embrace your uniqueness and dream big to achieve greatness.
- **Tucker: The Man and His Dream (1988)** – Biography/Innovation (PG)
    - Key Takeaway: Vision, resilience, and challenging the status quo lead to greatness. Follow your dreams.
- **Greater (2016)** – Football (PG)
    - Key Takeaway: Hard work and faith can create the impossible, underdogs can be leaders.
- **Field of Dreams (1989)** – Baseball (PG)
    - Key Takeaway: The power of dreams and belief in the impossible.
- **The Natural (1984)** – Baseball (PG)
    - Key Takeaway: Talent, destiny, and perseverance lead to greatness.
- **Soul Surfer (2011)** – Surfing (PG)
    - Key Takeaway: Courage and perseverance in the face of adversity.
- **The Miracle Season (2018)** – Volleyball (PG)
    - Key Takeaway: Playing through tragedy with heart and determination.

- **Rookie of the Year (1993)** – Baseball (PG)
  - Key Takeaway: Even when given an unexpected gift, hard work and humility are still essential.
- **The Longshots (2008)** – Football (PG)
  - Key Takeaway: Gender barriers fall when talent, dedication and support meet opportunity.
- **When the Game Stands Tall (2014)** – Football (PG)
  - Key Takeaway: The greatest achievement isn't winning streaks but building character that lasts beyond the field.
- **Queen of Katwe (2016)** – Chess (PG)
  - Key Takeaway: Strategic thinking and perseverance can help you overcome the most challenging circumstances.
- **Breaking Away (1979)** – Cycling (PG)
  - Key Takeaway: Finding your identity through sport can bridge social divides and open new opportunities.
- **Glory Road (2006)** – Basketball (PG)
  - Key Takeaway: Integration and unity create teams stronger than the sum of their parts.
- **The Greatest Game Ever Played (2005)** – Golf (PG)
  - Key Takeaway: Class barriers and social expectations can be overcome through excellence and focus.

  -

- **Dangal (2016)** – Wrestling (PG) {with English Subtitles}
  - Key Takeaway: Girls can excel in traditionally male sports with support and determination. GIRL POWER!
- **Safety (2020)** – Football (PG)
  - Key Takeaway: Determination, family responsibility, and community support can overcome seemingly impossible odds.
- **American Underdog (2021)** – Football (PG)
  - Key Takeaway: Never give up on your dreams, even when your path is unconventional.
- **Unstoppable (2024)** – Wrestling (PG)
  - Key Takeaway: Faith and determination can overcome even the most devastating injuries and setbacks.
- **The Heart of a Champion (2023)** – Multiple Sports (PG)
  - Key Takeaway: Athletic excellence in any sport begins with character development and personal discipline.

- **83 (2021)** – Cricket (PG) {with English Subtitles}
  - Key Takeaway: Bringing together diverse talents under inspiring leadership can achieve the impossible. How sports can unite a country.
- **Million Dollar Arm (2014)** – Baseball (PG)
  - Key Takeaway: Talent can be found in unexpected places, and perseverance transforms raw ability into excellence.
- **Madison (2005)** – Hydroplane Racing (PG)
  - Key Takeaway: A small town's determination and teamwork can overcome seemingly insurmountable challenges.
- **Akeelah and the Bee (2006)** – Spelling Competition (PG)
  - Key Takeaway: With support from your community, you can overcome self-doubt and achieve academic excellence.
- **The Ultimate Gift (2006)** – Inspirational Drama (PG)
  - Key Takeaway: The journey of personal growth often requires facing challenging "gifts" of work, problems, and responsibility.
- **The Ultimate Life (2013)** – Inspirational Drama (PG)
  - Key Takeaway: Building a legacy of purpose requires discovering what truly matters in life. How to build a life from your dreams.
- **The Ultimate Legacy (2015)** – Inspirational Drama (PG)
  - Key Takeaway: Mentorship and accountability transform individuals and create lasting impact across generations. Learning to "pay it forward".
-
  -
- **The Fire Inside (2024)** - Endurance Sports (PG)
  - Key Takeaway: Overcoming physical and emotional trauma through sport demonstrates the incredible resilience of the human spirit and the healing power of pursuing challenging goals.
- **From the Rough (2013)** - Golf (PG)
  - Key Takeaway: Breaking gender and racial barriers requires courage, innovation, and believing in others' potential when no one else will.
- **Rocky (1976)** – Boxing (PG)
  - Key Takeaway: Heart and determination matter more than natural talent.
- **Rocky II (1979)** – Boxing (PG)
  - Key Takeaway: Perseverance and belief in yourself can lead to triumph when given a second chance
- **Rocky III (1982)** – Boxing (PG)
  - Key Takeaway: Success can breed complacency; staying hungry and rediscovering your motivation is essential.

Key Things Athletes Should Know About Sleep

Sleep is one of the **most important recovery tools** for athletes. It affects **performance, muscle growth, reaction time, injury prevention, and mental focus**. Here's what every athlete needs to know:

1. **Athletes Need More Sleep Than the Average Person** 🕒
   - While most adults need **7-9 hours**, athletes should aim for **8-10 hours per night** for optimal recovery.
   - **Elite athletes** (like LeBron James & Roger Federer) reportedly sleep **10+ hours** per night!

2. **Sleep Boosts Muscle Recovery & Growth** 💪
   - During **deep sleep (slow-wave sleep)**, the body releases **growth hormone**, which repairs and rebuilds muscles.
   - Poor sleep leads to **slower muscle recovery**, increased soreness, and higher injury risk.

3. **Sleep Enhances Athletic Performance** 🚀
   - Studies show that **extra sleep improves speed, accuracy, reaction time, and endurance**.
   - Lack of sleep leads to **slower reflexes**, which is critical in sports like basketball, soccer, and football.

4. **Poor Sleep Increases Injury Risk** ⚠️
   - Athletes who sleep **less than 6 hours** are at a **30-40% higher risk of injury**.
   - Sleep deprivation leads to **slower reaction times and poor coordination**, increasing the risk of strains, sprains, and overuse injuries.

5. **Sleep Helps Regulate Stress & Mental Toughness** 🧠
   - Sleep improves **focus, decision-making, and emotional control**—essential for high-pressure moments.
   - Lack of sleep raises **cortisol (stress hormone)**, which increases anxiety and reduces motivation.

6. **Nap Strategically for Extra Recovery** 💤
   - Short **20-30 minute naps** can boost alertness and energy, especially if sleep-deprived.
   - **Avoid long naps (60+ minutes)** too late in the day, as they can interfere with nighttime sleep.

7. Optimize Sleep Quality (Not Just Quantity) 🌙
- ✅ **Keep a consistent sleep schedule** (sleep & wake at the same time daily).
- ✅ Make your room **dark, cool (60-67°F or 15-19°C), and quiet**.
- ✅ **Avoid screens (blue light)** 60 minutes before bed (it disrupts melatonin).
- ✅ **Limit caffeine after 2 PM**—it stays in your system for 6+ hours.
- ✅ Try **relaxation techniques** (breathing exercises, meditation, or reading).

8. Nutrition Affects Sleep 🍽
- **Avoid heavy meals & high sugar before bed**, as they can disrupt deep sleep.
- **Magnesium-rich foods** (bananas, almonds, dark chocolate) help relax muscles and improve sleep.
- **Tart cherry juice** naturally boosts melatonin and aids sleep.

9. Travel & Jet Lag? Adjust Sleep for Performance ✈
- If competing in different time zones, **adjust your sleep schedule** days before travel.
- Expose yourself to **natural sunlight** upon arrival to reset your body clock.

10. Recovery Sleep After a Game or Late Workout 🏆
- **Intense evening workouts can delay sleep** due to adrenaline & cortisol.
- Use a **warm shower, stretching, or deep breathing** to relax your body post-game.
- If sleep is cut short, a **30-90 minute nap the next day** can help restore recovery.

💧 **Pro Tip:**

> The Best Athletes Treat Sleep Like Training —
> It's The Most Important Part Of The Game Plan! 🏆

😴 HOW TO SET UP A PM SLEEP ROUTINE FOR ATHLETES 🏆

A **consistent nighttime routine** helps athletes fall asleep faster, improve sleep quality, and maximize recovery. Here's how to build a **high-performance PM sleep routine**:

✅ 60-90 Minutes Before Bed: Wind Down Mode 🌙

1. **Reduce Blue Light Exposure (TV, Phone, Laptop)** 📱
   - Blue light **suppresses melatonin**, making it harder to fall asleep.
   - Use **"Night Mode"** on devices or **blue-light-blocking glasses** if screen time is necessary.

2. **Lower Bright Lights** 💡
   - Dim overhead lights or use warm-colored lamps to signal **melatonin production**.

3. **Eat a Light, Sleep-Friendly Snack** 🍽 *(If Needed)*
   - Avoid **heavy meals, sugar, or caffeine** 2-3 hours before bed.
   - Best pre-sleep foods: **Bananas, almonds, yogurt, tart cherry juice, or a magnesium-rich snack**.

✅ 30-60 Minutes Before Bed: Relaxation Phase 🛁

4. **Take a Warm Shower or Bath** 🚿
   - A **warm shower** lowers core body temperature post-bath, signaling sleep time.

5. **Light Stretching, Foam Rolling, or Breathing Exercises** 🧘
   - Helps reduce muscle tension & activates the **parasympathetic nervous system** (rest & recovery mode).

6. **Read or Listen to Calming Music** 📖🎵
   - Avoid **intense/stressful content** (video games, action movies, work emails).
   - Try an **audiobook, podcast, or meditation app** (Calm, Headspace, or white noise).

✅ 10-30 Minutes Before Bed: Sleep Prep Mode 🛏

7. **Set Up Your Bedroom for Optimal Sleep** *(See Below!)*

8. **Try Sleep Supplements (If Needed)** 🌿
   - **Magnesium (glycinate)** - Helps relax muscles & nervous system.
   - **Tart cherry juice** - Naturally increases melatonin.
   - **Herbal teas** - Chamomile, valerian root, or passionflower.

9. **Set a Sleep-Wake Schedule** ⏰
   - Aim for **consistent sleep & wake times** (even on rest days).

🏠 IDEAL SLEEPING ENVIRONMENT FOR ATHLETES

☑ Keep the Room Cool (60-67°F or 15-19°C) ❄
- A cooler temperature **improves deep sleep** and prevents night sweats.

☑ Total Darkness (Use Blackout Curtains) 🌑
- Even small lights (from electronics, alarm clocks) **disrupt melatonin**.
- Use an **eye mask** if complete darkness isn't possible.

☑ Quiet or White Noise for Deep Sleep 🔊
- Use **earplugs, a fan, or a white noise machine** to block noise disturbances.

☑ Invest in a Quality Mattress & Pillows 🛏
- Choose a **medium-firm mattress** for spinal support and **cooling memory foam** if overheating is an issue.
- Pillows should support **neck alignment**—side sleepers need a higher pillow than back sleepers.

☑ No Screens - Work or Eating in Bed ❌📱
- Train your brain to associate **bed with sleep only**—not stress, TV, scrolling or eating meals. (even when sick - if possible. Rest on the couch & eat there if necessary

💧 Pro Tip:
If you **can't sleep after 20 minutes**, don't force it...
- ➤ Sit up, read a book - something relaxing - ❌NO screens❌
- ➤ Keep lights very dim and to a minimum
- ➤ Complete a muscle - tightening & relaxing sequence* from your toes all the way up to the top of your head, then try again.

📖 The Muscle - Tightening & Relaxing Sequence Secret Pro Athletes Use:
(complete this while staying in bed)

Starting with your toes; squeeze and tighten those muscles tightly and hold for 10-20 seconds and relax, then squeeze and tighten the muscles in your feet for 10-20 seconds and relax, then the muscles in your ankles for 10-20 seconds and relax, then your calves for 10-20 seconds and relax. Then squeeze and hold tight the muscles in your knees, hamstrings, and quads for 10-20 seconds and relax, then squeeze the muscles in your butt for 10-20 seconds and relax. Next squeeze and tighten your stomach muscles for 10-20 seconds and relax, then your chest muscles for 10-20 seconds and relax, then your back muscles for 10-20 seconds and relax. Then the muscles in your hands and fingers, squeeze them tightly for 10-20 seconds and relax, then your forearms for 10-20 seconds and relax, then your upper arms and biceps for 10-20 seconds and relax. Next the muscles in your neck for 10-20 seconds and relax, and then the muscles in your face and cheeks for 10-20 seconds and relax. Next tighten the muscles in your jaw for 10-20 seconds and relax. Then the muscles in your eyes and forehead – squeeze and tighten them for 10-20 seconds and relax them. Finally squeeze and relax the muscles on the top of your head for 10-20 seconds and then relax them.

You may not get all the way through your body before you fall asleep – that's the point and it's okay. If you can get all the way through – just start over again and you should fall asleep somewhere in the second sequence.

My Perfect Sleep Environment Checklist

- [ ] I use my bedroom only to sleep.
- [ ] I do not eat in my bedroom.
- [ ] I do not do any work in my bedroom.
- [ ] I do not have a television or a computer in my bedroom.
- [ ] I have taken all the electronics out of my room.
- [ ] I have blackout curtains over my window(s).
- [ ] I have a eye mask if I can't create complete darkness in my room.
- [ ] I have a totally quiet environment to sleep in.
- [ ] I have a fan or white noise machine to block out noise disturbances
- [ ] I have the perfect mattress for spinal support
- [ ] I have a cooling memory foam topper or mattress as overheating is an issue for me.
- [ ] I have the perfect pillow that supports my neck alignment.
- [ ] I keep my bedroom at a comfortable and cool temperature.
- [ ] My bed is the perfect size for my height. My feet don't hang over my bed.
- [ ] _____
- [ ] _____
- [ ] _____
- [ ] _____

Boost Memory & Brain Health by 226%—While You Sleep!

A **groundbreaking six-month study** from the **University of California, Irvine** revealed something incredible that athletes can take advantage of – immediately. Researchers took a group of participants, split them in half, and measured their memory and cognitive function both at the beginning and the end of the study. They also conducted MRI scans of their brains.

Here's where it gets amazing:
Half of the group used an **aromatherapy diffuser** in their bedroom every night for just **two hours**. Each night, a different **essential oil** scent was diffused—rotating through **rose, rosemary, eucalyptus, lemon, peppermint, orange, and lavender.**
The other group did not use any aromatherapy at all.
At the end of the study, the *results were shocking*:

- The aromatherapy group showed a **226% improvement** in memory and cognitive performance.

- Their brain scans showed **enhanced communication** in areas responsible for memory and thinking.

This is a **simple, passive,** and *powerful* way to protect your brain — especially as you age. If you're noticing early signs of cognitive difficulty, decline, or just want to stay sharp, we highly recommend starting this practice immediately.

Looking for a reliable diffuser? I've linked a few different types here as they are ones that I use at home, at the office, in my car, and when I travel...

ESSENTIAL OIL DIFFUSERS FOR YOUNG ATHLETES

A Smart & Simple Training & Wellness Tool for Focus, Recovery & Mood

What's a Diffuser? A diffuser releases tiny droplets of essential oils into the air—so you can breathe in their powerful, natural benefits.

Why Use One?

For athletes ages 7–15, diffusing oils can help:

- Boost focus & brain power
- Reduce stress before games
- Improve sleep & recovery
- Lift mood & motivation
- Support breathing (especially for asthma or allergies)

Best Diffuser Type:
☑ **Ultrasonic Diffuser**
— Easy to use
— Safe with water + oils
— Perfect for bedrooms, kitchens, locker rooms

Safety Tips

- Use **pure oils** only (CPTG®) *Adulterated oil brands will ruin diffusers quickly*
- Diffuse **30–120 min at a time**
- Clean weekly
- Avoid strong oils for very young children

If you found this helpful, please **connect with us** — attend one of our FREE weekly essential oils online events or our weekly Wednesday Essential Oils Q & A session by phone (or listen to the replay).

Please share this with your athletes, teams, coaches, and loved ones who could all benefit from this brain-boosting tip as well as the benefits of doTERRA essential oils. Let's help each other stay sharp and healthy, one breath at a time! Remember – **IT'S ALWAYS GAME TIME!**

Some Favorite Oils for Young Athletes

Goal	Oils
Focus	Lemon, Balance®, Thinker®
Calm Nerves	Lavender, Frankincense, Brave®
Clear Airways	Eucalyptus, Tea Tree, Breathe®
Sleep & Rest	Lavendar, Calmer®, Vetiver
Energy & Mood	Wild Orange, Peppermint, Bergamot

ESSENTIAL OILS FOR YOUNG ATHLETES:
A Guide for Athletes, Coaches, Parents & Medical Providers

What Are Essential Oils?
Essential oils are concentrated plant extracts that support the body and mind naturally. They can help young athletes with energy, focus, muscle recovery, breathing, and relaxation. We only recommend using **dōTERRA° CPTG° Essential Oils** due to their purity and testing procedures. *It's the only brand we use!*

Benefits for Young Athletes*
- **Energy & Focus** – Peppermint, Thinker,° Wild Orange, Steady°
- **Breathing & Stamina** – Breathe,° Eucalyptus, Peppermint
- **Muscle Recovery** – Lavender, Eucalyptus, Frankincense
- **Injury Support** – Rescuer, Stronger, Frankincense, Correct-X°
- **Stress & Sleep** – Calmer, Lavender,

How to Use Essential Oils Safely
☑ **Topical Use (On Skin)** – Always dilute with a carrier oil (e.g., coconut oil) before applying.
☑ **Aromatherapy (Inhalation)** – Diffuse in a room or apply to wrists for a quick scent boost.
☑ **Patch Test First** – Before using on the skin, test a small amount on the forearm to check for reactions.

YOU ARE HIGHLY ENCOURAGED TO ATTEND one of our FREE online educational programs or invite us to do one for your entire team...

Recommended Essential Oil Uses for Sports*
- **Before Training:** Peppermint, Brave,° & Thinker°
- **During Rest:** Eucalyptus, Peppermint for clear breathing
- **After Training:** Deep Blue,° Lavender or Lemongrass for muscle relaxation
- **Injury Recovery:** Tea tree, Fir Oil, Frankincense
- **Bedtime Recovery:** Calmer,° Lavender or Serenity° Sleep System for sleep

Excellent Essential Oil Blends for Young Athletes*
🏆 **Pre-Game Focus:** Balance,° Thinker,°
💪 **Muscle Recovery:** Deep Blue° stick
🗣 **Breathe:** Breathe°

⚠ Important Safety Notes for Parents & Medical Providers* ⚠
- Always monitor young athletes for skin sensitivities.
- Consult a healthcare provider for allergies or asthma concerns.
- Essential oils are complementary to medical care, not a replacement.

Do NOT Ingest –
Essential oils should not be swallowed unless directed by a healthcare professional.

Essential Oils for Athletes
A Natural Approach to Performance, Recovery, and Well-being

Dear Parents and Coaches,

As young athletes strive for excellence in their sport, it is essential to provide them with the best tools for performance, recovery, and overall well-being. Essential oils have been used for centuries to support physical and mental health, and in recent years, their benefits for athletes have become more widely recognized.

As an elite athlete who continues to compete at a high level, I attribute part of my longevity in sports to essential oils and scientifically backed nutritional supplements, which I have incorporated into my routine since the early 1990s.

These natural tools have helped me maintain endurance, recover faster, and optimize my overall health.

Why Consider Essential Oils for Athletes?

Essential oils can provide:

Enhanced Focus & Energy
Certain essential oils have powerful properties that can naturally sharpen mental clarity and sustain energy levels without the crash associated with synthetic stimulants. The right oils can help athletes enter their optimal performance zone, improving concentration during training and competition when it matters most.

Improve Respiratory Support
Proper breathing is fundamental to athletic performance. Selected essential oils support respiratory function by promoting clear airways and efficient oxygen exchange. This benefit is particularly valuable for endurance athletes, swimmers, and those training in challenging environmental conditions.

Faster Muscle Recovery
Recovery time is often what limits training progress. Specific essential oils contain natural compounds with anti-inflammatory and circulation-enhancing properties that can significantly reduce recovery windows between intense training sessions, allowing for more consistent progress with less downtime.

Support for Injuries & Soreness
The right essential oil blends can provide targeted comfort for training-related discomfort and support the body's natural recovery processes. When used properly, these natural solutions can complement traditional approaches to minor injury management, potentially reducing reliance on synthetic options.

Stress Management & Sleep Improvement
Peak performance depends on mental preparation and quality recovery. Certain essential oils have been shown to reduce anxiety levels and promote deeper, more restorative sleep—both critical elements that separate good athletes from great ones, especially during competitive seasons when pressure is highest.

Essential Oils: A Natural Approach to Performance, Recovery, & Well-being

Balanced Nutrition
Essential oils can support healthy digestive function, which is fundamental to nutrient absorption and energy production. Proper digestive health ensures athletes get the maximum benefit from their nutritional intake, creating a foundation for sustained performance and recovery.

Safety & Proper Use
- Essential oils should always be used properly, including dilution for topical application.
- Certain oils may need to be avoided for athletes with respiratory sensitivities or allergies.
- Essential oils are not a replacement for medical treatment but can be an effective complementary tool.
- Quality matters — not all essential oils on the market offer the same benefits or safety profiles.

Take Your Athlete's Performance to the Next Level
While this information provides an introduction to the benefits of essential oils for athletes, implementing an effective essential oil strategy requires proper knowledge about specific oils, appropriate applications, timing, sequence protocols, and safety considerations for athletes of all ages and in their respective sports.

For those serious about incorporating these powerful natural tools into your athletic program, I offer an exclusive **Essential Oils for Athletes Masterclass** designed specifically for coaches and parents. This comprehensive session covers:
- The science behind how essential oils affect athletic performance
- Step-by-step routines for pre-competition, training, and recovery
- Sport-specific practices for team and individual athletics
- Age-appropriate guidelines for athletes and their parents and coaches
- Quality considerations and how to identify effective products
- Customization strategies for different athletic needs and goals

By incorporating essential oils alongside proven training methods, proper nutrition, and recovery strategies, we can help athletes reach their highest potential while maintaining long-term health and wellness.

Space in the Masterclass is limited to ensure personalized attention. To reserve your spot or receive more information about how **essential oils can transform your athlete's performance naturally**, please connect with us at:
https://www.BarbV.Fun

Also follow me, Barb V, on Amazon to grab your copy of any or
All of my Athletic PLAYbooks...

Committed to your athletic success,

BARB V

https://www.SupterstarInTraining.com

Note: This information reflects my personal experience as an athlete, coach and educator, and is intended for educational purposes. Always consult with appropriate healthcare and medical providers before starting any new health regimen.

Stop Eating C.R.A.P.

Carbonated drinks

Refined sugars

Artificial sweeteners

Processed foods

Next time you eat anything, ask yourself: is this "C.R.A.P.?"
"Is this helping my brain, my energy, and my performances?"

Learning to read a food label is important, however, **READING THE INGREDIENT LIST is even more powerful!**

Nutrition Facts
Serving Size 1 ounce   Servings in bag 4

Amount Per Serving

Calories 155   Calories from Fat 93

	% Daily Value*
Total Fat 11g	16%
Saturated Fat 3g	15%
Trans Fat	
Cholesterol 0mg	0%
Sodium 148mg	6%
Total Carbohydrate 14g	5%
Dietary Fiber 1g	5%
Sugars 1g	
Protein 2g	
Vitamin A 0% • Vitamin C	9%
Calcium 1% • Iron	3%

*Percent Daily Values are based on a 2,000 calorie diet. Your daily values may be higher or lower depending on your calorie needs.

3 Popular Peanut butter labels:

Ingredients: Select roasted peanuts, sugar, hydrogenated vegetable oil, salt, fancy molasses

Ingredients: Freshly roasted peanuts, soybean oil, maltodextrin, icing sugar, hydrogenated vegetable oil, salt

Ingredients: Roasted peanuts, sugar, molasses, partially hydrogenated vegetable oil (soybean), fully hydrogenated vegetable oils (rapeseed and soybean), mono- and diglycerides, salt

Natural peanut butter generally consists of just <u>peanuts</u> and <u>salt</u>.

⭐ SUPERSTAR FUEL ⭐
WHY NUTRITION MATTERS

The Power Behind Every Practice, Play, and Your Personal Best

🏆 HEY SUPERSTAR!

You've got **BIG Dreams**. And your body is the vehicle that's going to get you there — in school, in your sport, and in life. But like any top-performing machine, you need the **right kind of fuel** to run at your best.

🍎 WHAT YOU EAT = HOW YOU FEEL, FOCUS, AND PERFORM

Just like a race car needs high-quality fuel, **your brain, muscles, and energy levels** depend on what you eat and drink every single day.

Eat well = feel strong, sharp, and ready to roll.

Eat junk = feel tired, cranky, and slow to recover.

🍽 FOOD AFFECTS YOUR:

- **Brain Power** – For faster thinking, better focus, and stronger memory
- **Energy** – So you can train hard, play hard, and still feel great afterward
- **Mood** – To stay calm, confident, and in control (even on hard days)
- **Muscles** – To get stronger, faster, and bounce back from soreness
- **Growth** – Because your body's still building every single day!

💪 BALANCED FUEL = MVP PERFORMANCE

A **balanced meal** has three key power sources:

1. **Carbohydrates** (like fruits, veggies, rice, oats, whole grains) for **quick energy**
2. **Proteins** (like eggs, chicken, fish, tofu, beans, yogurt) for **muscle repair**
3. **Healthy Fats** (like nuts, seeds, avocado, olive oil) for **long-lasting energy and brain power**

💬 COACH TIP:

> "If you want to play like a pro, you must fuel like one too.
> Champions are made in the kitchen just as much as on the field."

✅ SUPERSTAR CHALLENGE:

EVERY TIME YOU EAT SOMETHING, ask yourself:

> *"Is this helping my brain, my energy, and my game?"*

If the answer is YES –

...you're training **Your Body & Your Mindset** like a true **Superstar in Training!**

SUGAR

You know certain foods are good for you, but have you ever wondered exactly how they help your body? The following foods aid healthy brain development and offer nutritional benefits to you and your whole family. Brain foods rich in antioxidants, good fats, vitamins and minerals provide energy and aid in protecting against brain diseases. So when you focus on giving your body whole, nutritious foods benefiting both the gut and the brain, you're actually benefiting your mind and body while keeping them both in tip-top shape. Now a word on SUGAR...

High Sugar and Hidden Sugar Foods

Some foods are obvious sugar loads, but many foods may not be so obvious. If you want to know which foods have hidden sugar, read the labels. And, as always, eating real food in its original form, such as a piece of fruit instead of fruit juice, is better.

High Sugar Foods:

Sports drinks, sodas
Candy
Yogurt
Cereals
Dried fruits
Frozen dinners
Dried fruits
Fruit juices & other beverages,
Canned fruits

Chocolate milk
Flavored coffees
Iced tea
Energy drinks
BBQ sauce
Spaghetti sauce
Ketchup
Vitamin Water
Smoothies

Cakes, pies & doughnuts, pastries
Granola bars
Protein bars/energy bars
Canned baked beans
Breads

How to Reduce Sugar Intake

Reducing sugar intake is not as hard as you think, but if you're addicted, it can take some practice and commitment just like any change. The American Heart Association shares some great tips on how to reduce sugar. Put these ideas into practice on a regular basis, and in no time, you will reduce sugar and reduce your risk of diabetes, heart disease, metabolic syndrome and obesity.

- Remove sugar, syrup, "fake" honey and molasses from your cupboard and table.
- If you use sugar in your coffee, tea, cereal, pancakes, etc., cut back. Use half the amount you usually use to start and even less over time. And no artificial sweeteners! (I use Natural honey or CPTG™ Essential Oils)
- Drink water instead of flavored beverages and juices.
- Buy fresh fruits instead of fruits that are canned, especially those in syrups.
- Instead of adding sugar to your morning cereal, use fresh fruit, bananas or berries.
- When baking, cut the sugar by one third. Just try it! You probably won't even notice. (I use Natural honey)
- Try using spices, such as ginger, cinnamon or nutmeg, instead of sugar. (I use CPTG™ Essential Oils)
- Try unsweetened applesauce instead of sugar in recipes.
- Consider pure stevia but use in moderation. It's very sweet, so you don't need much.

©2017 Barb V   Nutrition for Athletes!   All Rights Reserved

HYDRATION

Hydrated athletes compete better than dehydrated ones

Your body is comprised of water and 75% of that is contained in muscles.

When you don't drink adequate fluids, your body temperature rises and the blood volume in your muscles decrease. Smaller muscles equal less strength.

Drink lots of liquid – WATER – throughout your day and during hard workouts and competitions.

Water lubricates your joints, helps you form saliva, and provides shock absorption

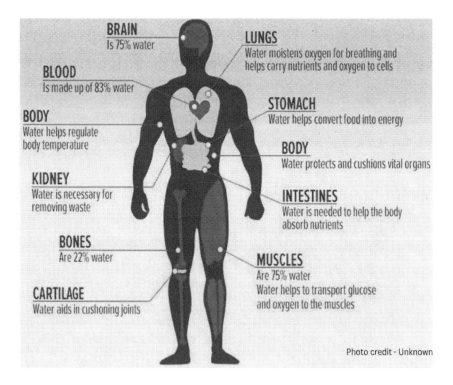

Active Athletes should be drinking 50% -75% of their body weight in ounces of water a day.

💧 HYDRATION TRUTHS AND PERFORMANCE SCIENCE
THE ELECTROLYTE MANIPULATION 🍬

Sports drinks claim advanced hydration but deliver compromised performance:

🧪 Osmotic Realities:
- Ideal fluid absorption requires proper osmolality (**275-295 mOsm/kg**)
- Commercial sports drinks average **338-382 mOsm/kg**, slowing absorption
- Excessive sugar content (**14-34g per 20 oz**) delays gastric emptying by **37%**
- Artificial colorings increase intestinal permeability **19%**
- Electrolyte ratios optimized for taste, not performance (sodium/potassium imbalance)

🍬 Hydration Efficiency Data:
- Water absorption decreased **29%** with commercial sports drinks
- Cellular hydration markers **21%** less favorable than natural alternatives
- Kidney filtration load increased **32%**, creating unnecessary stress
- Blood plasma volume expansion **18%** less effective than optimal hydration
- Electrolyte balance recovery delayed **41%** compared to proper protocols

🏸 Performance Measurements:
- Core temperature regulation **1.1°C / 2°F less effective** during intense exercise or
- Perceived thirst satisfaction **decreased 35%** despite greater fluid intake
- Cognitive function tests showed **27% greater decline** during extended activity
- Endurance capacity **decreased 15-19%** compared to optimal hydration
- Neuromuscular coordination **decreased 23% under heat stress**

🏃 Athletic Application Data:
- Tennis serve accuracy decreased **22%** with sports drink hydration vs. optimized protocol
- Basketball shooting percentage declined **17.3%** in final quarter
- Soccer sprint repeated ability decreased **24.6%** in second half
- Weightlifting force production decreased **12.8%** in final sets
- Cognitive sport decisions **31%** slower in crash phase

Understanding Your Pee
A Superstar Athlete's Guide

Why a SUPERSTAR's Pee Colors Matter
Your pee (urine) is one of your body's best ways of telling you how hydrated you are! For athletes, staying properly hydrated is super important for performance, energy levels, and preventing injuries. Let's learn how to read what your pee is trying to tell you!

The Pee Color Chart: Your Hydration Detector

Water Clear
Color: Clear like plain water
What it means: You're extremely overhydrated!
Athlete note: Okay before intense activity, but if it's always this clear, you might be drinking more water than you need, and that's not good.

Lemonade
Color: Pale yellow like lemonade
What it means: Perfect hydration!
Athlete note: This is your goal color most of the time - your body has the water it needs!

Apple Juice
Color: Transparent yellow like apple juice
What it means: Normal, but could use a bit more water
Athlete note: Drink a glass of water soon, especially before practice or games

Apple Cider
Color: Dark yellow like apple cider
What it means: You're dehydrated
Athlete note: Time to drink water! Your performance will start to decline at this level

Orange Juice
Color: Amber or honey-colored like orange juice
What it means: Severely dehydrated
Athlete note: Drink water now! You'll feel tired, your muscles won't work as well, and recovery will be slower

Tomato Juice
Color: Orange-brown like orange soda or cola
What it means: Seriously dehydrated
Athlete note: Your body needs water urgently - Tell parents & coaches - Seek Immediate Medical Assistance

SUPERSTAR Hydration / Pee Facts:
Your body is about 60% water
Even being just 2% dehydrated can make you 10-20% weaker and slower!
You should pee 4-7 times per day
The first pee of the day is usually darker (that's normal)
Your pee should be mostly odorless

When to Drink:
☐ First thing in the morning
☐ With every meal
☐ Before, during, and after practice or games
☐ When your pee looks darker than lemonade
☐ Even when you don't feel thirsty (thirst means you're already dehydrated!)

SUPERSTAR Hydration Check:
1. How many times have you peed today? _____
2. What color was your last pee? (Use the chart above) _____
3. Have you had water with your last meal? YES / NO
4. Did you bring a water bottle to practice/school today? YES / NO
If you pee less than 4 times a day or your pee is darker than apple juice, you need to drink more water!

Note: Tell a trusted adult if your pee is red, extremely dark, cloudy, or if it hurts when you pee. Some foods like beets and certain medications can change pee color temporarily and asparagus can make it smell different too (that's normal).

🏆 THE HIDDEN SCIENCE 🏆
WHAT PERFORMANCE PRODUCTS REALLY DO TO ATHLETES...

🧠 THE NEUROPHYSIOLOGY OF ENERGY DRINKS 🧠
WHAT HAPPENS IN YOUR BRAIN & NERVOUS SYSTEM

Energy drinks create a cascade of neurological events that directly impact athletic performance:

⏱ Initial 15-30 Minutes After Consumption:

- Caffeine blocks adenosine receptors, preventing normal fatigue signals
- Blood glucose spikes **30-45%**, triggering dopamine release
- Alpha and beta brain wave patterns show heightened activity **(+23%)**
- Decision speed temporarily increases by **8-12%**
- Visual processing improves **13%** (motion tracking, peripheral vision)

🧪 Performance Enhancement Illusion:

- Perceived energy increase is primarily CNS stimulation, not actual energy availability
- Studies show **87%** of the "energy" sensation is perception, not increased cellular ATP

⚠ The Critical Crash Phase (60-120 Minutes):

- Brain glucose metabolism plummets **27%** below baseline
- Dopamine receptors downregulate by **18%**, creating temporary insensitivity
- Prefrontal cortex (decision-making) activity decreases **31%**
- Motor cortex efficiency drops **17%**, affecting precision skills
- Visual-motor integration decreases **25-33%**

🏆 In-Game Performance Impact:
- 🏈 Quarterback completion percentage drops average of **14.2%** during crash phase
- 🏀 Basketball free throw accuracy decreases **18.3%** compared to proper hydration
- ⚽ Soccer passing accuracy declines **22.6%** in the final 30 minutes
- 📊 Reaction time slows from 203ms to 267ms **(31% decline)**
- 📉 Technique breakdown occurs **3.7x** more frequently in final quarter/period

📉 Longitudinal Neural Impact (Regular Consumption):
- Dopamine receptor sensitivity decreases **22%** after 6 weeks of regular use
- Natural energy regulation systems weaken, creating dependence loops
- Adenosine receptor upregulation leads to greater fatigue when not using
- CNS stimulation threshold increases **37%**, requiring more product for same effect

♥ CARDIOVASCULAR AND METABOLIC DISRUPTION HOW YOUR HEART AND ENERGY SYSTEMS SUFFER ⚡

The combination of caffeine, taurine, and sugar creates profound cardiac and metabolic stress:

♥ Immediate Cardiovascular Effects:
- Heart rate increases **8-11 BPM** at rest, **15-20 BPM** during activity
- Systolic blood pressure rises **5-8 mmHg**, creating unnecessary cardiac load
- Cardiac output becomes inefficient, pumping **12%** harder for same performance
- Heart rate variability (HRV) decreases **32%** (critical recovery marker)
- Microvascular constriction reduces oxygen delivery to working muscles by **18%**

⚡ Metabolic Consequences:
- Insulin response increases **40-70%** above normal
- Fat oxidation (burning) decreases **33%** during exercise
- Carbohydrate utilization efficiency drops **21%**
- Glycogen depletion occurs **27%** faster than with proper fueling
- Lactic acid threshold lowers by **0.5-1.0 mmol/L**

🏈 Game-Day Impact Data:
- VO2 max effectively decreases **7-11%** during crash phase
- Time to exhaustion shortens by **15-22%** in endurance scenarios
- Power output in final quarter/period decreases **19-26%**
- Required recovery between high-intensity bursts increases **41%**
- Perceived exertion increases **31%** for identical workload

📊 Six-Month Impact on Cardiovascular System:
- Resting heart rate increases average of **7 BPM**
- Cardiac efficiency markers decrease **12-18%**
- Endothelial function (blood vessel health) decreases **14%**
- Autonomic nervous system balance shifts **29%** toward sympathetic dominance
- Cardiac recovery time increases **35%** between training sessions

🏛 University Study Findings (D1 Athletes):
- Athletes consuming energy drinks 5+ times weekly showed **33% more overtraining symptoms**
- Resting morning heart rates averaged **11 BPM higher** than non-consumers
- **Sleep quality metrics decreased 28-37%** (critical for recovery)
- Respiratory rate **during sleep increased 15% (indicating stress response)**
- **Morning cortisol levels 41% higher** than recommended athletic ranges

THE PROTEIN BAR DECEPTION
SUGAR, INFLAMMATION,
AND RECOVERY HINDRANCE

Modern protein bars represent one of the greatest nutritional deceptions in sports:

🔍 Nutritional Reality vs. Marketing:
- Average "protein" bar contains **23g sugar/sugar alcohols vs 18g protein**
- **Glycemic impact equals or exceeds standard candy bars in 82%** of products tested
- Artificial sweeteners shown to alter gut microbiome **reducing protein utilization by 19%**
- **Low-quality protein** isolates have PDCAAS scores of 0.55-0.75 (vs. 1.0 for egg/whey)
- Essential amino acid **profiles are incomplete in 71% of plant-based bars**

🍬 Digestive and Hormonal Response:
- Sugar alcohols create osmotic imbalance, reducing nutrient absorption by **23%**
- Insulin/glucagon ratio **shifts toward fat storage** rather than muscle synthesis
- Artificial ingredients trigger **47% higher inflammatory** markers (IL-6, TNF-alpha)
- Gut barrier function **decreases 19%** with regular consumption
- Protein synthesis efficiency **decreases 22-31%** compared to whole food sources

⚙️ Recovery Impact Metrics:
- AMPK activation (recovery signaling) decreased **28%** vs. whole food protein
- Post-exercise inflammation resolution delayed **35%**
- Glycogen replenishment reduced **29%**
- Muscle protein synthesis rates **17-24%** lower than optimal nutrition
- Growth hormone response blunted by **32%** due to artificial ingredients

🏆 Performance Consequences (Next-Day Testing):
- Force production decreased **14.7%** following bar-based recovery
- Power endurance metrics **23.2%** lower than whole-food recovery
- Recovery heart rate **17.3%** higher at 24 hours post-exercise
- Neuromuscular recruitment patterns showed **19.6%** more fatigue indicators
- Protein utilization efficiency decreased **27%** when using bars for recovery

PROFESSIONAL ATHLETE REALITIES
WHAT THEY ACTUALLY USE VS.
WHAT THEY ENDORSE

The disconnect between endorsements and actual nutrition practices is striking:

Behind Closed Doors:
- 86% of professional athletes endorsing sugar-laden products use custom alternatives
- Average professional team employs 3-5 full-time nutrition specialists
- Individual nutrition plans revised weekly based on performance metrics
- Blood biomarker testing conducted 1-3x monthly to optimize fueling
- Supplement quality testing 14-21x more rigorous than consumer products

Professional Protocols Revealed:
- Pre-game fueling begins **4-6 hours** prior, with **3-4** specific nutrient timing windows
- Carbohydrate sources selected based on individual glucose response testing
- Protein quality standards require **9.6 on 10-point** bioavailability scale
- Hydration starts **24 hours** pre-competition with specific osmolality targets
- Recovery nutrition begins within **9 minutes** post-activity (not 30-60)

Recovery Science Used by Pros:
- Amino acid profiles customized to individual metabolic requirements
- Inflammation management uses specific antioxidant timing windows
- Circadian rhythm optimization incorporated into nutrition timing
- Sleep quality directly linked to carb/protein/fat ratios in evening meals
- Micronutrient testing identifies specific deficiencies affecting recovery

The Economics Exposed:
- Average endorsement contract: **$250,000-$5M** annually
- Cost of actual nutrition used: **$15,000-$30,000** annually
- **Products endorsed often contain ingredients banned from team facilities**
- 79% of endorsed products would fail team nutritionist standards
- Average career extension from proper nutrition: **2-4 years** - worth $$ Millions $$

🚀 YOUR PERFORMANCE SOLUTION
SCIENCE-BASED PROTOCOLS
ANY ATHLETE* CAN USE 🚀

Implementing elite-level nutrition doesn't require professional budgets:

🍽 Pre-Competition Fueling (2-4 hours before):

- Complex carbohydrate + lean protein combinations:
    - Sweet potato (200g) + chicken breast (100g)
    - Oatmeal (80g) + eggs (2 whole + 2 whites)
    - Brown rice (150g) + salmon (100g)
- Performance Impact: **41%** more stable energy, **32%** longer time to fatigue

*These are specifically created for a certain athlete in a particular sport… Your Values Will Differ!

💧 Hydration Protocol:

- Start 24 hours before: **5-7ml per kg** body weight plus foods with high water content
- 2 hours before: **500-600ml** water with pinch of salt and 1/4 lemon
- During: **150-250ml** water every 15-20 minutes (based on sweat rate)
- Post: Replacement of **125-150%** of weight lost plus natural electrolytes
- Performance Impact: **37%** better thermoregulation, **28%** improved endurance

🔄 Recovery Nutrition Science:

- **Timing Window:** Initial 0-30 minutes critical for 83% of recovery signaling
- **Protein Requirements:** 0.25-0.3g per kg body weight with leucine emphasis
- **Carbohydrate Needs:** 0.8-1.2g per kg for glycogen replenishment
- **Antioxidant Timing:** Specific compounds 2 hours post-exercise
- **Performance Impact:** 43% faster recovery, 35% reduced soreness, 27% improved next-day performance

CASE STUDIES AND SUCCESS STORIES
REAL RESULTS FROM ATHLETES
WHO MADE THE SWITCH

Documented transformations from commercial products to proper nutrition:

🏀 High School Basketball Player:
Before: Regular energy drink user, protein bar post-game
After: Proper hydration protocol, whole food recovery
Results:
- Vertical jump increased **3.2 inches**
- Fourth quarter scoring **+41%**
- Recovery time between games decreased **28%**
- Season scoring average increased **7.3 points**
- College scholarship offers increased from **2 to 7**

🏊 College Swimmer:
Before: Commercial sports drinks, meal replacement bars
After: Custom hydration, timed nutrition protocol
Results:
- 100m time improved **1.32 seconds**
- Training volume capacity increased **23%**
- Recovery markers improved **37%**
- Illness days decreased **78%**
- Qualified for national championships after previous misses

🏈 Professional Football Player:
Before: Energy drinks pre-game, marketed recovery products
After: Scientific fueling protocol, whole food emphasis
Results:
- Game-day GPS metrics showed **17%** more high-intensity distance
- Force production in 4th quarter improved **23%**
- Cognitive decision speed maintained throughout game
- Injury time decreased **65%** year-over-year
- Contract value increased **$2.8M** on renewal

YOUR NEXT STEPS

1. **Evaluate Your Current Practices:**
   Compare your nutrition to the science presented

2. **Implement Progressive Changes:**
   Start with pre/during/post fundamentals

3. **Track Performance Metrics:**
   Measure specific improvements

4. **Adjust Based on Results:**
   Personalize for your individual response

5. **Share Knowledge:**
   Help teammates benefit from science-based practices

Remember:

Every time you choose real nutrition over marketed products; you gain an edge that most competitors don't understand.

This is the difference between potential and achievement!

Understanding Your Poop

Why a SUPERSTAR's Poop Matters
Did you know your poop can tell you a lot about your health? Just like checking your pulse or tracking your sleep, looking at your poop gives you important information about how your body is working. For athletes, healthy digestion means better performance and faster recovery!

The Bristol Stool Scale: Your Poop Decoder

Doctors use something called the Bristol Stool Scale to categorize different types of poop. Here's what the different types mean for you as an athlete:

Type 1: Separate hard lumps (like nuts)
- What it means: You're probably dehydrated and need more water!
- Athlete alert: Hard to pass and might slow you down. Drink up!

Type 2: Sausage-shaped but lumpy
- What it means: Still not enough water or fiber
- Athlete alert: Your body isn't absorbing nutrients efficiently

Type 3: Sausage-shaped with cracks on the surface
- What it means: Getting better! This is normal for some people
- Athlete alert: You're doing okay, but could use more hydration

Type 4: Smooth and soft, like a snake or sausage
- What it means: Perfect! This is the ideal poop
- Athlete alert: Your digestion is working great - keep it up!

Type 5: Soft blobs with clear-cut edges
- What it means: Lacking some fiber, but passing easily
- Athlete alert: Your diet might need more whole foods

Type 6: Fluffy pieces with ragged edges, mushy
- What it means: Moving too quickly through your system
- Athlete alert: You might be nervous before competition or eating something that doesn't agree with you

Type 7: Entirely liquid, no solid pieces
- What it means: Your body is trying to get rid of something fast
- Athlete alert: If this happens during training or competition, you need to replace fluids and electrolytes!

A Superstar's Poop Checklist:
- ☐ Do you poop regularly? (Daily is usually best for athletes)
- ☐ Is your poop Type 3 or 4 most days?
- ☐ Does your poop sink rather than float?
- ☐ Is the color medium to dark brown?
- ☐ Does it take less than a minute or two to finish?

If you answered **YES** to most of these, your digestive system is probably working well!

Remember: Everyone's "normal" is a little different. Track your poop patterns in your journal to learn what's normal for you.

Note: Tell a trusted adult if your poop is black, white, or red, if you have severe pain, or if your pattern suddenly changes for more than a few days.

YOU ARE WHAT YOU EAT – ATE!

Understanding Your Poop

Yep, even your POOP tells a story.

Hey Superstars! Let's talk real for a second...
You've probably heard the saying "You are what you eat."
But guess what?

It goes even deeper:

"YOU ARE WHAT YOU EAT – ATE."

That means whatever your food ate, or whatever's hiding in it (like chemicals, sugar, fake colors, and processed junk), is now in YOU.
And here's the kicker...

Whatever goes into your body eventually has to come out.
And if you've been putting C.R.A.P. in (Carbonated drinks, Refined sugars, Artificial ingredients, Processed foods), your poop will absolutely reflect it!

IT MIGHT BE:
Too loose
Too hard
Too small
Too weirdly shaped or smelly
Or just... uncomfortable

That's your body's way of saying,

"HEY, HELP ME OUT! I NEED BETTER FUEL!"

As a young athlete, your poop can actually be a clue to your health, energy, hydration, and recovery.

If your poop is off, chances are you're not digesting well, not hydrated enough, or you're loading up on the wrong foods.

So remember:

Better IN = Better OUT = Better PERFORMANCE.

Flip to page 61 for more gross-but-great info on what your poop is telling you. Trust us — you'll be surprised how helpful it is.

STAY STRONG, EAT CLEAN, AND KEEP THINGS MOVING!

date

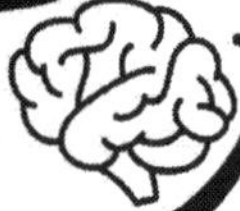

to do list

brain dump time...

random thoughts

think and make decision about

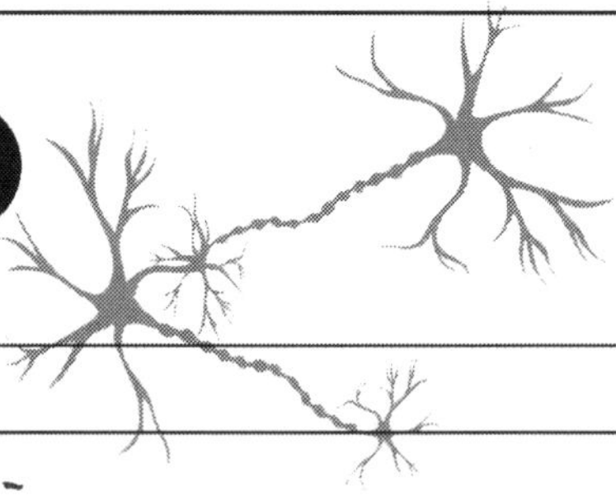

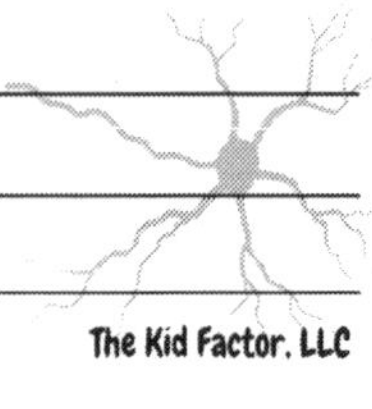

Section # 2
MONTHLY PLANNING, WEEKLY PLANNING, & 30-DAY CHALLENGES

MY MONTHLY PLANNER

Month: _____ Year: _____

Monday	Tuesday	Wednesday	Thursday	Friday	Saturday	Sunday

Notes:

30 DAY **CHALLENGE**

GOAL: ....

MY WHY: ....

START DATE: ....

REWARD: ....

1	2	3	4	5
6	7	8	9	10
11	12	13	14	15
16	17	18	19	20
21	22	23	24	25
26	27	28	29	30

©2025 Barb V All Rights Reserved

The Silent Assassins
HABITS & GOALS

The Kid Factor, LLC

MY WEEKLY PLANNER

WEEK OF:

Monday

Tuesday

Wednesday

Thursday

Friday

Saturday

Sunday

to-do

Notes

Start Date: __ / __ / __

My Goal's Target Date: __ / __ / __

How Long It Took Me To Attain My Goal
Number of Days: _____

MY HABIT & GOALS TRACKER

This Month's Habit to help me attain my Goals:

Circle each day you stick to your habit - cross off each day you don't...

01	02	03	04	05	06
07	08	09	10	11	12
13	14	15	16	17	18
19	20	21	22	23	24
25	26	27	28	29	30

Why I want to gain this habit:

What I learned this week:

This Week's Motivation - How I will reward myself...

My STAR rating for this week:
☆ ☆ ☆ ☆ ☆

My step-by-step action plan:

- ○
- ○
- ○
- ○
- ○
- ○

Due date:
__ / __
__ / __
__ / __
__ / __
__ / __
__ / __

Completed:

My Personal Review:

How I rate my week's efforts: ☆ ☆ ☆ ☆ ☆

Parent Notes:

Notes From My Coach:

©2025 Barb V All Rights Reserved   The F.I.X.ed Athlete Program   The Kid Factor, LLC
HABITS & GOALS

MY WEEKLY PLANNER

WEEK OF:

Monday

Tuesday

Wednesday

Thursday

Friday

Saturday

Sunday

to-do

Notes

Start Date: ___/___/___   My Goal's Target Date: ___/___/___   How Long It Took Me To Attain My Goal
Number of Days: _____

MY HABIT & GOALS TRACKER

This Month's Habit to help me attain my Goals:

Circle each day you stick to your habit - cross off each day you don't...

_____
_____
_____

01	02	03	04	05	06
07	08	09	10	11	12
13	14	15	16	17	18
19	20	21	22	23	24
25	26	27	28	29	30

Why I want to gain this habit:

What I learned this week:

This Week's Motivation - How I will reward myself...

My STAR rating for this week:
☆ ☆ ☆ ☆ ☆

My step-by-step action plan:
- ○
- ○
- ○
- ○
- ○
- ○

Due date: ___/___   Completed:
___/___
___/___
___/___
___/___
___/___

My Personal Review:

How I rate my week's efforts: ☆☆☆☆☆

Parent Notes:

Notes From My Coach:

©2025 Barb V All Rights Reserved   The F.I.X.ed Athlete Program   The Kid Factor, LLC
HABITS & GOALS

MY WEEKLY PLANNER

WEEK OF:

Monday

Tuesday

Wednesday

Thursday

Friday

Saturday

Sunday

to-do

Notes

Start Date: ___ / ___ / ___

My Goal's Target Date: ___ / ___ / ___

How Long It Took Me To Attain My Goal
Number of Days: _____

MY HABIT & GOALS TRACKER

This Month's Habit to help me attain my Goals:

Circle each day you stick to your habit - cross off each day you don't...

01	02	03	04	05	06
07	08	09	10	11	12
13	14	15	16	17	18
19	20	21	22	23	24
25	26	27	28	29	30

Why I want to gain this habit:

What I learned this week:

This Week's Motivation - How I will reward myself...

My STAR rating for this week:
☆ ☆ ☆ ☆ ☆

My step-by-step action plan:
- ○
- ○
- ○
- ○
- ○
- ○

Due date: ___ / ___
___ / ___
___ / ___
___ / ___
___ / ___
___ / ___

Completed:

My Personal Review:

How I rate my week's efforts: ☆ ☆ ☆ ☆ ☆

Notes From My Coach:

Parent Notes:

©2025 Barb V All Rights Reserved

The F.I.X.ed Athlete Program
HABITS & GOALS

The Kid Factor, LLC

MY WEEKLY PLANNER

WEEK OF:

Monday

Tuesday

Wednesday

Thursday

Friday

Saturday

Sunday

to-do

Notes

Start Date: __/__/__   My Goal's Target Date: __/__/__   How Long It Took Me To Attain My Goal
Number of Days: _____

MY HABIT & GOALS TRACKER

This Month's Habit to help me attain my Goals:

Circle each day you stick to your habit - cross off each day you don't...

01	02	03	04	05	06
07	08	09	10	11	12
13	14	15	16	17	18
19	20	21	22	23	24
25	26	27	28	29	30

Why I want to gain this habit:

What I learned this week:

This Week's Motivation - How I will reward myself...

My STAR rating for this week:
☆☆☆☆☆

My step-by-step action plan:
- ○
- ○
- ○
- ○
- ○
- ○

Due date:
__/__
__/__
__/__
__/__
__/__
__/__

Completed:

My Personal Review:

How I rate my week's efforts: ☆☆☆☆☆

Parent Notes:

Notes From My Coach:

©2025 Barb V All Rights Reserved   The F.I.X.ed Athlete Program   The Kid Factor, LLC
HABITS & GOALS

MY WEEKLY PLANNER

WEEK OF:

Monday

Tuesday

Wednesday

Thursday

Friday

Saturday

Sunday

to-do

Notes

Start Date: ___/___/___   My Goal's Target Date: ___/___/___   How Long It Took Me To Attain My Goal
Number of Days: _____

MY HABIT & GOALS TRACKER

This Month's Habit to help me attain my Goals:

Circle each day you stick to your habit - cross off each day you don't...

_____
_____
_____

01	02	03	04	05	06
07	08	09	10	11	12
13	14	15	16	17	18
19	20	21	22	23	24
25	26	27	28	29	30

Why I want to gain this habit:

What I learned this week:

This Week's Motivation - How I will reward myself...

My STAR rating for this week:
☆ ☆ ☆ ☆ ☆

My step-by-step action plan:
- ○
- ○
- ○
- ○
- ○
- ○

Due date:	Completed:
___/___	
___/___	
___/___	
___/___	
___/___	
___/___	

My Personal Review:

How I rate my week's efforts: ☆☆☆☆☆

Parent Notes:

Notes From My Coach:

MY MONTHLY PLANNER

Month: _____ Year: _____

Monday	Tuesday	Wednesday	Thursday	Friday	Saturday	Sunday

Notes:

_____
_____
_____
_____
_____
_____
_____

30 DAY **CHALLENGE**

GOAL: ....

MY WHY: ....

START DATE: ....

REWARD: ....

1 2 3 4 5
6 7 8 9 10
11 12 13 14 15
16 17 18 19 20
21 22 23 24 25
26 27 28 29 30

©2025 Barb V All Rights Reserved

The Silent Assassins
HABITS & GOALS

The Kid Factor, LLC

MY WEEKLY PLANNER

WEEK OF:

Monday

Tuesday

Wednesday

Thursday

Friday

Saturday

Sunday

To-do

Notes

Start Date: __/__/__   My Goal's Target Date: __/__/__   How Long It Took Me To Attain My Goal
Number of Days: _____

MY HABIT & GOALS TRACKER

This Month's Habit to help me attain my Goals:

Circle each day you stick to your habit - cross off each day you don't...

_____

01	02	03	04	05	06
07	08	09	10	11	12
13	14	15	16	17	18
19	20	21	22	23	24
25	26	27	28	29	30

Why I want to gain this habit:

What I learned this week:

This Week's Motivation - How I will reward myself...

My STAR rating for this week: ☆ ☆ ☆ ☆ ☆

My step-by-step action plan:
- ○
- ○
- ○
- ○
- ○
- ○

Due date: __/__/__ __/__/__ __/__/__ __/__/__ __/__/__ __/__/__

Completed:

My Personal Review:

How I rate my week's efforts: ☆☆☆☆☆

Notes From My Coach:

Parent Notes:

MY WEEKLY PLANNER

WEEK OF:

Monday

Tuesday

Wednesday

Thursday

Friday

Saturday

Sunday

to-do

Notes

Start Date: / /   My Goal's Target Date: / /   How Long It Took Me To Attain My Goal
Number of Days:_____

MY HABIT & GOALS TRACKER

This Month's Habit to help me attain my Goals:

Circle each day you stick to your habit - cross off each day you don't...

01	02	03	04	05	06
07	08	09	10	11	12
13	14	15	16	17	18
19	20	21	22	23	24
25	26	27	28	29	30

Why I want to gain this habit:

What I learned this week:

This Week's Motivation - How I will reward myself...

My STAR rating for this week:
☆ ☆ ☆ ☆ ☆

My step-by-step action plan:
- ○
- ○
- ○
- ○
- ○
- ○

Due date:
/ /
/ /
/ /
/ /
/ /
/ /

Completed:

My Personal Review:

How I rate my week's efforts: ☆☆☆☆☆

Parent Notes:

Notes From My Coach:

MY WEEKLY PLANNER

WEEK OF:

Monday

Tuesday

Wednesday

Thursday

Friday

Saturday

Sunday

To-do

Notes

Start Date: / /   My Goal's Target Date: / /   How Long It Took Me To Attain My Goal
Number of Days: _____

MY HABIT & GOALS TRACKER

This Month's Habit to help me attain my Goals:

Circle each day you stick to your habit - cross off each day you don't...

01	02	03	04	05	06
07	08	09	10	11	12
13	14	15	16	17	18
19	20	21	22	23	24
25	26	27	28	29	30

Why I want to gain this habit:

What I learned this week:

This Week's Motivation - How I will reward myself...

My STAR rating for this week:
☆ ☆ ☆ ☆ ☆

My step-by-step action plan:
- ○
- ○
- ○
- ○
- ○
- ○

Due date:
 / /
 / /
 / /
 / /
 / /
 / /

Completed:

My Personal Review:

How I rate my week's efforts: ☆ ☆ ☆ ☆ ☆

Parent Notes:

Notes From My Coach:

©2025 Barb V All Rights Reserved   The F.I.X.ed Athlete Program
HABITS & GOALS   The Kid Factor, LLC

MY WEEKLY PLANNER

WEEK OF:

Monday

Tuesday

Wednesday

Thursday

Friday

Saturday

Sunday

to-do

Notes

Start Date: __ / __ / __   My Goal's Target Date: __ / __ / __   How Long It Took Me To Attain My Goal
Number of Days: _____

MY HABIT & GOALS TRACKER

This Month's Habit to help me attain my Goals:

Circle each day you stick to your habit - cross off each day you don't...

_____
_____
_____

01	02	03	04	05	06
07	08	09	10	11	12
13	14	15	16	17	18
19	20	21	22	23	24
25	26	27	28	29	30

Why I want to gain this habit:

What I learned this week:

This Week's Motivation - How I will reward myself...

My STAR rating for this week:
☆ ☆ ☆ ☆ ☆

My step-by-step action plan:

- ○ _____
- ○ _____
- ○ _____
- ○ _____
- ○ _____
- ○ _____

Due date:

__ / __
__ / __
__ / __
__ / __
__ / __
__ / __

Completed:

_____
_____
_____
_____
_____
_____

My Personal Review:

How I rate my week's efforts: ☆☆☆☆☆

Parent Notes:

Notes From My Coach:

MY WEEKLY PLANNER

WEEK OF:

Monday

Tuesday

Wednesday

Thursday

Friday

Saturday

Sunday

to-do

Notes

Start Date: __/__/__   My Goal's Target Date: __/__/__   How Long It Took Me To Attain My Goal
Number of Days:_____

MY HABIT & GOALS TRACKER

This Month's Habit to help me attain my Goals:

Circle each day you stick to your habit -
cross off each day you don't...

01	02	03	04	05	06
07	08	09	10	11	12
13	14	15	16	17	18
19	20	21	22	23	24
25	26	27	28	29	30

Why I want to gain this habit:

What I learned this week:

This Week's Motivation - How I will reward myself...

My STAR rating for this week:
☆ ☆ ☆ ☆ ☆

My step-by-step action plan:
- ○
- ○
- ○
- ○
- ○
- ○

Due date:
__/__
__/__
__/__
__/__
__/__
__/__

Completed:

My Personal Review:

How I rate my week's efforts: ☆☆☆☆☆

Notes From My Coach:

Parent Notes:

©2025 Barb V All Rights Reserved   The F.I.X.ed Athlete Program   The Kid Factor, LLC
HABITS & GOALS

MY MONTHLY PLANNER

Month: _____ Year: _____

Monday	Tuesday	Wednesday	Thursday	Friday	Saturday	Sunday
☐	☐	☐	☐	☐	☐	☐
☐	☐	☐	☐	☐	☐	☐
☐	☐	☐	☐	☐	☐	☐
☐	☐	☐	☐	☐	☐	☐
☐	☐	☐	☐	☐	☐	☐

Notes:

30 DAY **CHALLENGE**

GOAL:

MY WHY:

START DATE:

REWARD:

1	2	3	4	5
6	7	8	9	10
11	12	13	14	15
16	17	18	19	20
21	22	23	24	25
26	27	28	29	30

©2025 Barb V All Rights Reserved

The Silent Assassins
HABITS & GOALS

The Kid Factor, LLC

MY WEEKLY PLANNER

WEEK OF:

Monday

Tuesday

Wednesday

Thursday

Friday

Saturday

Sunday

to-do

Notes

Start Date: ___/___/___ My Goal's Target Date: ___/___/___ How Long It Took Me To Attain My Goal
Number of Days: _____

MY HABIT & GOALS TRACKER

This Month's Habit to help me attain my Goals:

Circle each day you stick to your habit - cross off each day you don't...

01	02	03	04	05	06
07	08	09	10	11	12
13	14	15	16	17	18
19	20	21	22	23	24
25	26	27	28	29	30

Why I want to gain this habit:

What I learned this week:

This Week's Motivation - How I will reward myself...

My STAR rating for this week:
☆ ☆ ☆ ☆ ☆

My step-by-step action plan:
- ○
- ○
- ○
- ○
- ○
- ○

Due date: ___/___/___
___/___/___
___/___/___
___/___/___
___/___/___
___/___/___

Completed:

My Personal Review:

How I rate my week's efforts: ☆☆☆☆☆

Parent Notes:

Notes From My Coach:

MY WEEKLY PLANNER

WEEK OF:

Monday

Tuesday

Wednesday

Thursday

Friday

Saturday

Sunday

to-do

Notes

Start Date: __/__/__ My Goal's Target Date: __/__/__ How Long It Took Me To Attain My Goal Number of Days:_____

MY HABIT & GOALS TRACKER

This Month's Habit to help me attain my Goals:

_____
_____
_____

Circle each day you stick to your habit - cross off each day you don't...

01	02	03	04	05	06
07	08	09	10	11	12
13	14	15	16	17	18
19	20	21	22	23	24
25	26	27	28	29	30

Why I want to gain this habit:

What I learned this week:

This Week's Motivation - How I will reward myself...

My STAR rating for this week:
☆ ☆ ☆ ☆ ☆

My step-by-step action plan:
○ _____
○ _____
○ _____
○ _____
○ _____
○ _____

Due date:
__/__
__/__
__/__
__/__
__/__
__/__

Completed:

My Personal Review:

How I rate my week's efforts: ☆☆☆☆☆

Notes From My Coach:

Parent Notes:

©2025 Barb V All Rights Reserved   The F.I.X.ed Athlete Program   The Kid Factor, LLC
HABITS & GOALS

MY WEEKLY PLANNER

WEEK OF:

Monday

Tuesday

Wednesday

Thursday

Friday

Saturday

Sunday

to-do

Notes

Start Date: __ / __ / __   My Goal's Target Date: __ / __ / __   How Long It Took Me To Attain My Goal
Number of Days: _____

MY HABIT & GOALS TRACKER

This Month's Habit to help me attain my Goals:

Circle each day you stick to your habit - cross off each day you don't...

01	02	03	04	05	06
07	08	09	10	11	12
13	14	15	16	17	18
19	20	21	22	23	24
25	26	27	28	29	30

Why I want to gain this habit:

What I learned this week:

This Week's Motivation - How I will reward myself...

My STAR rating for this week:
☆ ☆ ☆ ☆ ☆

My step-by-step action plan:
-
-
-
-
-
-

Due date:
__ / __
__ / __
__ / __
__ / __
__ / __
__ / __

Completed:

My Personal Review:

How I rate my week's efforts: ☆ ☆ ☆ ☆ ☆

Notes From My Coach:

Parent Notes:

MY WEEKLY PLANNER

WEEK OF:

Monday

Tuesday

Wednesday

Thursday

Friday

Saturday

Sunday

to-do

Notes

Start Date: ___/___/___ My Goal's Target Date: ___/___/___ How Long It Took Me To Attain My Goal
Number of Days:_____

MY HABIT & GOALS TRACKER

This Month's Habit to help me attain my Goals:

Circle each day you stick to your habit - cross off each day you don't...

....
....
....

01	02	03	04	05	06
07	08	09	10	11	12
13	14	15	16	17	18
19	20	21	22	23	24
25	26	27	28	29	30

Why I want to gain this habit:

What I learned this week:

This Week's Motivation - How I will reward myself...

My STAR rating for this week:
☆ ☆ ☆ ☆ ☆

My step-by-step action plan:

- ○
- ○
- ○
- ○
- ○
- ○

Due date: ___/___ ___/___ ___/___ ___/___ ___/___ ___/___

Completed:

My Personal Review:

How I rate my week's efforts: ☆ ☆ ☆ ☆ ☆

Notes From My Coach:

Parent Notes:

©2025 Barb V All Rights Reserved   The F.I.X.ed Athlete Program   The Kid Factor, LLC
HABITS & GOALS

MY WEEKLY PLANNER

WEEK OF:

Monday

Tuesday

Wednesday

Thursday

Friday

Saturday

Sunday

to-do

Notes

Start Date: ___ / ___ / ___

My Goal's Target Date: ___ / ___ / ___

How Long It Took Me To Attain My Goal
Number of Days: _____

MY HABIT & GOALS TRACKER

This Month's Habit to help me attain my Goals:

Circle each day you stick to your habit - cross off each day you don't...

_____
_____
_____

01	02	03	04	05	06
07	08	09	10	11	12
13	14	15	16	17	18
19	20	21	22	23	24
25	26	27	28	29	30

Why I want to gain this habit:

What I learned this week:

This Week's Motivation - How I will reward myself...

My STAR rating for this week:
☆ ☆ ☆ ☆ ☆

My step-by-step action plan:

- ○ _____
- ○ _____
- ○ _____
- ○ _____
- ○ _____
- ○ _____

Due date:

___ / ___
___ / ___
___ / ___
___ / ___
___ / ___
___ / ___

Completed:

My Personal Review:

How I rate my week's efforts: ☆ ☆ ☆ ☆ ☆

Parent Notes:

Notes From My Coach:

©2025 Barb V All Rights Reserved

The F.I.X.ed Athlete Program
HABITS & GOALS

The Kid Factor, LLC

date

brain dump time...

to do list

random thoughts

think and make decision about

Section # 3
PERSONAL DEVELOPMENT ACTIVITIES & ATHLETE'S PLAYbook

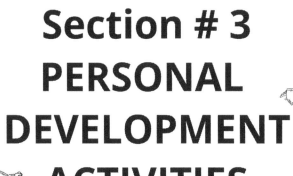

I'mPossible

⭐ SUPERSTAR TIME SYSTEM ⭐
🏋 Train Your Time Like You Train Your Body 🏋

Great athletes and high achievers don't do everything — they do the *right* things at the *right* time. Here's The SUPERSTAR's In Training all-in-one system to **decide** *what to do*, *when to do it*, and *how to win your day*. Use this system every day to plan your week, month, season, and year. You'll be amazed where you will be even before you complete this book!

STEP 1: 🌀 FILTER With the 5 D's
Before anything gets your time, ask:

TASK	ACTION	EXAMPLES
☑ Do it	If it's quick & important, do it now	Fill water bottle, stretch, respond to coach
🍀 Delegate it	Can someone help? Let them	Ask for help prepping gear or timing sprints
✖ Delete it	Is it useless or distracting? Cut it	Random scrolling, gossip, extra YouTube time
⏳ Delay it	Important but not urgent? Schedule it	Video games after training, Netflix post-study
🎨 Design it	Big or long-term? Break it into steps	School project, meal prep, workout plan

Use this to clear your plate before you fill it.

STEP 2: 📋 PLAN – PRIORITIZE – PERFORM

Now that you've cleared out distractions, let's lock in your **top 3 actions** for the day:

Priority	ACTIVITY	Time Blocked
Must Do		
Should Do		
Could Do		

> **Plan**: Think clearly about what matters most for your body, brain, and sport.

> **Prioritize**: Order your goals by impact and importance.

> **Perform**: Start with #1. Focus. Finish. Move on. Repeat.

⚡ PRO TIP ⚡

Before your day starts, sort everything through the 5 D's.
PROFESSIONAL ATHLETES & HIGH PERFORMERS TYPICALLY DO THIS THE NIGHT BEFORE...

Then, write your top 3 and attack your day like it's game time.

My Day –

My focus for today is:
_____
_____
_____

Date	What Time I Went To Bed Last Night?
	What Time Did I Wake Up Today?
I had _____ hours of sleep	

Today's practice was...

3 things I want to accomplish today...

1. ....
2. ....
3. ....

What I learned today?

What challenged me today?

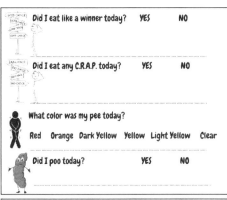

Did I eat like a winner today? YES   NO

Did I eat any C.R.A.P. today? YES   NO

What color was my pee today?
Red   Orange   Dark Yellow   Yellow   Light Yellow   Clear

Did I poo today? YES   NO

WHAT I ATE TODAY?

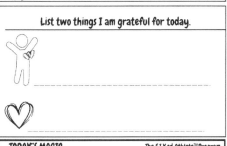

List two things I am grateful for today.

What's my mindset today?

Who and How did I serve or help somebody today?

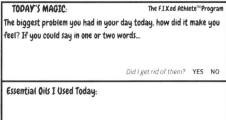

TODAY'S MAGIC: The F.I.X.ed Athlete™ Program
The biggest problem you had in your day today, how did it make you feel? If you could say in one or two words...

Did I get rid of them? YES   NO

Essential Oils I Used Today:

What I'm looking forward to tomorrow?

WRITE YOUR "Dear Future Me" LETTER
Tell Me What You Liked BEST About This Book...

Instructions: A **DEAR FUTURE ME** letter...

Writing to yourself helps you connect with your goals, reflect on your strengths, and set a vision for the kind of person and athlete you're becoming. When you read this again at the end, you'll be amazed at how far you've come! The challenges you've overcome and the amazing things you have accomplished in a short period of time...

TURN TO page #286
to write yourself your amazing letter...

What to Include in Your Letter:
You don't need to get it "perfect." Just be honest. Talk to yourself like a trusted coach or best friend...
Consider answering some of these prompts in your letter:
- Here's who I am right now...
- This is what I hope to achieve over the next 90 days...
- One thing I really want to improve is...
- I believe I can become...
- When things get tough, I'll remind myself that...
- A strength I want to build on is...
- I'm excited about...
- My biggest dream is...

Writing a "Dear Future Me" letter teaches powerful personal development lessons for young athletes and anyone committed to growth.

1. Self-Awareness
This is your opportunity to pause and reflect on who you are right now — your habits, emotions, mindset, goals, and challenges. This deepens your understanding of yourself in the moment.

2. Goal Setting & Vision
You can clarify what you want — not just what others expect. This activity helps you to focus on your own dreams and visualize what success looks like, on your terms.

3. Accountability
By writing down your hopes, goals, and intentions, you're making a promise to yourself. That future version of you becomes someone you want to show up as and for.

4. Emotional Regulation
It builds emotional intelligence by letting you express your fears, worries, hopes, and confidence — and it gives you a safe place to work through them. The next 90 days will be incredible!

5. Perspective Over Time
When you re-read the letter later, you will see how much you've grown. Things that once felt hard might now feel easy — and that's empowering. This is a SUPER POWER opportunity - take full advantage of it.

6. Motivation During Tough Times
Your own words can become your fuel. A letter filled with belief, dreams, and encouragement can be exactly what you need on a hard day, after a difficult practice, after losing an important competition, or even after getting a poor grade in school.

7. Identity & Ownership
You start to understand: "**I am the author of my story!**" You're not just reacting to life — you're designing your own life.

So turn to page **#286** and
WRITE TO YOUR FUTURE SUPERSTAR SELF!

My Day —

My focus for today is:
_____
_____
_____

Date	What Time I Went To Bed Last Night?
	What Time Did I Wake Up Today?
I had _____ hours of sleep	

Today's practice was...

3 things I want to accomplish today...
1. ....
2. ....
3. ....

What I learned today?

What challenged me today?

Did I eat like a winner today?   YES   NO

Did I eat any C.R.A.P. today?   YES   NO

What color was my pee today?
Red   Orange   Dark Yellow   Yellow   Light Yellow   Clear

Did I poo today?   YES   NO

WHAT I ATE TODAY?

List two things I am grateful for today.

What's my mindset today?

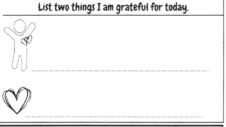

Who and How did I serve or help somebody today?

TODAY'S MAGIC: *The F.I.X.ed Athlete™ Program*
The biggest problem you had in your day today, how did it make you feel? If you could say in one or two words...

Did I get rid of them?   YES   NO

Essential Oils I Used Today:

What I'm looking forward to tomorrow?

A SUPERSTAR'S POWER CENTER
ORGANIZING YOUR BEDROOM

HEY SUPERSTAR

Every elite athlete needs a space that helps them recover, focus, train, and dream big. Your room is more than just where you sleep — it's your power center.
This week, you'll take full ownership and set it up like a champion. Let's GO!

This Week's Challenge:

WHY THIS MATTERS
A clean, organized room helps your brain focus, your body recover, and your mindset stay sharp. Champions know: outer order = inner calm.

☑ SUPERSTAR POWER CENTER CHECKLIST
Color in the box next to each one when you're done!

ZONE 1: SLEEP + RECOVERY
(review the Sleep pages in Section #1)
- ☐ Bed is made and fresh
- ☐ Clean sheets + comfy pillow
- ☐ No electronics in bed zone at night
- ☐ Room is dark, cool temperature, and quiet at bedtime

ZONE 2: SCHOOL + STUDY
- ☐ Desk or quiet spot for homework
- ☐ Pens, pencils, and supplies ready
- ☐ Backpack packed and organized
- ☐ Tomorrow's outfit ready

ZONE 3: TRAINING GEAR
- ☐ Sport bag packed (use your other checklist!)
- ☐ Uniform, shoes, water bottle, towel, gear
- ☐ Practice schedule posted or noted
- ☐ Dirty gear in laundry, not on the floor

ZONE 4: DREAMS + FOCUS
- ☐ Vision board or inspiration poster on display
- ☐ Journal or reflection notebook nearby
- ☐ No clutter in sight = clear mind
- ☐ One personal item that motivates you

🏆 **Your Superstar Challenge: 15-Minute Room Reset** 🏆

Set a timer for 15 minutes every **SUNDAY & WEDNESDAY**.

Use that time to reset all four zones, toss trash, straighten up, and make sure you're set up for a winning week!

✏ Sketch Your Dream Room Layout!
(Draw or map out how you'd set up your ultimate Superstar's room — label your zones!)

My Day -

My focus for today is:
_____
_____
_____

Date	What Time I Went To Bed Last Night?
	What Time Did I Wake Up Today?
I had _____ hours of sleep	

Today's practice was...

3 things I want to accomplish today...

1. _____
2. _____
3. _____

What I learned today?

What challenged me today?

Did I eat like a winner today?   YES   NO

Did I eat any C.R.A.P. today?   YES   NO

What color was my pee today?
Red   Orange   Dark Yellow   Yellow   Light Yellow   Clear

Did I poo today?   YES   NO

WHAT I ATE TODAY?

List two things I am grateful for today.

What's my mindset today?

😊 😴 🙁 😐 😠 🤢 ☹️

Who and How did I serve or help somebody today?

TODAY'S MAGIC: The F.I.X.ed Athlete™ Program

The biggest problem you had in your day today, how did it make you feel? If you could say in one or two words...

Did I get rid of them?   YES   NO

Essential Oils I Used Today:

What I'm looking forward to tomorrow?

The SUPERSTAR In Training - Fitness Challenge

Tracking your baseline and progress over time helps you see just how far you've come—and where to focus your efforts next. It's not about being perfect; it's about getting stronger, faster, and more confident with every rep, jump, sprint, and skill. As a SUPERSTAR In Training, your goal is always to progress forward – both inside and out.

📅 TESTING DAY:

Time of Day: _____

Today's Body Weight (lbs): _____

🎖 SELECT YOUR LEVEL

Pick the level based on your age group. Compete only with yourself—and go for that personal best!

LEVEL	AGE GROUP	INTENSITY
⭐ Level 1	Ages - & Under	Foundation Training (Fun Form & Focus)
⭐⭐ Level 2	Ages 10 – 12	Challenge Training (Speed & Strength)
⭐⭐⭐ Level 3	Ages 13 +	Elite Training (Power & Performance)

💪 THE SUPERSTAR FITNESS CHALLENGES 💪

In each of the following activities, record your **best of 3 attempts** for each test. You may decide to select any of the times, distances, or object you want in the Sprint, Jump Rope, and throw. Be honest. Be tough. Be proud.

TEST	Attempt #1	Attempt #2	Attempt #3	PERSONAL BEST
Push-Ups (Max reps)				
Sit-Ups (Max reps)				
Jump Rope (Reps in 1 – 2 - 5 minutes)				
Burpees (Reps in 1 minute)				
Plank Hold (Seconds)				
Wall Sit (Seconds)				
Sprint – 40 / 50 / 100 -yard dash (Seconds)				
Standing Throw (Ft/In) Baseball, Softball, Football				
High Jump Touch (Wall mark)				
Broad Jump (Ft/In)				
Leg Raise Hold – 6 in. (Seconds)				

My Day —

My focus for today is:
_____
_____
_____
_____

Date	What Time I Went To Bed Last Night?
	What Time Did I Wake Up Today?
I had _____ hours of sleep	

Today's practice was...

3 things I want to accomplish today...

What I learned today?

What challenged me today?

Did I eat like a winner today?   YES   NO

Did I eat any C.R.A.P. today?   YES   NO

What color was my pee today?

Red   Orange   Dark Yellow   Yellow   Light Yellow   Clear

Did I poo today?   YES   NO

WHAT I ATE TODAY?

List two things I am grateful for today.

What's my mindset today?

Who and How did I serve or help somebody today?

TODAY'S MAGIC: The F.I.X.ed Athlete™ Program

The biggest problem you had in your day today, how did it make you feel? If you could say in one or two words...

Did I get rid of them?   YES   NO

Essential Oils I Used Today:

What I'm looking forward to tomorrow?

HEY SUPERSTAR

Show Us How A-Maze-Ing You Are!

Are you ready to work your focus, concentration, spatial awareness, problem solving, perpetual speed, flow-state control, and some hand-eye coordination? All of these skills are needed by athletes and working the following mazes, you will strengthen these skills today...

Solutions on page #301

112

My Day –

My focus for today is:
_____
_____
_____

Date _____

What Time I Went To Bed Last Night? _____

What Time Did I Wake Up Today? _____

I had _____ hours of sleep

Today's practice was...

3 things I want to accomplish today...

1. _____
2. _____
3. _____

What I learned today?

What challenged me today?

Did I eat like a winner today?   YES   NO

Did I eat any C.R.A.P. today?   YES   NO

What color was my pee today?

Red   Orange   Dark Yellow   Yellow   Light Yellow   Clear

Did I poo today?   YES   NO

WHAT I ATE TODAY?

List two things I am grateful for today.

What's my mindset today?

Who and How did I serve or help somebody today?

TODAY'S MAGIC: The F.I.X.ed Athlete™ Program

The biggest problem you had in your day today, how did it make you feel? If you could say in one or two words...

Did I get rid of them?   YES   NO

Essential Oils I Used Today:

What I'm looking forward to tomorrow?

AS AN ATHLETE, YOU NEED TO KNOW YOUR BODY PARTS & WHAT THEY DO.

INSTRUCTIONS:
- Fill in each region of your body. Stick to the color assigned so that you begin associating each part with its unique role.
- Label Each Area by writing the name next to it with a line or arrow.
- **Bonus Challenge:** After coloring, write down which movements or sports actions use each part.

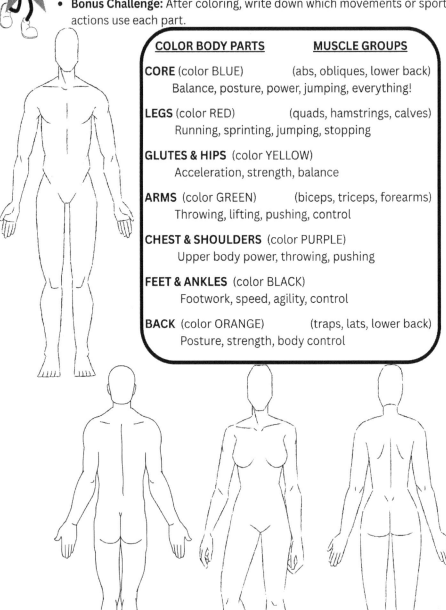

COLOR BODY PARTS	**MUSCLE GROUPS**
CORE (color BLUE)	(abs, obliques, lower back)
Balance, posture, power, jumping, everything!	
LEGS (color RED)	(quads, hamstrings, calves)
Running, sprinting, jumping, stopping	
GLUTES & HIPS (color YELLOW)	
Acceleration, strength, balance	
ARMS (color GREEN)	(biceps, triceps, forearms)
Throwing, lifting, pushing, control	
CHEST & SHOULDERS (color PURPLE)	
Upper body power, throwing, pushing	
FEET & ANKLES (color BLACK)	
Footwork, speed, agility, control	
BACK (color ORANGE)	(traps, lats, lower back)
Posture, strength, body control	

MyDay –

My focus for today is:
_____
_____
_____

Date	What Time I Went To Bed Last Night?
	What Time Did I Wake Up Today?
I had _____ hours of sleep	

Today's practice was...

3 things I want to accomplish today...
1. _____
2. _____
3. _____

What I learned today?

What challenged me today?

Did I eat like a winner today?   YES   NO

Did I eat any C.R.A.P. today?   YES   NO

What color was my pee today?

Red   Orange   Dark Yellow   Yellow   Light Yellow   Clear

Did I poo today?   YES   NO

WHAT I ATE TODAY?

List two things I am grateful for today.

What's my mindset today?

Who and How did I serve or help somebody today?

TODAY'S MAGIC: The F.I.X.ed Athlete™ Program
The biggest problem you had in your day today, how did it make you feel? If you could say in one or two words...

Did I get rid of them?   YES   NO

Essential Oils I Used Today:

What I'm looking forward to tomorrow?

SCHULTE TABLES

How To Use Schulte Tables for Athletes

Reaction Training:
Start at 1 and touch the numbers in ascending or descending order as quickly as possible.
Scan the table horizontally and vertically to find all the numbers in order as quickly as possible
Time yourself or have a coach time you to track progress.

- **Focus and Awareness:**

Instead of touching the numbers, verbally call out each number as you find it.
Increase the challenge by calling out the next number but touching the previous one (e.g., say "2" but touch "1").

Cognitive Flexibility:
Try finding the numbers or letters in a reverse order (25 to 1) or (Z to A).
Alternatively, you can find odd numbers first and then even numbers.

Game Options:

Find Odd / Even numbers

Name the sporting equipment

Name the letters

Create your own tables

Challenge team members and friends Play for speed & accuracy

Skip by multiples. 2s, 3s, 4s, 4s, 5s, and so on through the 10 x 10 tables

Memorize rows and columns; see how many you can recite without error

MAKE IT FUN AND CHALLENGING!

My Fastest Time: _____

5	8	24	3	17
19	4	11	22	6
1	13	21	9	25
10	18	7	16	2
23	15	14	20	12

My Fastest Time: _____

A	M	H	R	K
I	B	X	U	G
P	Y	C	J	N
L	S	D	O	Q
E	W	T	F	V

My Fastest Time: _____

7	24	13	19	2
20	11	5	16	8
3	22	9	14	25
17	6	21	1	10
12	18	4	23	15

My Fastest Time: _____

My Fastest Time: _____

F	J	N	D	K
G	C	T	W	H
M	X	R	Z	U
O	V	E	Y	A
B	S	I	L	P

My Fastest Time: _____

C	10	3	E	J
H	2	A	I	5
L	6	B	4	7
D	11	8	M	F
K	1	G	9	12

# MyDay

My focus for today is:
_____
_____
_____

Date _____
What Time I Went To Bed Last Night? _____
What Time Did I Wake Up Today? _____
I had _____ hours of sleep

Today's practice was...

3 things I want to accomplish today...

What I learned today?

What challenged me today?

Did I eat like a winner today?   YES   NO

Did I eat any C.R.A.P. today?   YES   NO

What color was my pee today?
Red   Orange   Dark Yellow   Yellow   Light Yellow   Clear

Did I poo today?   YES   NO

WHAT I ATE TODAY?

List two things I am grateful for today.
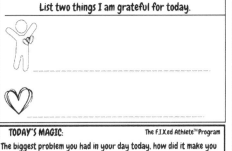

What's my mindset today?

Who and How did I serve or help somebody today?
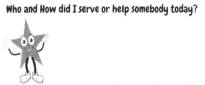

TODAY'S MAGIC: The F.I.X.ed Athlete™ Program
The biggest problem you had in your day today, how did it make you feel? If you could say in one or two words...

Did I get rid of them?   YES   NO

Essential Oils I Used Today:

What I'm looking forward to tomorrow?

HEY SUPERSTAR SUGAR SWAP CHALLENGE
Unlock Your True Power by Cutting Back on Sugar!

The average kid in the U.S. eats over 17 teaspoons of added sugar per day. (That's like drinking 3–4 sodas every day!) Too much sugar can harm your memory, focus, and decision-making.→ That affects your play, your studies, and your mindset! "THEY" even hide added sugar in peanut butter!

This Week's Challenge:

⚠️ SUGAR HURTS YOUR GAME

MOST ATHLETES DON'T REALIZE THIS — BUT EATING TOO MUCH ADDED SUGAR CAN SLOW YOU DOWN, MAKE YOU TIRED FASTER, AND EVEN AFFECT HOW YOUR BRAIN WORKS.

- SUGAR GIVES YOU A QUICK ENERGY SPIKE... THEN A CRASH.
- SUGAR CRASHES INCREASE MENTAL ERRORS DURING COMPETITION.
- → YOU MIGHT FEEL TIRED, DIZZY, OR IRRITABLE MID-PRACTICE.
- SUGAR CAN CAUSE INFLAMMATION IN YOUR MUSCLES.
- → RECOVERY IS SLOWER, SORENESS LASTS LONGER.
- TOO MUCH SUGAR CAN HARM YOUR MEMORY, FOCUS, AND DECISION-MAKING.
- → THAT AFFECTS YOUR PLAY, YOUR STUDIES, AND YOUR MINDSET!
- SUGAR CONTRIBUTES TO CHRONIC INFLAMMATION, WHICH CAUSES LONGER RECOVERY TIMES, MORE SORENESS, AND HIGHER RISK OF OVERUSE INJURIES.

👀 THE SCARY TRUTH:

- A STUDY OF ELITE YOUTH ATHLETES SHOWED THAT THOSE WITH DIETS HIGH IN SUGAR HAD MORE FREQUENT DIGESTIVE ISSUES, MUSCLE CRAMPS, & DEHYDRATION EPISODES — ESPECIALLY DURING HEAT TRAINING OR TOURNAMENTS.
- ADDED SUGAR IS HIDING IN *SPORTS DRINKS, KETCHUP, GRANOLA BARS, CEREAL, CRACKERS, AND EVEN YOGURT!

  TOO MUCH SUGAR CAN RAISE YOUR RISK OF:
  - EARLY FATIGUE
  - ACNE AND SKIN ISSUES
  - BRAIN FOG AND MOOD SWINGS
  - TYPE 2 DIABETES
  - LONG-TERM BRAIN AGING

🏆 TAKE THE SUGAR SWAP CHALLENGE! 🏆

SUGAR BOMB 🍭	SMARTER SWAP	YOUR CHOICE ✅
SODA OR SPORTS DRINK	WATER WITH LEMON OR FRUIT-INFUSED WATER	☐ _____
CANDY	FROZEN GRAPES, DRIED FRUIT (NO SUGAR ADDED)	☐ _____
SWEET BREAKFAST CEREAL	OATMEAL WITH BANANA + PEANUT BUTTER WITH NO SUGAR	☐ _____
FLAVORED YOGURT	PLAIN GREEK YOGURT + BERRIES + HONEY	☐ _____
GRANOLA BAR (WITH CORN SYRUP)	NUT & SEED MIX, OR HOMEMADE ENERGY BITES	☐ _____
STORE-BOUGHT SMOOTHIE	DIY SMOOTHIE: BANANA, SPINACH, FROZEN FRUIT	☐ _____
CHOCOLATE MILK	UNSWEETENED COCONUT MILK + COCOA + APPLE	☐ _____

🎯 THIS WEEK'S CHALLENGE:

- ✅ CHOOSE AT LEAST 2 SUGAR SWAPS A DAY
- ✅ TRACK HOW YOU FEEL BEFORE AND AFTER PRACTICE FOR 7 DAYS.
- ✅ EACH DAY, WRITE HOW YOUR BODY AND BRAIN FEEL:

  MY NOTES: (write these on your "My Day" pages)
  - ☀ I NOTICED I HAD MORE...
  - ⚡ I FELT LESS...
  - 💪 I WANT TO KEEP SWAPPING SUGAR BECAUSE...

YOUR BODY IS A MACHINE – SUGAR IS JUNK FUEL.

MyDay –

My focus for today is:

_____
_____
_____

Date

What Time I Went To Bed Last Night?

What Time Did I Wake Up Today?

I had _____ hours of sleep

Today's practice was...

3 things I want to accomplish today...

1. _____
2. _____
3. _____

What I learned today?

What challenged me today?

Did I eat like a winner today?   YES   NO

Did I eat any C.R.A.P. today?   YES   NO

What color was my pee today?
Red   Orange   Dark Yellow   Yellow   Light Yellow   Clear

Did I poo today?   YES   NO

WHAT I ATE TODAY?

List two things I am grateful for today.

What's my mindset today?

Who and How did I serve or help somebody today?

TODAY'S MAGIC: The F.I.X.ed Athlete™ Program

The biggest problem you had in your day today, how did it make you feel? If you could say in one or two words...

Did I get rid of them?   YES   NO

Essential Oils I Used Today:

What I'm looking forward to tomorrow?

HEY SUPERSTAR
SUGAR, YOUR BRAIN & YOUR PERFORMANCES...

DO YOU KNOW WHAT SUGAR IS DOING TO YOUR BRAIN & PERFORMANCES?

Your Challenge:
Here's a 15-question crossword puzzle designed to help athletes learn more about sugar, its effects on performance, and make healthier choices. This is perfect for building your memory & recall, vocabulary development, learning and analytical thinking, pattern recognition, skill acquisition, and strategic thinking... while reinforcing lessons through play and cognitive engagement. ALL skills SUPERSTAR Athletes need to take their play to the next level...

Across:

1. THIS POPULAR TREAT IS HIGH IN ADDED SUGAR.
2. TOO MUCH SUGAR CAN AFFECT YOUR _____ HEALTH LONG TERM.
3. SUGAR MAY MAKE YOU FEEL TIRED OR _____
4. SUGAR CAN ALSO BE CALLED THIS ON A LABEL _____
5. A COMMON SUGARY DRINK.
6. SUGAR HUDES IN SNACKS UNDER THIS WORD THAT STARTS WITH "M."
7. INSTEAD OF SUGAR, ATHLTESE SHOULD FUEL WITH WHOLE _____
8. ATHLETES SHOULD STOP EATING THESE FOUR CATEGORIES OF POOR PERFORMANCE FOODS.

Down:

1. NATURAL SUGAR FROUND IN FRUIT.
2. SUGAR GIVES YOU A QUICK _____ BUT THEN A CRASH.
3. ATHLETES NEED THIS TYPE OF ENERGY, NOT SUGAR SPIKES.
4. A NATURAL SWEETENER MADE BY BEES.
5. THIS FORM OF SYRUP IS USED IN MANY PROCESSED FOODS.
6. SUGAR MESSES WITH YOU _____ FUNCTION AND FOCUS.
7. THIS IS THE BEST DRINK FOR HYDRATION.

Solutions on page #301

MyDay –

My focus for today is:

_____
_____
_____

Date	What Time I Went To Bed Last Night?
	What Time Did I Wake Up Today?
I had _____ hours of sleep	

Today's practice was...

3 things I want to accomplish today...

1. _____
2. _____
3. _____

What I learned today?

What challenged me today?

- Did I eat like a winner today? YES NO
- Did I eat any C.R.A.P. today? YES NO
- What color was my pee today?
  Red   Orange   Dark Yellow   Yellow   Light Yellow   Clear
- Did I poo today? YES NO

WHAT I ATE TODAY?

List two things I am grateful for today.

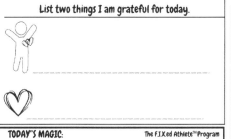

What's my mindset today?

Who and How did I serve or help somebody today?

TODAY'S MAGIC: The F.I.X.ed Athlete™ Program

The biggest problem you had in your day today, how did it make you feel? If you could say in one or two words...

Did I get rid of them? YES NO

Essential Oils I Used Today:

What I'm looking forward to tomorrow?

Interview a Teacher About Their Athletic Journey
Develop Excellent Communication & Story Telling Skills

Instructions: Today, your mission is to interview a teacher at your school who played sports in high school, college, professionally, or just for fun. You'll ask them about their athletic journey, the lessons they learned, and how it shaped who they are today. This activity teaches two important superstar skills:
- How to be an amazing interviewer – someone who listens deeply, asks great questions, and learns from others.
- How to be confidently interviewed – because as you grow in your sport, others will want to hear your story too!

Step-by-Step:
1. Prepare your questions.
Write 5–7 thoughtful questions to ask.

Example questions:
- What sport did you play, and how did you get started?
- What was your toughest moment, and how did you overcome it?
- What was the best lesson sports ever taught you?
- Did playing sports help you in your life or career?
- What advice would you give to young athletes like me?

2. Request the interview.
Politely ask a teacher if you may interview them. You can do it in person or write a short, respectful note. Be sure to thank them either way!

3. Set the tone.
Start with a smile, introduce yourself, and explain why you chose them. Speak clearly, sit up straight, and show curiosity.

4. Listen like a pro.
Make eye contact, nod, and take notes if you want to remember something. Let them finish their answers before jumping to the next question.

5. Wrap it up with gratitude.
End with a thank-you and ask for a photo to remember the moment!

Bonus Tip for Future Superstars:
As your career grows, coaches, reporters, and fans will want to know your story. Every great athlete becomes a great communicator—learning how to tell their story, inspire others, and stay humble. ★*This activity gets you ready for your future.* ★

My Day –

My focus for today is:
_____
_____
_____

Date	What Time I Went To Bed Last Night?
	What Time Did I Wake Up Today?
I had _____ hours of sleep	

Today's practice was...

3 things I want to accomplish today...

What I learned today?

What challenged me today?

Did I eat like a winner today?   YES   NO

Did I eat any C.R.A.P. today?   YES   NO

What color was my pee today?
Red   Orange   Dark Yellow   Yellow   Light Yellow   Clear

Did I poo today?   YES   NO

WHAT I ATE TODAY?

List two things I am grateful for today.

What's my mindset today?

Who and How did I serve or help somebody today?

TODAY'S MAGIC: The F.I.X.ed Athlete™ Program
The biggest problem you had in your day today, how did it make you feel? If you could say in one or two words...

Did I get rid of them?   YES   NO

Essential Oils I Used Today:

What I'm looking forward to tomorrow?

123

HEY SUPERSTAR JUGGLING MAKES YOU A BETTER ATHLETE!
BUILD YOUR BRAIN – BOOST YOUR GAME!

Did you know that learning to juggle literally changes your brain? Scientists have used fMRI scans and found that juggling increases Gray Matter in the areas of the brain responsible for:
- Motor Control
- Memory
- Spatial Reasoning

That means juggling helps you become smarter, quicker, more focused, and more in control of your body and mind—a true Superstar in Training!

This Week's Challenge:
WHY JUGGLING? START LEARNING HOW TO JUGGLE – BETTER!

ATHLETIC + COGNITIVE BENEFITS OF JUGGLING

When you juggle, you're strengthening:
- ☑ Focus and Concentration
- ☑ Hand-Eye Coordination
- ☑ Reaction Time
- ☑ Pattern Recognition
- ☑ Adaptability and Flow State
- ☑ Kinesthetic and Spatial Awareness
- ☑ Mental Resilience and Emotional Control
- ☑ Memory Recall and Perceptual Speed

◎ Your Juggling Challenge

Step 1: Start With Silks or Scarves

Light scarves or silks fall slowly, giving you time to learn the rhythm.
- Grab 3 lightweight scarves (or even tissues!)
- Stand tall, eyes forward, feet shoulder-width apart
- Toss one scarf gently in an arc to your opposite hand
- Add a second scarf, alternating hands
- Then try adding a third—slow and steady wins!

"Drop it? No problem! Pick it up and go again. Every drop is data!"

Step 2: Graduate to Ping Pong Balls or Tennis Balls

Once you've got the rhythm with scarves:
- Try with one ball — toss and catch in each hand
- Add a second, then a third
- Aim for smooth patterns, not speed

Visualization Tip:

Imagine a triangle in front of your chest — the balls or scarves travel in a figure-8 pattern, not straight lines!

Track Your Progress:

Track your progress on your "**MY DAY**" pages... If you practice this everyday, IMAGINE how good you will be 10 weeks from now!

Day 1 Successes: _____
What I'm Working On: _____
My Best Time Juggling Without a Drop: _____ seconds
Goal for Next Week: _____

✷ Challenge:

Teach someone else how to juggle by the end of the week!
If you can teach it, you've mastered it.

MyDay –

My focus for today is:
_____
_____
_____

Date _____

What Time I Went To Bed Last Night? _____

What Time Did I Wake Up Today? _____

I had _____ hours of sleep

Today's practice was...

3 things I want to accomplish today...
1. ....
2. ....
3. ....

What I learned today?

What challenged me today?

Did I eat like a winner today?   YES   NO

Did I eat any C.R.A.P. today?   YES   NO

What color was my pee today?
Red   Orange   Dark Yellow   Yellow   Light Yellow   Clear

Did I poo today?   YES   NO

WHAT I ATE TODAY?

List two things I am grateful for today.

What's my mindset today?

Who and How did I serve or help somebody today?

TODAY'S MAGIC: The F.I.X.ed Athlete™ Program
The biggest problem you had in your day today, how did it make you feel? If you could say in one or two words...

Did I get rid of them?   YES   NO

Essential Oils I Used Today:

What I'm looking forward to tomorrow?

HEY SUPERSTAR HIDDEN SUGARS WORDSEARCH

Eat like a Champion! Feel like a Champion! Perform like a Champion!

Your Challenge:
Athletes who regularly consume added sugar experience slower reaction times and lower endurance than those who fuel with whole foods.
Find the following 25 of more than 101 words food manufactures use to hide sugar in products. **ALWAYS READ THE INGREDIENT LABEL!**

E	M	C	W	R	N	S	U	G	A	R	A	K	I	I	C	G	S	A
U	K	O	O	D	E	X	T	R	O	S	E	S	X	P	A	Y	B	P
O	C	U	L	R	B	K	S	Y	R	U	P	V	I	G	T	V	H	N
F	E	K	C	A	N	E	J	U	I	C	E	K	G	L	A	F	P	P
F	R	F	C	L	S	S	R	I	C	E	S	Y	R	U	P	V	U	P
R	M	U	R	R	B	S	Y	I	B	E	C	T	L	C	W	R	O	T
U	J	G	C	C	D	J	E	R	D	V	L	Z	F	O	Y	E	M	Z
I	Y	R	C	T	O	Z	H	S	U	A	O	E	N	S	R	B	Y	L
T	Q	A	M	A	O	C	R	Y	M	P	S	P	E	E	M	Z	J	C
J	X	P	B	Z	R	S	O	Y	B	O	H	L	A	G	A	V	E	O
U	T	E	D	E	Y	A	E	N	T	R	P	O	V	R	L	U	R	R
I	O	J	W	P	E	L	M	C	U	A	O	U	N	E	T	S	R	N
C	T	U	J	L	R	T	U	E	M	T	R	W	M	E	S	D	A	S
E	P	I	J	A	Y	R	S	Z	L	E	S	O	N	N	Y	U	W	Y
A	U	C	B	T	F	O	Y	U	J	D	C	U	Y	S	R	C	S	R
D	W	E	I	H	T	T	Y	V	G	C	A	V	G	E	U	P	U	U
B	C	A	G	L	O	N	L	O	V	A	Y	N	A	A	P	G	G	P
D	S	I	A	H	J	A	C	V	B	N	R	B	J	B	R	C	A	E
Y	H	M	A	S	U	C	R	O	S	E	G	C	F	A	Z	X	R	R

SUGAR
SUCROSE
GLUCOSE
FRUCTOSE
CORN SYRUP
DEXTROSE
CANE JUICE

MALTOSE
RICE SYRUP
AGAVE
CORN SYRUP HONEY
MAPLE SYRUP
BROWN SUGAR
FRUIT JUICE

MOLASSES
BARLEY MALT
CARAMEL
HIGH FRUCTOSE
EVAPORATED CANE
RAW SUGAR
COCONUT SUGAR

SYRUP
GRAPE JUICE
BEET SUGAR
MALT SYRUP

Solutions on page #302

MyDay –

My focus for today is:
_____
_____
_____

Date
What Time I Went To Bed Last Night?
What Time Did I Wake Up Today?
I had _____ hours of sleep

Today's practice was...

3 things I want to accomplish today...

What I learned today?

What challenged me today?

Did I eat like a winner today?   YES   NO

Did I eat any C.R.A.P. today?   YES   NO

What color was my pee today?
Red   Orange   Dark Yellow   Yellow   Light Yellow   Clear

Did I poo today?   YES   NO

WHAT I ATE TODAY?

List two things I am grateful for today.

What's my mindset today?

Who and How did I serve or help somebody today?

TODAY'S MAGIC: The F.I.X.ed Athlete™ Program
The biggest problem you had in your day today, how did it make you feel? If you could say in one or two words...

Did I get rid of them?   YES   NO

Essential Oils I Used Today:

What I'm looking forward to tomorrow?

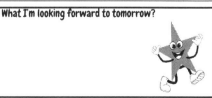

Tell Others What You've Learned About Sugar This Week!

Using the comic strip layout below draw and tell a short story about how sugar can kill your athletic performances and how companies hide added sugar into so many different food products. Review the Nutrition & C.R.A.P. material in Section #1 of this book for help.

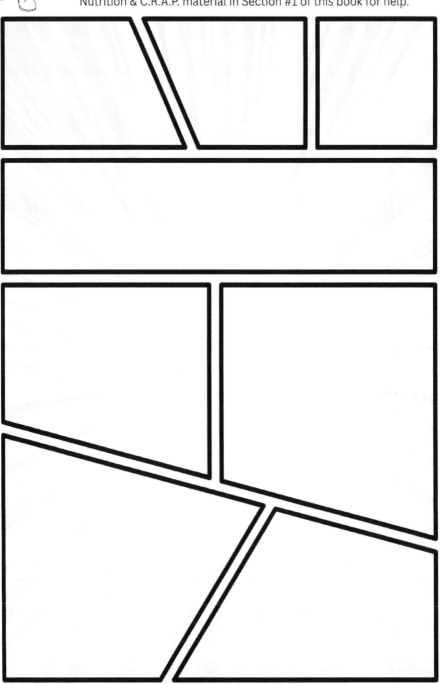

MyDay –

My focus for today is:
_____
_____
_____

Date _____
What Time I Went To Bed Last Night? _____
What Time Did I Wake Up Today? _____
I had _____ hours of sleep

Today's practice was...

3 things I want to accomplish today...

What I learned today?

What challenged me today?

Did I eat like a winner today? YES NO

Did I eat any C.R.A.P. today? YES NO

What color was my pee today?

Red   Orange   Dark Yellow   Yellow   Light Yellow   Clear

Did I poo today? YES NO

WHAT I ATE TODAY?

List two things I am grateful for today.

What's my mindset today?

Who and How did I serve or help somebody today?

TODAY'S MAGIC: The F.I.X.ed Athlete℠ Program
The biggest problem you had in your day today, how did it make you feel? If you could say in one or two words...

Did I get rid of them? YES NO

Essential Oils I Used Today:

What I'm looking forward to tomorrow?

SUGAR WORD SCRAMBLE

HEY SUPERSTAR

EAT LIKE A CHAMPION!   SKIP THE C.R.A.P.   PERFORM LIKE A CHAMPION!

Your Challenge:
The food industry uses a variety of names for sugar, often to disguise it in ingredient lists. Can you unscramble these words? If you need help, we've added a word list below... to make it a bit more challenging, some of the words in the word list, are not included in this word scramble...

The food industry continues to find creative ways to label sugar, often using scientific, exotic, or less familiar names use this word list to assist you with the ones we've included with the sugar word scramble:

Acesulfame	Cyclamate	Fructose	Maltitol	Saccharin
Advantame	Dextran	Glucose Syrup	Maltodextrin	Sorbitol
Alitame	Dextrin	Isomalt	Maltose	Sucralose
Aspartame	Erythritol	Lactitol	Mannitol	Turbinado
Caramel	Ethyl Maltol	Malt	Neotame	Xylitol

1) ASPEARTME
2) LOSEARUSC
3) ACARSINCH
4) UFLAMEACES
5) AMEENOT
6) EAAADMTV
7) MEALAIT
8) TILLOYX
9) LOBSTORI
10) LAMTTOLI
11) TINMANLO
12) SALTOMI
13) CLLATTOI
14) ANXDERT
15) NTDEIRX
16) CAALEMR
17) CUTOESRF
18) LAMT
19) AODBINURT
20) MALTECCYE

Answers on page #302

130

My Day —

My focus for today is:
_____
_____
_____

Date	What Time I Went To Bed Last Night?
	What Time Did I Wake Up Today?
I had _____ hours of sleep	

Today's practice was...

3 things I want to accomplish today...
1. _____
2. _____
3. _____

What I learned today?

What challenged me today?

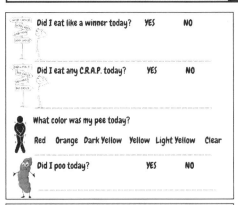

Did I eat like a winner today?   YES   NO

Did I eat any C.R.A.P. today?   YES   NO

What color was my pee today?
Red   Orange   Dark Yellow   Yellow   Light Yellow   Clear

Did I poo today?   YES   NO

WHAT I ATE TODAY?

List two things I am grateful for today.

What's my mindset today?

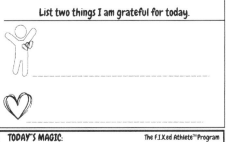

Who and How did I serve or help somebody today?

TODAY'S MAGIC: The F.I.X.ed Athlete™ Program
The biggest problem you had in your day today, how did it make you feel? If you could say in one or two words...

Did I get rid of them?   YES   NO

Essential Oils I Used Today:

What I'm looking forward to tomorrow?

THE POWER OF POSITIVE WORDS & SELF-TALK
UnLEASH Your SUPERPOWERS by Eliminating Negative Words!

Research shows that a child can hear the word "NO" more than 400 times a day before their 1st birthday. That's more than 146,000 times in 1-year. This week we will blend learning, neuroscience, performance psychology, and communication skills to train your brain to win the power over negative words and thoughts.

This Week's Challenge:

The Power of Positive Words & Self-Talk

Reset Your Inner Voice – Be Your Own #1 Teammate

Did you know?

Some experts believe the average child hears over 400 negative statements a day—things like:
- "No, don't do that!"
- "You're not ready."
- "You messed up again."
- "That's not how you do it."

This adds up really fast. It can sneak into our own self-talk — what we say to ourselves in our heads.

But here's the secret of champions:
- ☀ **Positive self-talk changes your brain.**
- ☀ **Positive words boost performance.**
- ☀ **Positive energy makes you a better teammate, athlete, and person.**

Train your brain like you train your body.

Use only positive self-talk and words—to yourself AND others—for the entire week.

Each day this week, write these on your **MY DAY** pages
1. **My Power Statement Today:**
2. **Write one positive sentence to say to yourself all day.** Example: *"I am focused and fierce!"*
3. **One Positive Thing I Said to Someone Else:** *Compliment, encouragement, support*

A Negative Thought I Caught and Flipped: What did I think or almost say? How did I flip it to something helpful? *Example:*
✗ *"I'm not good at this."* → ✅ *"I'm still learning. I'll get better if I keep trying."*

Optional - try this: **Science Experiment!**
Try this 2-day Experiment:
Day 1: Let negative thoughts & feelings go wild in your head **(don't say them—just notice them)**.
Day 2: Replace every one with a positive word or phrase.
   (If you are a member of The F.I.X.ed Athlete Program, work with your F.I.X. Code Coach & Extract Them!)

Then ask:
- Which day felt better?
- Which day helped you perform stronger?

Why This Matters *The Science Corner*
When you use positive self-talk, your brain:
1. **Rewires negative patterns into confident ones**
2. **Activates the prefrontal cortex, which helps with focus, problem-solving, and staying calm**
3. **Improves performance and reduces muscle tension**
4. **Boosts your mood and makes teammates want to be around you**
5. **Reduces stress and allows you to perform better.**

End of Week Challenge:
- Write your favorite power phrase from the week. Decorate it and hang it where you'll see it daily.
- Write a letter to a younger athlete, friend or sibling encouraging them to use positive self-talk, just like you did this week.

This week you're not just training for sport—you're training your brain for life.

SUPERSTARS don't let negativity live in their minds rent-free.
YOU are the landlord of your mind.
Keep it full of Great Thoughts, Powerful Energy, & Winning Words!

CONTINUE THIS NEW SKILL FOR THE REST OF YOUR LIFE!

My Day —

My focus for today is:
_____
_____
_____

Date	What Time I Went To Bed Last Night?
	What Time Did I Wake Up Today?
I had _____ hours of sleep	

Today's practice was...

3 things I want to accomplish today...
1. _____
2. _____
3. _____

What I learned today?

What challenged me today?

Did I eat like a winner today?   YES   NO

Did I eat any C.R.A.P. today?   YES   NO

What color was my pee today?
Red   Orange   Dark Yellow   Yellow   Light Yellow   Clear

Did I poo today?   YES   NO

WHAT I ATE TODAY?

List two things I am grateful for today.

What's my mindset today?

Who and How did I serve or help somebody today?

TODAY'S MAGIC: The F.I.X.ed Athlete™ Program
The biggest problem you had in your day today, how did it make you feel? If you could say in one or two words...

Did I get rid of them?   YES   NO

Essential Oils I Used Today:

What I'm looking forward to tomorrow?

THE POWER OF FEELINGS

Using the comic strip layout below and then going to page #224, select 9 negative feeling words from that page and write one in each of the empty boxes below. Focus on ones that you have felt.
NEXT: Draw a **SUPERSTAR** that feels the opposite of that negative feeling word. Then draw a line through the negative feeling word.
I did the first one for you in box #1

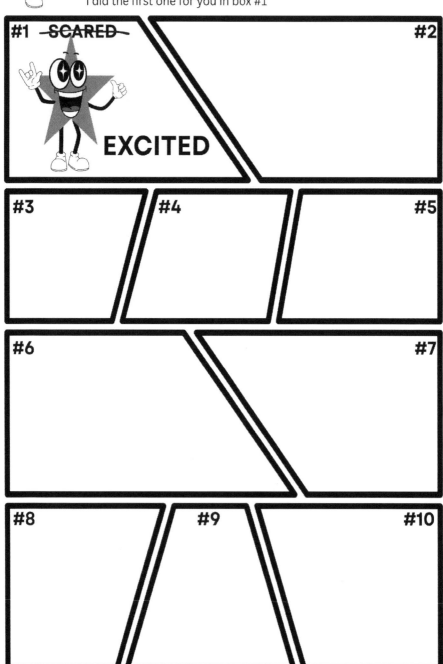

MyDay –

My focus for today is:

_____
_____
_____

Date

What Time I Went To Bed Last Night?

What Time Did I Wake Up Today?

I had _____ hours of sleep

Today's practice was...

3 things I want to accomplish today...

1.
2.
3.

What I learned today?

What challenged me today?

Did I eat like a winner today?   YES   NO

Did I eat any C.R.A.P. today?   YES   NO

What color was my pee today?

Red   Orange   Dark Yellow   Yellow   Light Yellow   Clear

Did I poo today?   YES   NO

WHAT I ATE TODAY?

List two things I am grateful for today.

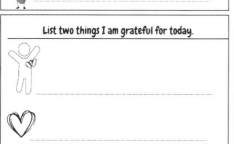

What's my mindset today?

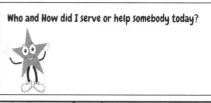

Who and How did I serve or help somebody today?

TODAY'S MAGIC: The F.I.X.ed Athlete™ Program

The biggest problem you had in your day today, how did it make you feel? If you could say in one or two words...

Did I get rid of them?   YES   NO

Essential Oils I Used Today:

What I'm looking forward to tomorrow?

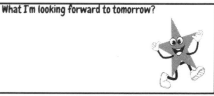

COMMUNICATION IN TRAINING

Instructions:
Today's challenge is all about lifting others up while reflecting on your own greatness, too! You're going to write and send a letter to a friend that includes 22 positive statements:
- 12 kind, encouraging, or awesome things about THEM
- 8 positive truths about YOU
- 2 uplifting statements about your journey as an ATHLETE

Write your letter on paper, decorate it if you'd like, and make sure you send it! You never know how much a positive message can mean to someone.

Examples:
- **About Them:**
  - You are always a great listener.
  - I admire your creativity.
  - You work really hard in school.
  - You have a contagious laugh.
- **About You:**
  - I have a strong work ethic.
  - I bounce back after setbacks.
  - I'm getting better at staying focused.
- **About Your Athletics:**
  - I've been training hard and I'm getting better at _____.
  - I'm becoming stronger, faster, and smarter in my sport.

This Matters:
- ☑ Positive communication builds stronger friendships.
- ☑ Focusing on strengths boosts your confidence and your friend's, too!
- ☑ Science shows that practicing gratitude and positivity improves your brain health, emotional well-being, and athletic performance.

Now go write that letter—and deliver some serious good vibes!

MyDay-

My focus for today is:

_____
_____
_____

Date	What Time I Went To Bed Last Night?
	What Time Did I Wake Up Today?
I had _____ hours of sleep	

Today's practice was...

3 things I want to accomplish today...

What I learned today?

What challenged me today?

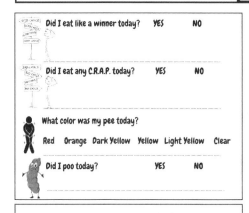

WHAT I ATE TODAY?

List two things I am grateful for today.

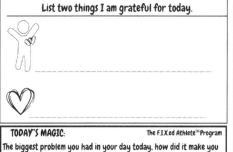

What's my mindset today?

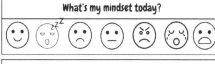

Who and How did I serve or help somebody today?

TODAY'S MAGIC: The F.I.X.ed Athlete™ Program
The biggest problem you had in your day today, how did it make you feel? If you could say in one or two words...

Did I get rid of them?   YES   NO

Essential Oils I Used Today:

What I'm looking forward to tomorrow?

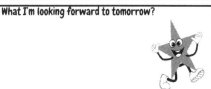

CLEAN YOUR SPACE – CLEAR YOUR MIND!
HEY SUPERSTAR ATHLETIC SECRETS OF SUPERSTARS!

Every elite athlete needs a space that helps them recover, focus, train, and dream big. Your room & lockers are power centers. We talk about controlling the controllables. Your spaces are 100% controllable. They reflect and affect your mental state.

This Week's Upgrade:

THE FOUR-BOX SYSTEM:
FOR EACH SPACE YOU ORGANIZE, USE THESE CATEGORIES:
1. **KEEP (IN SIGHT):** Essential daily items that support performance
2. **STORE (OUT OF SIGHT):** Important but not needed daily
3. **DONATE/DISCARD:** Items that create mental drag without adding value
4. **UNCERTAIN:** Items to revisit after a 7-day cooling off period

ATHLETIC PERFORMANCE CONNECTION
PROFESSIONAL TEAMS UNDERSTAND THE ORGANIZATION-PERFORMANCE LINK:
CONTROL YOUR CONTROLLABLES!

Performance Research: A 2021 study in Sports Medicine found that athletes who implemented organization systems experienced:
- 17% reduction in pre-competition anxiety
- 22% improvement in on-time arrival to training
- Significant increase in coach-reported preparation quality

THE 15-MINUTE METHOD
This research-backed approach prevents overwhelm:
1. Set a timer for exactly 15 minutes
2. Focus on one small area completely
3. Stop when the timer ends—even mid-task
4. Recognize progress, not perfection

This method leverages the Psychology of Small Wins
to Build Momentum Without Triggering Avoidance Behaviors!

CLEARER THINKING
=
BETTER PERFORMANCES !

My Day –

My focus for today is:
_____
_____
_____

Date	What Time I Went To Bed Last Night?
	What Time Did I Wake Up Today?
I had _____ hours of sleep	

Today's practice was...

3 things I want to accomplish today...

1. ....
2. ....
3. ....

What I learned today?

What challenged me today?

Did I eat like a winner today?   YES   NO

Did I eat any C.R.A.P. today?   YES   NO

What color was my pee today?

Red   Orange   Dark Yellow   Yellow   Light Yellow   Clear

Did I poo today?   YES   NO

WHAT I ATE TODAY?

List two things I am grateful for today.

What's my mindset today?

Who and How did I serve or help somebody today?

TODAY'S MAGIC: The F.I.X.ed Athlete™ Program

The biggest problem you had in your day today, how did it make you feel? If you could say in one or two words...

Did I get rid of them?   YES   NO

Essential Oils I Used Today:

What I'm looking forward to tomorrow?

The Penalty Box

Each player takes alternate turns writing the numbers 1 - 10 in the Hockey Pucks of their choice, in order: 1,2,3,4,etc....

Once all numbers are written, one circle will remain blank as this puck becomes The Penalty Box, which cancels out its neighboring pucks and points.

The player with the highest remaining sum of numbers after The Penalty Box removes its neighbors - WINS!

5+3+8+7+10+2+1= 36

4+8+9+10+6+5+7= 41

WINNER

MyDay-

My focus for today is:
_____
_____
_____
_____

Date	What Time I Went To Bed Last Night?
	What Time Did I Wake Up Today?
I had _____ hours of sleep	

Today's practice was...

3 things I want to accomplish today...

What I learned today?

What challenged me today?

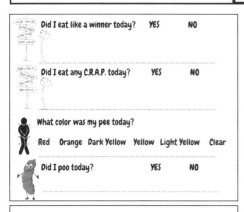

Did I eat like a winner today?   YES   NO

Did I eat any C.R.A.P. today?   YES   NO

What color was my pee today?
Red   Orange   Dark Yellow   Yellow   Light Yellow   Clear

Did I poo today?   YES   NO

WHAT I ATE TODAY?

List two things I am grateful for today.

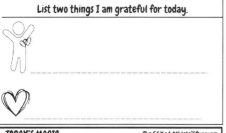

What's my mindset today?

Who and How did I serve or help somebody today?

TODAY'S MAGIC: The F.I.X.ed Athlete™ Program

The biggest problem you had in your day today, how did it make you feel? If you could say in one or two words...

Did I get rid of them?   YES   NO

Essential Oils I Used Today:

What I'm looking forward to tomorrow?

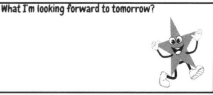

FINISH THE STORY
How The F.I.X. Code Can Build Confidence.

Instructions:
Read each of the short stories and then write out what you would do in that situation.... These scenarios can be used as writing prompts, discussion starters, or role-playing exercises. They'll help you develop the critical skills of active listening, problem-solving, and empathy while building stronger communication and team dynamics.

- **The Call That Changed Everything**

"Practice was rough. I felt off. My teammates were faster, sharper, stronger. I started to wonder if I'd ever catch up. That's when I called My F.I.X.ed Athlete's Coach. I didn't know what to say at first, but they just listened... and then they reminded me of something really important."

☞ Finish the story by sharing what the coach said, how it helped shift your mindset, and what you did next that made you proud. Reflect on what it means to ask for help and use support to grow stronger.

- **Self-Doubt: "Am I Good Enough?"**

"All the other athletes looked so confident. I started to wonder if I even belonged there. But then I took a deep breath and remembered something I had forgotten..."

☞ Finish the story by showing how you moved past the doubt and found your strength.

- **Sadness; The Stormy Day Inside**

"Nothing felt right that day. Not my practice, not my mood, not even my favorite song. I felt like there was a storm inside me... until I found a way to calm it down."

☞ Explain what helped you feel better and what you learned about dealing with tough feelings.

- **Losing a Competition: "My Best Loss I Ever Had"**

"We lost the final match. I sat there staring at my shoes, trying not to cry, when someone came over and said something that changed how I felt about losing..."

☞ Share what they said and how it helped you grow stronger or better.

- **Confidence: "The Game-Changer Inside Me"**

"Everyone was watching as I stepped onto the field. My heart was pounding, but then I remembered the one thing that always brings me confidence..."

☞ Now describe what that thing is, how it helped you rise in that moment, and what you learned about believing in yourself.

My Day -

My focus for today is:
_____
_____
_____

Date

What Time I Went To Bed Last Night?

What Time Did I Wake Up Today?

I had _____ hours of sleep

Today's practice was...

3 things I want to accomplish today...

What I learned today?

What challenged me today?

Did I eat like a winner today?   YES   NO

Did I eat any C.R.A.P. today?   YES   NO

What color was my pee today?

Red   Orange   Dark Yellow   Yellow   Light Yellow   Clear

Did I poo today?   YES   NO

WHAT I ATE TODAY?

List two things I am grateful for today.

What's my mindset today?

Who and How did I serve or help somebody today?

TODAY'S MAGIC: The F.I.X.ed Athlete™ Program

The biggest problem you had in your day today, how did it make you feel? If you could say in one or two words...

Did I get rid of them?   YES   NO

Essential Oils I Used Today:

What I'm looking forward to tomorrow?

WHAT WOULD YOU DO?
Conflict Resolution

Instructions:
Read each of the short stories and then write out what you would do in that situation.... These scenarios can be used as writing prompts, discussion starters, or role-playing exercises. They'll help you develop the critical skills of active listening, problem-solving, and empathy while building stronger communication and team dynamics.

1. The Misunderstanding with a Teammate
During practice, you feel like a teammate isn't passing the ball to you when you're open. You're getting frustrated because you believe they're ignoring you on purpose, but you haven't said anything. At the same time, your teammate seems upset and keeps looking at you with a scowl.
How would you approach the situation?
Do you confront your teammate right away?
Do you give them space and then talk later?
How can you both clear up the misunderstanding?
What can you say to make sure both sides are heard?

2. The Coach's Decision
You worked hard all season, but during the final game, the coach decides to put someone else in for a critical play instead of you. You're disappointed and feel like your efforts were ignored. You don't agree with the decision and are angry.
How would you approach your coach?
What would you say to express your feelings respectfully?
How can you show that you're a team player even when you're not the one chosen?
How do you handle your disappointment without letting it affect the team?

3. Competing for a Position
You and a teammate are both competing for the same position on the team, and it's creating tension. You both feel like you're the right choice, and it's affecting the way you communicate and work together. This tension is now spilling over into practices and even personal conversations.
How would you handle the situation?
How can you communicate with your teammate without causing further tension?
What would you do to ensure that your relationship stays positive, regardless of who gets the position?
How can you still support each other and improve together, even in competition?

4. The Disagreement with a Referee
During a game, the referee makes a call that you believe is wrong. It's a critical moment in the game, and you feel frustrated and want to argue. Your teammates and coach are also upset, but the game is still ongoing.
How would you handle your frustration?
How can you stay calm in the moment and not let your emotions take over?
What would you say to your coach or teammates to maintain control of the situation?
How can you refocus and encourage your team, despite the bad call?

5. The Negative Team Member
One of your teammates is constantly negative, and it's bringing down the whole team's energy. They often complain about the drills, the coach, or even other teammates. This negativity is starting to affect your own mindset and the way the team practices and plays together.
How would you handle this teammate?
Do you talk to them directly? If so, how do you express your concerns without causing an argument?
How can you encourage them to see things more positively without making them feel attacked?
How can you help the team stay united and positive while handling this challenge?

My Day

My focus for today is:
_____
_____
_____

Date _____
What Time I Went To Bed Last Night? _____
What Time Did I Wake Up Today? _____
I had _____ hours of sleep

Today's practice was...

3 things I want to accomplish today...

What I learned today?

What challenged me today?

Did I eat like a winner today?   YES   NO

Did I eat any C.R.A.P. today?   YES   NO

What color was my pee today?
Red   Orange   Dark Yellow   Yellow   Light Yellow   Clear

Did I poo today?   YES   NO

WHAT I ATE TODAY?

List two things I am grateful for today.

What's my mindset today?

Who and How did I serve or help somebody today?

TODAY'S MAGIC: The F.I.X.ed Athlete™ Program
The biggest problem you had in your day today, how did it make you feel? If you could say in one or two words...

Did I get rid of them?   YES   NO

What I'm looking forward to tomorrow?

Essential Oils I Used Today:

MY HERO'S JOURNEY
Unleashing My Inner Hero

HEY SUPERSTAR

A Journey into Becoming Your Own Hero

This week, you're not just writing a story — you're starting a mission of self-discovery.

Great athletes aren't just built by training harder. They grow by knowing who they want to become — and then becoming that person step by step.

This Week's Challenge:

PART 1: RESEARCH POTENTIAL HEROES

START BY LOOKING OUTSIDE YOURSELF:

1. **CHOOSE 5 PEOPLE WHO YOU CONSIDER HEROES**
   ATHLETES, LEADERS, COACHES, OLYMPIANS, OR FAMILY MEMBERS
2. **WRITE DOWN WHAT MAKES EACH ONE A HERO TO YOU.**
   - WHAT TRAITS DO THEY HAVE?
   - HOW DO THEY ACT WHEN THINGS ARE TOUGH?
   - WHAT HABITS OR CHOICES DO THEY MAKE DAILY?
   - HOW DO THEY TREAT OTHERS?

PART 2: TURN THE FOCUS INWARD

NOW THAT YOU'VE IDENTIFIED THE TRAITS OF YOUR HEROES, LOOK AT YOURSELF. ANSWER THESE:

- WHICH OF THOSE TRAITS DO YOU ALREADY HAVE?
- WHICH ONES DO YOU WANT TO GROW INTO?
- WHAT WOULD IT LOOK LIKE IF YOU BECAME YOUR OWN HERO?

HERO	SPORT / ROLE	TRAIT YOU ADMIRE	TRAIT IN ACTION
Tina Lilak	Finnish Javelin Thrower	Focused on only one track and field event	1984 Olympic Games single event took only 5 of her 6 throws

PART 3: WRITE YOUR HERO STORY

"THE PERSON I WANT TO BECOME IS ALWAYS 10 YEARS AHEAD OF ME..."

NOW IMAGINE:

- WHERE ARE YOU?
- WHAT KIND OF ATHLETE ARE YOU?
- WHAT DO YOU STAND FOR?
- WHAT HAVE YOU OVERCOME?
- HOW DID YOU GET THERE?

INCLUDE SCENES, EMOTION, AND VISION — MAKE YOUR STORY VIVID AND REAL.
YOU'RE WRITING THE BLUEPRINT FOR WHO YOU'RE BECOMING.

PART 4: WHY YOU MUST BE YOUR HERO

HEROES ARE INSPIRING — BUT WE DON'T NEED TO COPY ANYONE ELSE.

YOU WERE MADE TO BE AN ORIGINAL, NOT A COPY. THAT'S WHY...

- BEING YOUR OWN HERO MEANS YOU'RE IN CHARGE OF YOUR OWN GROWTH.
- YOU'LL NEVER RUN OUT OF MOTIVATION — THERE'S ALWAYS A NEXT LEVEL OF YOU TO REACH.
- YOU'LL STAY FOCUSED ON BECOMING INSTEAD OF JUST WINNING.
- YOU'LL CHASE EXCELLENCE, NOT PERFECTION — AND THAT'S THE REAL KEY TO GREATNESS.

REFLECTION PROMPT:

"WHAT DECISION CAN I MAKE THIS WEEK THAT MY FUTURE HERO-SELF WILL BE PROUD OF?"

THIS IS A CHALLENGE TO REVISIT OFTEN.
YOUR DEFINITION OF A HERO WILL GROW AS YOU GROW.
KEEP THIS JOURNAL ENTRY OR VISION PAGE SOMEWHERE VISIBLE AND RETURN TO IT EACH SEASON.

MyDay –

My focus for today is:
_____
_____
_____

Date	What Time I Went To Bed Last Night?
	What Time Did I Wake Up Today?
I had _____ hours of sleep	

Today's practice was...

3 things I want to accomplish today...
1. _____
2. _____
3. _____

What I learned today?

What challenged me today?

Did I eat like a winner today?   YES   NO

Did I eat any C.R.A.P. today?   YES   NO

What color was my pee today?
Red   Orange   Dark Yellow   Yellow   Light Yellow   Clear

Did I poo today?   YES   NO

WHAT I ATE TODAY?

List two things I am grateful for today.

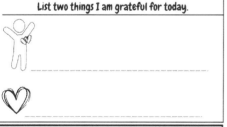

What's my mindset today?

Who and How did I serve or help somebody today?

TODAY'S MAGIC: The F.I.X.ed Athlete™ Program
The biggest problem you had in your day today, how did it make you feel? If you could say in one or two words...

Did I get rid of them?   YES   NO

Essential Oils I Used Today:

What I'm looking forward to tomorrow?

Trivia Time: Are you ready to test your knowledge, learn new things, engage your analytical thinking, memory, and recall? All skills that will make you a better athlete and a powerful **SUPERSTAR In Training**!

Today's subject: # Essential Oils for Athletes

Need Help? Review the Essential Oil pages earlier in this book: 59, 60, and 61.

1) Lavender
2) Frankincense
3) Peppermint
4) Wild Orange
5) Basil
6) Cedarwood
7) Deep Sleep
8) Post-Workout Support
9) Muscle Recovery
10) Deep Blue Stick
11) Reducing Inflammation
12) Calm Nervous System
13) Injury Recovery Support
14) Recovery Time
15) Natural Tools for Recovery

A. Assists with earaches, oily hair, wounds, and is an anti-inflammatory

B. Supports cellular repair and stress relief

C. Helps relieve tension and muscle tightness

D. Known for calming properties and sleep enhancement

E. Improves recovery between intense workouts

F. Anti-inflammatory oil that stimulates the conscious mind, opens airways, helps with charley horses, heat issues

G. Contains natural compounds that promote healing

H. Uplifting, assists with anxiety, fears, nervousness, and sluggish digestion

I. Promotes circulation and faster healing

J. Slows the nervous system and helps athletes recharge

K. Blend for muscle soreness, pain, tension headaches, bruises, bone pain

L. Helps reduce over-reliance on synthetic pain relievers

M. Essential after long or intense training

N. Required for long-term training success

O. Restorative rest for peak muscle function and brain reset

Answer Key: 1-D | 2-B | 3-F | 4-H | 5-A | 6-J | 7-O | 8-M | 9-E | 10-K | 11-I | 12-J | 13-G | 14-N | 15-L

MyDay -

My focus for today is:
_____
_____
_____

Date	What Time I Went To Bed Last Night?
	What Time Did I Wake Up Today?
I had _____ hours of sleep	

Today's practice was...

3 things I want to accomplish today...

1.
2.
3.

What I learned today?

What challenged me today?

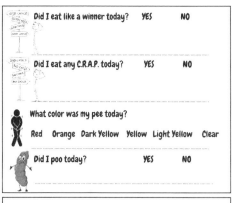

WHAT I ATE TODAY?

List two things I am grateful for today.

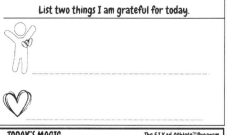

What's my mindset today?

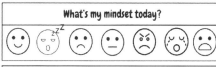

Who and How did I serve or help somebody today?

TODAY'S MAGIC: The F.I.X.ed Athlete™ Program

The biggest problem you had in your day today, how did it make you feel? If you could say in one or two words...

Did I get rid of them?   YES   NO

Essential Oils I Used Today:

What I'm looking forward to tomorrow?

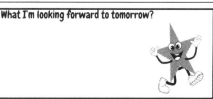

Interview a Champion
Learn from Those Who've Been There!

Instructions: Choose a coach, teacher, neighbor, or family friend who competed at the college, Olympic, or professional level in any sport. Ask if you can interview them to learn about their journey, mindset, and habits that helped them succeed.

What to Do:
1. Prepare your questions ahead of time. Use the sample list below or create your own.
2. Be respectful of their time. Ask for 15–20 minutes.
3. Take notes or record the interview (with permission).
4. After the interview, write a short reflection about what you learned and how you'll apply it to your own journey.
5. **Send a Thank-You** note or message to **show your appreciation!**

Sample Interview Questions:
- What sport did you compete in, and at what level?
- How did you first get started in your sport?
- What was your biggest challenge, and how did you overcome it?
- What did your daily or weekly training look like?
- What was your mindset before big competitions?
- What role did coaches, teammates, or family play in your success?
- How did you stay motivated during tough times?
- What advice would you give to young athletes today?
- What are you most proud of from your athletic career?
- What lessons from sports have helped you in your life now?

Goal: Learn firsthand what it takes to be a high-level athlete—and use that wisdom to become a Superstar in Training!

Write your quesitons:

Write your reflections:

MyDay –

My focus for today is:
_____
_____
_____

Date _____

What Time I Went To Bed Last Night? _____

What Time Did I Wake Up Today? _____

I had _____ hours of sleep

Today's practice was...

3 things I want to accomplish today...
1. _____
2. _____
3. _____

What I learned today?

What challenged me today?

Did I eat like a winner today?   YES   NO

Did I eat any C.R.A.P. today?   YES   NO

What color was my pee today?
Red   Orange   Dark Yellow   Yellow   Light Yellow   Clear

Did I poo today?   YES   NO

WHAT I ATE TODAY?

List two things I am grateful for today.

What's my mindset today?

Who and How did I serve or help somebody today?

TODAY'S MAGIC: The F.I.X.ed Athlete™ Program
The biggest problem you had in your day today, how did it make you feel? If you could say in one or two words...

Did I get rid of them?   YES   NO

Essential Oils I Used Today:

What I'm looking forward to tomorrow?

151

CREATING SUSTAINABLE SYSTEMS
HABITS & ROUTINES REDUCE EFFORT

HEY SUPERSTAR

Now that your spaces are organized, you'll need to establish routines to maintain clarity with minimal efforts.

DAILY CHECKLISTS...

DAILY CHECKLIST:
1. Implement the 5-Minute Reset Ritual (see below)
2. Practice the "One Touch Rule" for incoming items
3. Remove one non-essential item from your primary spaces
4. Continue tracking focus, stress, and performance metrics
5. Note relationships between maintained order and mental clarity
6. Document your personal "organization rules" for future reference

THE 5-MINUTE RESET RITUAL:
- Set a timer for exactly 5 minutes before bed
- Return items to their designated homes
- Clear primary surfaces completely
- Prepare tomorrow's essentials
- Take a mental snapshot of the ordered space

ELITE PERFORMANCE CONNECTION

Top performers across sports integrate environmental organization into their success routines:

> "My preparation starts with my environment.
> A clear space leads to clear performance.
> It's a non-negotiable part of my routine."
> - **Tom Brady**, 7-time Super Bowl champion

Performance Research:
A longitudinal study in the Journal of Applied Sport Psychology found that athletes who maintained organized spaces for 21+ days showed:
- **Enhanced pre-sleep quality (critical for recovery)**
- **Lower reported pre-competition anxiety**
- **Improved coach-rated "mental readiness" scores**
- **Greater consistency across multiple performances**

THE MINDFULNESS CONNECTION

Organization is a form of mindfulness practice:

- **Present-Moment Awareness:** The reset ritual trains your brain to notice details in your environment
- **Non-Judgmental Observation:** You learn to see spaces objectively, just as you need to view performance without emotional attachment
- **Intentional Action:** Small, consistent organization actions build the same mental muscles needed for deliberate practice

REFLECTION QUESTIONS & FUTURE PLANNING
- How has your relationship with your environment changed?
- What differences have you noticed in your preparation or performance?
- Which organizational habits feel sustainable long-term?
- How might you apply these same principles to organizing your training plan, nutrition, or recovery routines?

Remember: The ultimate goal is creating an environment that supports your best thinking and performance without requiring constant attention.

Your organization system should give you mental energy, not consume it.

 **MyDay -**

Date	What Time I Went To Bed Last Night?
	What Time Did I Wake Up Today?
I had _____ hours of sleep	

My focus for today is:
_____
_____
_____

Today's practice was...

3 things I want to accomplish today...

What I learned today?

What challenged me today?

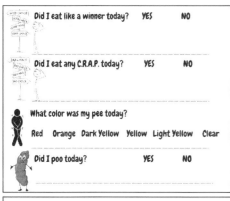

WHAT I ATE TODAY?

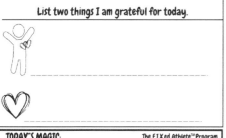

List two things I am grateful for today.

What's my mindset today?

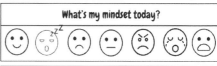

Who and How did I serve or help somebody today?

TODAY'S MAGIC: The F.I.X.ed Athlete™ Program
The biggest problem you had in your day today, how did it make you feel? If you could say in one or two words...

Did I get rid of them? YES   NO

Essential Oils I Used Today:

What I'm looking forward to tomorrow?

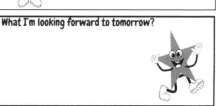

GOAT in SPORTS
Greatest Of All Time – Who Is Your Hero?

Hey Superstar

Your Challenge:
Here's a 20-question crossword puzzle designed to help you learn more about some of the Greatest Of All Time (GOAT) in their given sport. This crossword puzzle is perfect for building your memory & recall, vocabulary development, learning and analytical thinking, pattern recognition, skill acquisition, and strategic thinking... while reinforcing lessons through play and cognitive engagement. ALL skills SUPERSTAR Athletes need to take their play to the next level...

Across:

1. BRAZILIAN LEGEND, 3-TIME WORLD CUP WINNER
2. GOLF LEGEND KNOWN FOR WEARING RED ON SUNDAYS
3. SPANISH BADMINTON GOAT AND OLYMPIC GOLD MEDALIST
4. F1 DRIVER WITH A RECORD-TYING 7 WORLD CHAMPIONSHIPS
5. AIR JORDAN – WIDELY CONSIDERED THE BEST BASKETBALL PLAYER EVER
6. NEW ZEALAND RUGBY LEGEND WHO CHANGED THE GAME
7. AMERICAN SPRINTER WITH THE MOST OLYMPIC MEDALS IN TRACK & FIELD HISTORY
8. RUSSIAN WRESTLING BEAST NICKNAMED "THE EXPERIMENT"
9. JAPANESE JUDO GOAT WITH 3 OLYMPIC GOLDS
10. HOLDS THE MOST GRAND SLAM TITLES IN THE OPEN ERA (FEMALE)

Down:

1. NFL QUAETERBACK WITH THE MOST SUPER BOWL WINS
2. KNOWN AS THE GREATEST WNBA PLAYER OF ALL TIME, HER NICKNAME IS "WHITE MAMBA"
3. THREE-TIME OLYMPIC GOLD MEDALIST IN BEACH VOLLEYBALL, TEAMED UP WITH MISTY MAY-TREANOR
4. CHINESE TABLE TENNIS QUEEN WITH FOUR OLYMPIC GOLD MEDALS
5. DOMINANT U.S. GYMNAST WITH MORE MEDALS THAN MOST COUNTRIES
6. KENYAN MARATHONER AND WORLD RECORD HOLDER
7. AMERICAN SWIMMING LEGEND WITH MULTIPLE OLYMPIC GOLDS
8. TWO-TIME WOMEN'S WORLD CUP WINNER AND GOAL-SCORING MACHINE
9. U.S. SNOWBOARDER WITH 3 OLYMPIC GOLDS
10. TRIATHLON GOAT WITH 8 IRONMAN WORLD CHAMPIONSHIPS (FIRST NAME ONLY)

Solution on page #303

My Day –

My focus for today is:
_____
_____
_____

Date
What Time I Went To Bed Last Night?
What Time Did I Wake Up Today?
I had _____ hours of sleep

Today's practice was...

3 things I want to accomplish today...

1. _____
2. _____
3. _____

What I learned today?

What challenged me today?

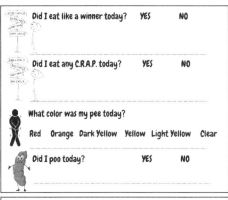

Did I eat like a winner today? YES   NO

Did I eat any C.R.A.P. today? YES   NO

What color was my pee today?

Red   Orange   Dark Yellow   Yellow   Light Yellow   Clear

Did I poo today?   YES   NO

WHAT I ATE TODAY?

List two things I am grateful for today.

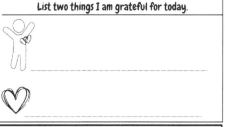

What's my mindset today?

Who and How did I serve or help somebody today?

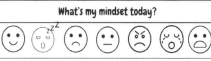

TODAY'S MAGIC: The F.I.X.ed Athlete™ Program
The biggest problem you had in your day today, how did it make you feel? If you could say in one or two words...

Did I get rid of them?   YES   NO

Essential Oils I Used Today:

What I'm looking forward to tomorrow?

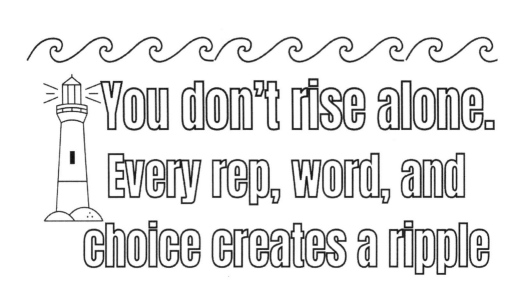

MyDay -

My focus for today is:
_____
_____
_____

Date
What Time I Went To Bed Last Night?
What Time Did I Wake Up Today?
I had _____ hours of sleep

Today's practice was...

3 things I want to accomplish today...

What I learned today?

What challenged me today?

Did I eat like a winner today?   YES   NO

Did I eat any C.R.A.P. today?   YES   NO

What color was my pee today?
Red   Orange   Dark Yellow   Yellow   Light Yellow   Clear

Did I poo today?   YES   NO

WHAT I ATE TODAY?

List two things I am grateful for today.

What's my mindset today?

Who and How did I serve or help somebody today?

TODAY'S MAGIC: The F.I.X.ed Athlete™ Program
The biggest problem you had in your day today, how did it make you feel? If you could say in one or two words...

Did I get rid of them?   YES   NO

Essential Oils I Used Today:

What I'm looking forward to tomorrow?

CREATE & COLOR
WHAT DO YOU WANT TO ME KNOWN FOR?

On page #156 you colored the motivational quote and on page #240 you will create a team banner. Today you will write your own personal quote that you want to be known for. Make it your own. You can combine several sayings that you like, but make this one ALL YOU! **Color It. Decorate It. Share It!** Share it with your coach and team. Let them know who YOU ARE and what you want to be known for. After writing your quote, read it every day this week. Let it guide your actions, your thoughts, and your efforts. Post it somewhere visible or write it on your water bottle, gear, or journal.

You're not just an athlete —
You're A Leader In The Making!

YOUR CHALLENGE:

A quotation is a powerful way to share an idea, belief, or value in just a few words. The best quotes stick in our minds, inspire action, and help others understand what we stand for. Great athletes, leaders, and changemakers are often remembered by the quotes that shaped their lives and motivated others.

Your quote should be:
- Original (written by you!)
- Short and powerful (1–2 sentences max)
- Positive, strong, and inspiring
- Something you believe in and want to live by

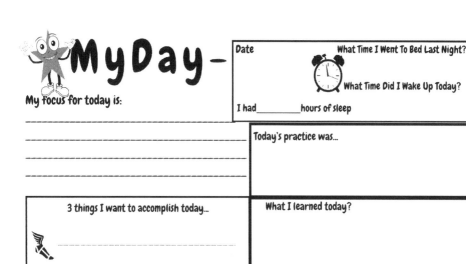

MyDay –

My focus for today is:

_____
_____
_____

Date	What Time I Went To Bed Last Night?
	What Time Did I Wake Up Today?
I had _____ hours of sleep	

Today's practice was...

3 things I want to accomplish today...

What I learned today?

What challenged me today?

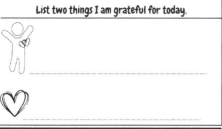

Did I eat like a winner today?   YES   NO

Did I eat any C.R.A.P. today?   YES   NO

What color was my pee today?

Red   Orange   Dark Yellow   Yellow   Light Yellow   Clear

Did I poo today?   YES   NO

WHAT I ATE TODAY?

List two things I am grateful for today.

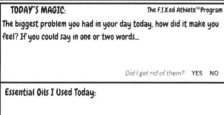

What's my mindset today?

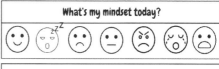

Who and How did I serve or help somebody today?

TODAY'S MAGIC: The F.I.X.ed Athlete™ Program

The biggest problem you had in your day today, how did it make you feel? If you could say in one or two words...

Did I get rid of them?   YES   NO

Essential Oils I Used Today:

What I'm looking forward to tomorrow?

Growth Activity:

Create Your Vision Board
See It! – Believe It! – Become It!

Vision boards are powerful tools that help you "see" your goals and dreams. Many top athletes use them because our brains respond strongly to images. When you regularly look at pictures of your goals, your mind starts working toward them even when you're not thinking about it!

The power of visualization lies in its ability to bridge the conscious and unconscious mind. When an athlete consciously creates vivid mental images of successful performance, these images can penetrate the unconscious mind, influencing beliefs, attitudes, and automatic responses.

🏆 Why Make a Vision Board? ✨

A vision board helps you picture your goals, stay motivated, and train your mind like a champion. What you see daily, you move toward.

   💨 It builds focus   🖌 Boosts confidence   ◎ Helps you commit to your goals

✨ What You'll Need:

Poster board or paper, scissors, glue, tape, magazines or printed images, markers or pens, pictures of YOU Motivational Words, quotes, numbers & items that motivate you. I have several and they are framed and hanging in my gym along with motivational posters. Another one hangs in my office, my bedroom, and in my car, and on my home screen of my phone.

✎ Steps to Build Your Board:

1. Think Big – What do you want to achieve in your sport, school, and life?
2. Find Images & Words – Choose photos, quotes, and symbols that show your dreams.
3. Put It All Together – Place them on your board to tell your story. Include:
4. ☑ A picture of YOU
5. ☑ 3 goals
6. ☑ 1-2 athletes you admire
7. ☑ Powerful words (e.g., Focus, Gold, Fearless)
8. Hang It Up – Put it where you'll see it every day (locker, wall, notebook).
9. Use It – Look at it daily and say: **"I am becoming this athlete."**

Every champion starts with a vision. A Vision Board is a powerful tool used by top athletes to train your mind, set big goals, and see your future self winning — long before it happens.

When you see your goals every day, your brain starts to believe they're possible — and you begin taking actions that bring them to life.

🎖 Famous Athletes Who Use Vision Boards:

- Michael Phelps (Swimming): Used vision boards and visualization to plan each gold medal.
- Serena Williams (Tennis): Pictured her wins and success long before she achieved them.
- Conor McGregor (MMA): Created a vision board with private jets, world titles — and made it real.
- Kerri Walsh Jennings (Beach Volleyball): Put Olympic gold on her board and earned it three times.
- Allyson Felix (Track & Field): Visualized her comeback and family life while chasing medals.

If they can do it, so can you!

👤 Who Should Make a Vision Board?

Any athlete who wants to:
- Set clear goals for sports and life
- Boost motivation and mental strength
- Improve focus during training and competition
- Build a winner's mindset and develop daily discipline

Whether you're a beginner or going pro, this is for YOU.

❗ Where to Put It:

Somewhere you see it DAILY:
Bedroom wall   -   Locker   -   Inside your journal   -   Home gym or training space
As your phone/computer background (if digital)

   💨 **Your brain needs to SEE the vision daily to BELIEVE it!** 💨

☑ Activate It

When it's done:
- Hang it up
- Take a picture of it
- Share with your coach or teammates
- Look at it every morning and before competitions
- Speak it out loud: **"I am becoming this athlete!"**

   ◎ **Vision without action is just a dream — but vision + action = destiny!** ◎

MyDay -

My focus for today is:
_____
_____
_____

Date

What Time I Went To Bed Last Night?

What Time Did I Wake Up Today?

I had _____ hours of sleep

Today's practice was...

3 things I want to accomplish today...

1. ....
2. ....
3. ....

What I learned today?

What challenged me today?

Did I eat like a winner today?   YES   NO

Did I eat any C.R.A.P. today?   YES   NO

What color was my pee today?
Red   Orange   Dark Yellow   Yellow   Light Yellow   Clear

Did I poo today?   YES   NO

WHAT I ATE TODAY?

List two things I am grateful for today.

What's my mindset today?

Who and How did I serve or help somebody today?

TODAY'S MAGIC: The F.I.X.ed Athlete™ Program
The biggest problem you had in your day today, how did it make you feel? If you could say in one or two words...

Did I get rid of them?   YES   NO

Essential Oils I Used Today:

What I'm looking forward to tomorrow?

SLEEP, YOUR BRAIN & YOUR PERFORMANCES...
DO YOU KNOW THE POWER OF A GREAT NIGHT SLEEP?

SHHHH...
SUPERSTAR In Training
- Sleeping

Your Challenge:
Use this 20-question crossword puzzle designed to help athletes learn more about the power of getting good sleep, its effects on performance, and how you can make better sleep choices. Are you using the secrets that professional athletes and high achievers use to elevate their performances?

Across:

1. The number of hours of sleep young athletes should aim for each night
2. A nightly routine that helps the body and brain prepare for sleep
3. What blue light from screens can block, making it hard to fall asleep
4. What you should turn off an hour before bed for better sleep
5. A deep state of rest your body enteres that helps with muscle recovery
6. Which doTERRA calming oil is recommended at bedtime for relaxation for young athletes?
7. The best environment for a good night's sleep is cool and _____
8. The F.I.X. Code skill that invites intention and reflection to imporve sleep habits
9. A special page or activity written to clear the mind, often at the end of the day or a long week
10. The best type of curtains to use in your bedroom

Down:

1. The natural oil known to help calm the mind and promotes sleep
2. A feeling like worry or sadness that might interfere with quality sleep
3. Managing frustration and pressure under intense rally situations is know as emotional _____
4. When you train hard and sleep well, your body builds this while you rest
5. A guided method that uses scent and memory to rewire the brain
6. The Muscle ☐ Tightening & Relaxing Sequence Secret _____ Athletes use when they have difficulty falling asleep
7. What your body uses sleep time to do, especially after hard training
8. Feeling this before bed may cause your body to stay tense
9. What your brain builds and repairs during deep, uninterrupted sleep
10. The name of the program designed to help athletes manage feelings and become SUPERSTARs and CHAMPIONs inside and out

Solutions on page #304

MyDay -

My focus for today is:
_____
_____
_____

Date

What Time I Went To Bed Last Night?

What Time Did I Wake Up Today?

I had _____ hours of sleep

Today's practice was...

3 things I want to accomplish today...

What I learned today?

What challenged me today?

Did I eat like a winner today?   YES   NO

Did I eat any C.R.A.P. today?   YES   NO

What color was my pee today?

Red   Orange   Dark Yellow   Yellow   Light Yellow   Clear

Did I poo today?   YES   NO

WHAT I ATE TODAY?

List two things I am grateful for today.

What's my mindset today?

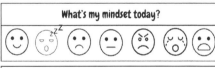

Who and How did I serve or help somebody today?

TODAY'S MAGIC: The F.I.X.ed Athlete™ Program

The biggest problem you had in your day today, how did it make you feel? If you could say in one or two words...

Did I get rid of them?   YES   NO

Essential Oils I Used Today:

What I'm looking forward to tomorrow?

SUPER GRATITUDE IN TRAINING

DID YOU KNOW?

Research shows that practicing gratitude can significantly improve both mental and physical health—especially in young athletes. Studies from institutions like Harvard Medical School and UC Berkeley's Greater Good Science Center reveal that people who regularly express gratitude experience better sleep, stronger immune systems, more optimism, and increased motivation and resilience—key traits for athletic performance.

Gratitude activates the brain's reward center (the ventral tegmental area), releases dopamine, and helps reduce stress hormones like cortisol. That means **saying "thank you" isn't just polite—it's a performance enhancer!**

Take a few quiet minutes to think about someone who supports you—your coach, parent, or a fan. On a sheet of paper or a card, write a short letter thanking them for something specific they've done to help you grow as an athlete. Be kind, be real, and let them know what their support means to you. Sign your name proudly, put it in an envelope, add a stamp, and mail it!

Bonus Challenge: *Write and send one gratitude letter each week for the next 10 weeks!*

Use the space below to practice before you write your official letter or card...

My Day

My focus for today is:
_____
_____
_____

Date _____
What Time I Went To Bed Last Night? _____
What Time Did I Wake Up Today? _____
I had _____ hours of sleep

Today's practice was...

3 things I want to accomplish today...
1. _____
2. _____
3. _____

What I learned today?

What challenged me today?

Did I eat like a winner today?   YES   NO

Did I eat any C.R.A.P. today?   YES   NO

What color was my pee today?
Red   Orange   Dark Yellow   Yellow   Light Yellow   Clear

Did I poo today?   YES   NO

WHAT I ATE TODAY?

List two things I am grateful for today.

What's my mindset today?

Who and How did I serve or help somebody today?

TODAY'S MAGIC: The F.I.X.ed Athlete™ Program
The biggest problem you had in your day today, how did it make you feel? If you could say in one or two words...

Did I get rid of them?   YES   NO

Essential Oils I Used Today:

What I'm looking forward to tomorrow?

HEY SUPERSTAR INCREASE YOUR REFLEX – REACTION TIME
Train Your Quick-Thinking Muscles

These activities are designed to be engaging and fun while secretly training crucial athletic skills such as:

- **Response Inhibition**
- **Quick Decision-Making**
- **Sport-Specific Focus**
- **Visual Recognition**
- **Predictive Skills**
- **Focus**
- **Concentration**
- **Visual Scanning**
- **Reaction Time**
- **Emotional Regulation**
- **Visual Discrimination**
- **Motor Planning**
- **Visual Perception**
- **Numerical Processing**

Circle the word ON
X-out the word GO

ON	ON	GO	ON	GO
GO	GO	ON	GO	ON
ON	ON	GO	GO	GO
ON	GO	ON	ON	GO
ON	ON	GO	GO	ON

Circle the number 02
cross out the number 2
scratch out the number 22

2	02	22	02	22
22	22	02	2	02
02	2	22	22	2
02	2	02	2	22
2	02	22	22	02

Circle the word ON
Put a box around NO

ON	ON	NO	NO	NO
NO	NO	ON	NO	ON
ON	ON	NO	NO	NO
ON	NO	ON	ON	NO
ON	ON	NO	NO	ON

Circle the BASKETBALLS
Put a box around the SOCCER BALLS

Circle the SETTERS
X-out the VOLLEYBALL
Put a box around the SPIKER

DESIGN YOUR OWN

DESIGN YOUR OWN

DESIGN YOUR OWN

My Day –

My focus for today is:
_____
_____
_____

Date _____

What Time I Went To Bed Last Night?

What Time Did I Wake Up Today?

I had _____ hours of sleep

Today's practice was...

3 things I want to accomplish today...

1. _____
2. _____
3. _____

What I learned today?

What challenged me today?

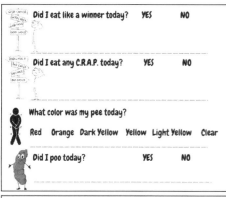

Did I eat like a winner today?   YES   NO

Did I eat any C.R.A.P. today?   YES   NO

What color was my pee today?
Red   Orange   Dark Yellow   Yellow   Light Yellow   Clear

Did I poo today?   YES   NO

WHAT I ATE TODAY?

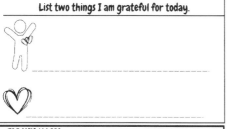

List two things I am grateful for today.

What's my mindset today?

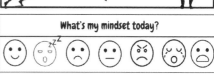

Who and How did I serve or help somebody today?

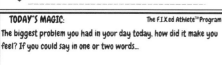

TODAY'S MAGIC: The F.I.X.ed Athlete™ Program

The biggest problem you had in your day today, how did it make you feel? If you could say in one or two words...

Did I get rid of them?   YES   NO

Essential Oils I Used Today:

What I'm looking forward to tomorrow?

HEY SUPERSTAR
Show Us How A-Maze-Ing You Are!

Are you ready to work your focus, concentration, spatial awareness, problem solving, perpetual speed, flow-state control, and some hand-eye coordination? All of these skills are needed by athletes and working the following mazes, you will strengthen these skills today...

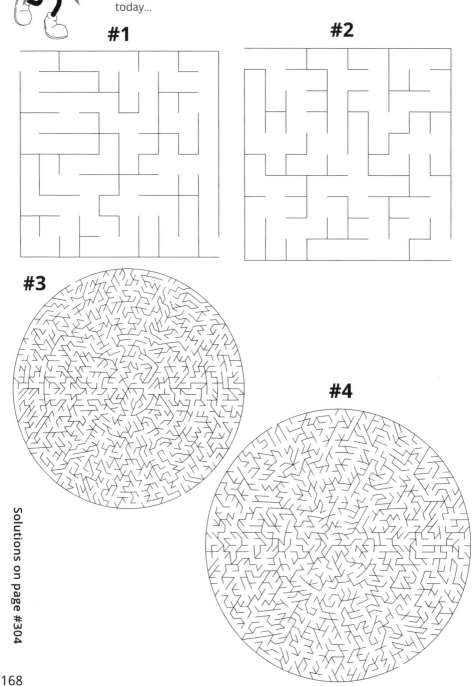

My Day -

My focus for today is:

_____
_____
_____

Date

What Time I Went To Bed Last Night?

What Time Did I Wake Up Today?

I had _____ hours of sleep

Today's practice was...

3 things I want to accomplish today...

_____

_____

_____

What I learned today?

What challenged me today?

Did I eat like a winner today?   YES   NO

Did I eat any C.R.A.P. today?   YES   NO

What color was my pee today?

Red   Orange   Dark Yellow   Yellow   Light Yellow   Clear

Did I poo today?   YES   NO

WHAT I ATE TODAY?

List two things I am grateful for today.

_____

_____

What's my mindset today?

Who and How did I serve or help somebody today?

TODAY'S MAGIC: The F.I.X.ed Athlete™ Program

The biggest problem you had in your day today, how did it make you feel? If you could say in one or two words...

Did I get rid of them? YES   NO

Essential Oils I Used Today:

What I'm looking forward to tomorrow?

HEY SUPERSTAR 5 Minutes to Greatness...

Imagine this: There are five minutes left in the game. Your team is losing, and it feels like the crowd is holding its breath. Everyone's looking around... wondering if someone will step up. That's when YOU decide to believe something amazing is possible.

Your Challenge:
Use the Wishful Thinking strategy to finish this story. Write what you wish would happen next — even if it seems impossible. Let your imagination lead.
Think: A Big Play   A Bold Speech   A Surprising Moment   A Total Team Comeback

 Think it.   ✍ Write it.   🔥 Make it unforgettable

My Day

My focus for today is:
_____
_____
_____

Date _____

What Time I Went To Bed Last Night? _____

What Time Did I Wake Up Today? _____

I had _____ hours of sleep

Today's practice was...

3 things I want to accomplish today...
- _____
- _____
- _____

What I learned today?

What challenged me today?

Did I eat like a winner today?   YES   NO

Did I eat any C.R.A.P. today?   YES   NO

What color was my pee today?

Red   Orange   Dark Yellow   Yellow   Light Yellow   Clear

Did I poo today?   YES   NO

WHAT I ATE TODAY?

List two things I am grateful for today.

What's my mindset today?

Who and How did I serve or help somebody today?

TODAY'S MAGIC: The F.I.X.ed Athlete™ Program

The biggest problem you had in your day today, how did it make you feel? If you could say in one or two words...

Did I get rid of them?   YES   NO

Essential Oils I Used Today:

What I'm looking forward to tomorrow?

COMPETITION

Are you ready for some strategic thinking, decision-making, pattern recognition, anticipation, adaptability skills and some 1:1 competition? All skills that are necessary to have as they make you a better athlete and a more powerful **SUPERSTAR In Training**! Today you will play my Penalty Box game (directions on page 140) and some Tic-Tac-Toe games.

My Day

My focus for today is:

_____
_____
_____

Date _____

What Time I Went To Bed Last Night? _____

What Time Did I Wake Up Today? _____

I had _____ hours of sleep

Today's practice was...

3 things I want to accomplish today...

1. _____
2. _____
3. _____

What I learned today?

What challenged me today?

Did I eat like a winner today?   YES   NO

Did I eat any C.R.A.P. today?   YES   NO

What color was my pee today?

Red   Orange   Dark Yellow   Yellow   Light Yellow   Clear

Did I poo today?   YES   NO

WHAT I ATE TODAY?

List two things I am grateful for today.

What's my mindset today?

Who and How did I serve or help somebody today?

TODAY'S MAGIC: The F.I.Xed Athlete™ Program

The biggest problem you had in your day today, how did it make you feel? If you could say in one or two words...

Did I get rid of them?   YES   NO

Essential Oils I Used Today:

What I'm looking forward to tomorrow?

HEY SUPERSTAR HYDRATION TRUTHS & PERFORMANCE MARKETING VERSUS SCIENCE

Learn the science behind sports drinks, hydration, and performance so you can fuel like a champion — not just follow the hype. Commercial sports drinks often promise "advanced hydration," but research shows they may hurt performance more than help. What will you drink next?

PART 1: DID YOU KNOW?

OSMOTIC TRUTHS
- Ideal absorption occurs with 275–295 mOsm/kg osmolality.
- Most sports drinks are 338–382 mOsm/kg — too high!
- Too much sugar delays hydration and makes you feel sluggish.
- Artificial colors damage your gut, increasing leakiness by 19%.
- Electrolytes are optimized for taste, not athletic performance.

HYDRATION EFFICIENCY
- Water absorption is 29% lower with sports drinks.
- 21% less effective at cellular hydration vs. natural hydration (like water + fruit + pinch of salt).
- Sports drinks stress kidneys 32% more.
- Plasma volume expansion (what keeps you cool & strong) is 18% weaker with sports drinks.
- Electrolyte recovery is 41% slower.

PERFORMANCE BREAKDOWNS
- You'll overheat faster: 2°F higher core temp.
- Feel thirstier: 35% less thirst satisfaction.
- Brain fog kicks in: Cognitive function drops 27%.
- Endurance drops by 15–19%.
- Coordination drops by 23% in hot conditions.

ATHLETIC IMPACT
- Tennis serve accuracy ↓ 22%
- Basketball shooting in Q4 ↓ 17.3%
- Soccer sprint repeat ↓ 24.6%
- Lifting power ↓ 12.8%
- Sport decision speed ↓ 31%

PART 2: Sports Drink or Science? (True/False Challenge)

Circle T or F for each:

1. Sports drinks have ideal osmolality for fast absorption.	T / F
2. A little sugar speeds up hydration.	T / F
3. Artificial colors can hurt your gut health.	T / F
4. Electrolytes in sports drinks are designed to help athletes, not just taste.	T / F
5. Sports drinks reduce kidney stress.	T / F
6. Sports drinks help you stay cooler in intense heat.	T / F
7. Sports drinks improve decision-making in long events.	T / F
8. Water with fruit, a pinch of sea salt, and a squeeze of lemon makes a great hydration solution.	T / F

What will YOU use to hydrate before, during, and after sports?
(Circle one or write your own)
- Water + Fruit + Salt
- Coconut Water
- Homemade Electrolyte Mix
- Sports Drink
- Other: _____

WRITE A HYDRATION GOAL FOR YOUR NEXT PRACTICE OR COMPETITION:

✎ "I WILL..." _____

MyDay-

My focus for today is:
_____
_____
_____
_____

Date _____

What Time I Went To Bed Last Night?

What Time Did I Wake Up Today?

I had _____ hours of sleep

Today's practice was...

3 things I want to accomplish today...
1. _____
2. _____
3. _____

What I learned today?

What challenged me today?

Did I eat like a winner today?   YES   NO

Did I eat any C.R.A.P. today?   YES   NO

What color was my pee today?
Red   Orange   Dark Yellow   Yellow   Light Yellow   Clear

Did I poo today?   YES   NO

WHAT I ATE TODAY?

List two things I am grateful for today.

What's my mindset today?

Who and How did I serve or help somebody today?

TODAY'S MAGIC: The F.I.X.ed Athlete™ Program
The biggest problem you had in your day today, how did it make you feel? If you could say in one or two words...

Did I get rid of them?   YES   NO

Essential Oils I Used Today:

What I'm looking forward to tomorrow?

SUPERSTAR'S WELLNESS QUIZ

Hey SUPERSTAR

Are you ready to test your knowledge, learn new things, engage your analytical thinking, memory, and recall? All skills that will make you a better athlete and a powerful **SUPERSTAR In Training**!

Topic Areas: Nutrition, CRAP, Sugar, Sports Drinks, Hydration, Urine/Hydration, Essential Oils

Instructions: Answer True or False. Then, check the answer key to see how you did!

SCORING GUIDE:
23-25 Correct: Elite Wellness Warrior - You're crushing the game mentally and physically!
19-22 Correct: Strong Start - Great job! You're building awesome habits.
15-18 Correct: Solid Knowledge - Time to sharpen your focus on better choices.
Below 15: Time-Out! - Let's revisit the facts and fuel up your mind.

1) C.R.A.P. stands for Carbonated drinks, Refined sugars, Artificial sweeteners, and Processed foods.
2) C.R.A.P. foods give your body long-lasting fuel for training and competition.
3) Eating colorful fruits and vegetables helps boost performance and recovery.
4) Sugar is a great pre-game energy source because it gives quick energy without any downside.
5) The average child hears the word "no" or other negative words hundreds of times per day.
6) Learning to use positive self-talk can improve both mental focus and athletic performance.
7) All sports drinks are better for hydration than water.
8) You should only drink water when you're thirsty during sports.
9) A pale yellow urine color usually means you are well-hydrated.
10) Dark yellow or brownish urine could mean you're dehydrated.
11) Essential oils can be used for focus, relaxation, or recovery by athletes.
12) Peppermint oil may help with energy and breathing during workouts.
13) Lemon essential oil can help detox the body and improve your mood.
14) Using lavender oil can help with sleep and stress recovery.
15) Sugar is hidden in many foods using names like corn syrup, dextrose, or fructose.
16) Watermelon, cucumbers, and oranges can help hydrate your body.
17) C.R.A.P. foods help your brain and body recover after tough practices.
18) You should drink soda or energy drinks right before a game.
19) Doing kind things for others, like making snacks or thanking first responders, builds character.
20) Urine that smells strong and is dark yellow means you are fully hydrated.
21) Essential oils are a substitute for healthy food and hydration.
22) Gratitude and giving back can help reduce stress and improve emotional strength.
23) Your body needs electrolytes like sodium and potassium, especially during long practices or games.
24) Overusing the word "no" can create negative habits and hurt communication.
25) Positive habits around food, hydration, and self-talk build the foundation for lifelong success.

My Day –

My focus for today is:

_____
_____
_____
_____

Date	What Time I Went To Bed Last Night?
	What Time Did I Wake Up Today?

I had _____ hours of sleep

Today's practice was…

3 things I want to accomplish today…

1. _____
2. _____
3. _____

What I learned today?

What challenged me today?

Did I eat like a winner today?   YES   NO

Did I eat any C.R.A.P. today?   YES   NO

What color was my pee today?

Red   Orange   Dark Yellow   Yellow   Light Yellow   Clear

Did I poo today?   YES   NO

WHAT I ATE TODAY?

List two things I am grateful for today.

_____
_____

What's my mindset today?

Who and How did I serve or help somebody today?

TODAY'S MAGIC: The F.I.X.ed Athlete™ Program

The biggest problem you had in your day today, how did it make you feel? If you could say in one or two words…

Did I get rid of them?   YES   NO

Essential Oils I Used Today:

What I'm looking forward to tomorrow?

Hey Superstar: Fuel & Share A Snack Challenge

Activity: Make a Homemade, Healthy Snack to Share with a neighbor or your team. This week, you're challenged to fuel your body and fuel someone else's day by preparing a healthy snack and sharing it.

Purpose:
You've been learning how proper nutrition helps you play your best, recover faster, and stay focused. But being a great athlete isn't just about how you perform — it's about how you show up for others too.

WHY THIS MATTERS:

✓ **Showing Gratitude Makes You Stronger Inside and Out**
When you take the time to thank those who support you — like teammates, coaches, family, or neighbors — you build stronger relationships, stay humble, and feel more positive energy.

✓ **Doing Good for Others Builds Team Spirit and Leadership**
Being generous and thoughtful teaches you to lead by example, be a great teammate, and earn respect — all of which are key parts of athletic excellence and life success.

✓ **Kindness is Contagious**
When you go out of your way to care for someone, it encourages others to do the same. That's how we build stronger teams, communities, and champions — from the inside out.

YOUR CHALLENGE:

1. Choose a Healthy Snack Recipe:
2. Pick something that includes:

   A natural carbohydrate (like fruit, oats, or whole grains)
   A protein or healthy fat (like nut butter, seeds, or yogurt)
   Optional: An electrolyte source (like citrus, banana, or sea salt)

SNACK IDEAS:

Nutty Energy Balls
Apple Slices with Pure Peanut Butter
Mini Hummus & Veggie Cups
Banana - Oat & Chia Seed Muffins
Meat Sticks & Cheese Wedges

Reflect & Write:
On the opposite page answer:
1. Who did you share your snack with, and why?
2. How did they respond?
3. How did you feel after doing it?
4. What does gratitude mean to you as an athlete?

MAKE IT AT HOME:

- Prep your snack safely and cleanly, and ask an adult to help if needed.
- Package It to Share... *(make sure to avoid allergies)*
- Use small containers, bags, or cups.
- Include a positive message like:

    "Fuel up — you matter!"
    "Made with hustle and heart!"
    "Here's to your next win — you've got this!"

GIVE IT AWAY:

Share it with a neighbor
Bring it to your team practice
Give it to a coach, teacher, trainer, or teammate
Surprise someone who might need a boost

SUPERSTAR'S REMINDER:

TRUE GREATNESS IS MORE THAN MEDALS OR STATS.

IT'S ABOUT CHARACTER.

GRATITUDE AND KINDNESS MAKE YOU NOT JUST A BETTER ATHLETE — BUT A BETTER HUMAN BEING!

My Day —

My focus for today is:
_____
_____
_____
_____

Date
What Time I Went To Bed Last Night?
What Time Did I Wake Up Today?
I had _____ hours of sleep

Today's practice was...

3 things I want to accomplish today...
- _____
- _____
- _____

What I learned today?

What challenged me today?

Did I eat like a winner today?   YES   NO

Did I eat any C.R.A.P. today?   YES   NO

What color was my pee today?
Red   Orange   Dark Yellow   Yellow   Light Yellow   Clear

Did I poo today?   YES   NO

WHAT I ATE TODAY?

List two things I am grateful for today.

What's my mindset today?

Who and How did I serve or help somebody today?

TODAY'S MAGIC: The F.I.X ed Athlete™ Program
The biggest problem you had in your day today, how did it make you feel? If you could say in one or two words...

Did I get rid of them?   YES   NO

Essential Oils I Used Today:

What I'm looking forward to tomorrow?

HEY SUPERSTAR CREATE YOUR OWN OBSTACLE COURSE

Athletes face obstacles every day—on the field, in the classroom, and in life. But every challenge is a chance to grow stronger, smarter, and more resilient.

Now it's your turn to **design your own Mini-Obstacle Course** using whatever you have around you—your home, room, backyard, or neighborhood. But this isn't just about jumping over chairs or running cones—this is a course that tests your physical strength, mental focus, and personal character.

Your Challenge

Step 1: Physical Obstacles
Challenge your body. Use your space and creativity!
Examples: Sprints from one side of the room to the other, jumping over a line 10 times, balancing on one foot, crawling under a table, 10 push-ups between each stop.

Step 2: Mental Obstacles
These train your focus, memory, or calm under pressure.
Examples: Recite your goals while doing jumping jacks. Do math or spelling out loud while holding a plank. Practice breathing techniques between tasks. Visualize your best performance before the next round.

Step 3: Character Obstacles
These build who you are when no one's looking—your resilience, kindness, leadership, and integrity.
*Examples: Say something positive about yourself at each station. Write or say how you'd support a teammate after a loss. Do one task with your non-dominant hand to practice patience.
Push through a task even when it's uncomfortable—then reflect: What did I learn about myself?*

YOUR FINISH LINE

Once you've completed your course, ask yourself:

What was the hardest obstacle—and why?

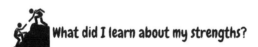

What did I learn about my strengths?

How did I grow from this challenge?

MyDay –

My focus for today is:
_____
_____
_____

Date
What Time I Went To Bed Last Night?
What Time Did I Wake Up Today?
I had _____ hours of sleep

Today's practice was...

3 things I want to accomplish today...

What I learned today?

What challenged me today?

Did I eat like a winner today?   YES   NO

Did I eat any C.R.A.P. today?   YES   NO

What color was my pee today?
Red   Orange   Dark Yellow   Yellow   Light Yellow   Clear

Did I poo today?   YES   NO

WHAT I ATE TODAY?

List two things I am grateful for today.

What's my mindset today?

Who and How did I serve or help somebody today?

TODAY'S MAGIC: The F.I.X.ed Athlete™ Program
The biggest problem you had in your day today, how did it make you feel? If you could say in one or two words...

Did I get rid of them?   YES   NO

Essential Oils I Used Today:

What I'm looking forward to tomorrow?

Schulte Tables for Athletes
Letter & Number Table

A	8	38	51	23	37	P	27	7	F
16	O	20	E	15	53	45	41	U	50
I	28	T	47	Q	6	19	58	63	46
9	1	11	34	70	62	Z	B	2	67
24	31	L	56	H	72	49	10	54	42
G	36	W	43	66	30	40	V	26	71
29	14	57	22	52	N	73	55	74	21
R	39	K	60	3	69	12	59	C	64
4	33	44	S	25	18	J	32	35	13
X	D	48	17	Y	65	5	61	68	M

My Time: ____ Date: __/__   My Time: ____ Date: __/__

My Time: ____ Date: __/__   My Time: ____ Date: __/__

My Time: ____ Date: __/__   My Time: ____ Date: __/__

My Time: ____ Date: __/__   My Time: ____ Date: __/__

My Time: ____ Date: __/__   My Time: ____ Date: __/__

My Time: ____ Date: __/__   My Time: ____ Date: __/__

My Day —

My focus for today is:

_____
_____
_____
_____

Date
What Time I Went To Bed Last Night?
What Time Did I Wake Up Today?
I had _____ hours of sleep

Today's practice was...

3 things I want to accomplish today...

_____
_____
_____

What I learned today?

What challenged me today?

Did I eat like a winner today?   YES   NO

Did I eat any C.R.A.P. today?   YES   NO

What color was my pee today?

Red   Orange   Dark Yellow   Yellow   Light Yellow   Clear

Did I poo today?   YES   NO

WHAT I ATE TODAY?

List two things I am grateful for today.

What's my mindset today?

Who and How did I serve or help somebody today?

TODAY'S MAGIC: The F.I.X.ed Athlete™ Program

The biggest problem you had in your day today, how did it make you feel? If you could say in one or two words...

Did I get rid of them?   YES   NO

Essential Oils I Used Today:

What I'm looking forward to tomorrow?

Story Starter: "Describe a time your extra effort inspired someone else. What might've happened if you held back?"

Think back to a moment — maybe during a tough practice, a big game, or even off the field — when you pushed a little harder than expected. Maybe you stayed late, cheered louder, helped a teammate who was struggling, or gave 110% even when no one was watching.

Tell the story:
- Where were you?
- What did you do differently?
- Who noticed — and how did they react?

Now imagine the same situation, but this time you hold back. You stay quiet. You don't give the extra rep. What might've happened instead? How do you think your actions created a ripple — in your team, your coach, or even in someone who never told you they were watching?

My Day

My focus for today is:
_____
_____
_____

Date _____
What Time I Went To Bed Last Night? _____
What Time Did I Wake Up Today? _____
I had _____ hours of sleep

Today's practice was...

3 things I want to accomplish today...
1. _____
2. _____
3. _____

What I learned today?

What challenged me today?

Did I eat like a winner today?   YES   NO

Did I eat any C.R.A.P. today?   YES   NO

What color was my pee today?
Red   Orange   Dark Yellow   Yellow   Light Yellow   Clear

Did I poo today?   YES   NO

WHAT I ATE TODAY?

List two things I am grateful for today.

What's my mindset today?

Who and How did I serve or help somebody today?

TODAY'S MAGIC: The F.I.X.ed Athlete™ Program
The biggest problem you had in your day today, how did it make you feel? If you could say in one or two words...

Did I get rid of them?   YES   NO

Essential Oils I Used Today:

What I'm looking forward to tomorrow?

ESSENTIAL OILS WORDSEARCH
WHAT OILS DO YOU USE AS AN ATHLETE?

HEY SUPERSTAR

Your Challenge:
Find all 20 of the most popular essential oils our young athletes are using on a daily basis or weekly to elevate their SUPERSTAR status.

```
G X O M C Z S N T P U B Z T D K L
R U D N M A V B L J X S J F H T D
R E L A V E N D E R E D C C T A D
D C S P M E T H I N K E R A H M G
V O W C K D I F F U S E R L B E A
A R K W U L C R L F H P A M R R X
K R H B Q E B A S I L B W E A D D
Y E K I R M R N S J N L W R V L Y
W C H W Y O Q K U T X U C D E L F
J T E Y X N H I S E R E N I T Y X
F X Q S T G D N N U B O H N Y T J
P E Y T E R Y C P E U S N X B Y J
K Z U N A A Y E M M A E G G F O Y
S R E U T S S N B R P T V A E H V
R I G R R S W S R T H I G C I R N
D N R P E P P E R M I N T U R H Y
O N B R E A T H E V F L E M O N R
```

DIFFUSER	LEMON	THINKER	BREATHE
LEMONGRASS	TEA TREE	TAMER	CORRECTX
PEPPERMINT	DEEP BLUE	STRONGER	TERRASHIELD
FRANKINCENSE	BRAVE	CALMER	SERENITY
LAVENDER	RESCUER	ONGUARD	BASIL

Solutions on page #305

My Day —

My focus for today is:
_____
_____
_____

Date	What Time I Went To Bed Last Night?
	What Time Did I Wake Up Today?

I had _____ hours of sleep

Today's practice was...

3 things I want to accomplish today...

1. _____
2. _____
3. _____

What I learned today?

What challenged me today?

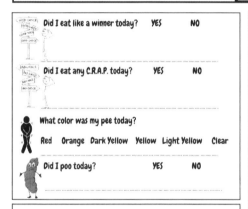

Did I eat like a winner today? YES NO

Did I eat any C.R.A.P. today? YES NO

What color was my pee today?

Red   Orange   Dark Yellow   Yellow   Light Yellow   Clear

Did I poo today? YES NO

WHAT I ATE TODAY?

List two things I am grateful for today.

What's my mindset today?

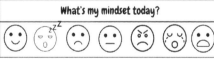

Who and How did I serve or help somebody today?

TODAY'S MAGIC: The F.I.X.ed Athlete™ Program

The biggest problem you had in your day today, how did it make you feel? If you could say in one or two words...

Did I get rid of them? YES NO

Essential Oils I Used Today:

What I'm looking forward to tomorrow?

HEY SUPERSTAR CREATE A WEEKLY MEAL PLAN
Fuel Your Body. Fire Up Your Brain. Finish Strong

Your body is your powerhouse. Just like you train your muscles and your mindset, you need to fuel them with smart food choices. This week, you're the Head Coach of Nutrition—and you're creating your very own weekly meal plan! Use the food section of your training pages to PLAN & Track your progress

This Week's Challenge:

☑ STEP 1: KNOW YOUR POWER ZONES
You'll need food for 3 main times every day:
Meals: Breakfast 🍳, Lunch 🥪, Dinner 🍽
Snacks: Before Practice/Competition, During (if needed), After Practice/Recovery

☑ STEP 2: THE MAGIC FORMULA
Use this formula to plan every day:
- **Before Practice or Game:** A small snack with healthy carbs + a little protein
  (ex: banana + peanut butter)
- ⚡ **During:** Water & easy-to-digest snacks only if long practice
  (ex: orange slices, pretzels)
- ◎ **After Practice or Game:** Protein + carbs to recover
  (ex: protein smoothie, yogurt + granola, turkey sandwich)

☑ STEP 3: PLAN YOUR WEEK
Use a simple table or grid to plan each day's: **Breakfast   Lunch   Dinner**
  Pre-Practice Snack After-Practice Recovery Snack
  Remember any: "On-the-Go" needs (weekend games, travel, tournaments)

☑ STEP 4: BALANCE YOUR PLATE
At every meal, ask:
- 🍎 Do I have a fruit or veggie?
- 🍗 Do I have protein? (meat, eggs, yogurt, beans, nuts)
- 🍠 Do I have a healthy carb? (sweet potatoes, quinoa)
- 💧 Am I drinking enough water?

☑ STEP 5: SUPERSTAR TIP:
Plan snacks the night before and pack them in your bag.

Ask your parents or coaches to review your plan -

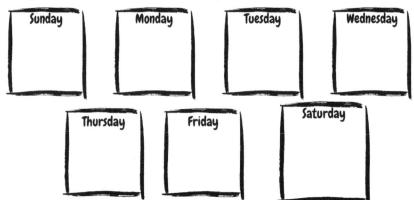

MyDay —

My focus for today is:

_____
_____
_____

Date	What Time I Went To Bed Last Night?
	What Time Did I Wake Up Today?
I had _____ hours of sleep	

Today's practice was...

3 things I want to accomplish today...

1.
2.
3.

What I learned today?

What challenged me today?

Did I eat like a winner today?   YES   NO

Did I eat any C.R.A.P. today?   YES   NO

What color was my pee today?

Red   Orange   Dark Yellow   Yellow   Light Yellow   Clear

Did I poo today?   YES   NO

WHAT I ATE TODAY?

List two things I am grateful for today.

What's my mindset today?

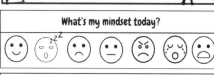

Who and How did I serve or help somebody today?

TODAY'S MAGIC: The F.I.X.ed Athlete™ Program

The biggest problem you had in your day today, how did it make you feel? If you could say in one or two words...

Did I get rid of them?   YES   NO

Essential Oils I Used Today:

What I'm looking forward to tomorrow?

HEY SUPERSTAR BUILDING YOUR FIRM FOUNDATION
Proper Foot Care Can Lead To Excellent Performances

Your Challenge: Here's 28-questions to help athletes learn more about proper foot care. Healthy feet provide the foundation for balance, power, and agility in every movement. Preventing injuries like blisters, sprains, and infections ensures athletes can train consistently and perform at their highest level without setbacks.

Across:
1. FOOTWEAR SHOULD BE PROPERLY _____ TO AVOID BLISTERS
2. THESE OCCUR WHEN SOES RUB THE WRONG WAY
3. WHEN YOUR TOENAIL GROWS INTO THE SKIN
4. SOAKING YOUR FEET IN WARM WATER HELPS THIS
5. STRETCH THIS PART OF THE FOOT TO HELP PREVENT PLANTAR FASCIITIS
6. IMPORTANT TO DO AFTER WASHING FEET
7. THESE FOOT BONES GIVE YOUR FOOT STRUCTURE AND MOVEMENT
8. WORN-OUT _____ CAN CAUSE FOOT AND ANKLE INJURIES
9. SKIN BETWEEN TOES SHOULD BE KEPT _____ TO AVOID FUNGUS
10. A FOOT INJURY THAT CAUSES SHARP HEEL PAIN
11. THESE CAN BE USED IN SHOES TO SUPPORT ARCHES
12. WHAT ATHLETES SHOUD CHECK DAILY FOR CUTS, SWELLING, OR BLISTERS
13. BEFORE AND AFTER WORKSOUTS, ALWAYS DO THIS WITH YOUR FEET
14. RAISED PART OF YOUR FOOT THAT NEEDS SUPPORT

Down:
1. THICK SKIN THAT FORMS FROM FRICTION
2. COMMON INJURY FROM NOT WARMING UP PROPERLY
3. NEVER WALK BAREFOOT IN THESE PUBLIC PLACES
4. WEARING SHOES THAT ARE TOO SMALL CAUSE THIS FOOT CONDITION
5. TYPE OF FUNGUS THAT CAUSES ITCHING AND CRACKING BETWEEN TOES
6. ALSAYS DO THIS TO YOUR TOENAILS TO AVOID SNAGGING
7. RUNNING SHOES SHOULD BE REPLACED EVERY _____ MILES
8. ACRONYM FOR TREATING MINOR INJURIES (REST, ICE, COMPRESSION, ELEVATION)
9. SHOULD BE CUT STRAIGHT ACROSS TO PREVENT INGROWN NAILS
10. CHOOSE SOCKS MADE FROM THIS MATERIAL TO AVOID SWEAT BUILDUP
11. THE TYPE OF DOCTOR WHO SPECIALIZES IN FOOT CARE
12. THE NUMBER OF TOES ON EACH FOOT
13. A BAD SMELL CAN BE CAUSED BY THIS BUILD-UP IN SHOES
14. PRACTICE GOOD _____ TO AVOID INFECTIONS

Answers on page #305

My Day –

My focus for today is:
_____
_____
_____

Date

What Time I Went To Bed Last Night?

What Time Did I Wake Up Today?

I had _____ hours of sleep

Today's practice was...

3 things I want to accomplish today...

What I learned today?

What challenged me today?

Did I eat like a winner today?   YES   NO

Did I eat any C.R.A.P. today?   YES   NO

What color was my pee today?
Red   Orange   Dark Yellow   Yellow   Light Yellow   Clear

Did I poo today?   YES   NO

WHAT I ATE TODAY?

List two things I am grateful for today.

What's my mindset today?

Who and How did I serve or help somebody today?

TODAY'S MAGIC: The F.I.X.ed Athlete™ Program
The biggest problem you had in your day today, how did it make you feel? If you could say in one or two words...

Did I get rid of them?   YES   NO

Essential Oils I Used Today:

What I'm looking forward to tomorrow?

HEY SUPERSTAR Game Changer Gratitude Mission

ACTIVITY:
Do Something Kind for a First Responder or Emergency Worker

PURPOSE:
As a young athlete, you train to be strong in body — but the strongest athletes also have strong hearts. This week's mission is about giving back to some of the quiet heroes in your community: First Responders — including Police Officers, Firefighters, Paramedics, EMTs, and Hospital Room Staff

These are the people who show up when someone's hurt — and many of them have helped athletes just like you on the sidelines, at games, during accidents, or in emergencies. They often work long hours, face danger, and do it all without ever being thanked by the people they serve.

WHY THIS MATTERS:

✓ **Gratitude in Action**
Saying thank you is important — showing thank you is powerful. It builds character and makes the world better.

✓ **Real-Life MVPs Help Athletes Every Day**
When an athlete is injured, passes out, or needs urgent help, First Responders are often the ones who step in. Your appreciation may one day come full circle.

✓ **Teamwork Is Bigger Than Sports**
You're part of a larger team — the human team. Just like teammates lift each other up, we lift up our community too.

YOUR CHALLENGE:

- **PICK ONE GROUP OF FIRST RESPONDERS NEAR YOU:**
  - FIREFIGHTERS
  - POLICE OFFICERS
  - PARAMEDICS/EMTS
  - EMERGENCY ROOM DOCTORS, NURSES, AND STAFF

- **CREATE AND DELIVER A SMALL ACT OF KINDNESS:**

  Here are some great options:

  ☑ **HEALTHY SNACK PACKS:**
  Include items like trail mix, fruit cups, water bottles, or granola bars. Add a note of encouragement or thanks.

  ☑ **HANDWRITTEN CARDS OR POSTERS**
  Write a message like:
  "Thank you for helping athletes like me stay safe."
  "You're the MVPs when things go wrong."
  "We notice what you do — and we're grateful."

  ☑ **CARE BASKET FROM THE TEAM**
  Gather small items (snacks, coffee, thank-you notes, mini gift cards) and decorate a box or bag with your team colors.

- **MAKE THE DELIVERY:**
  Ask a parent or coach to help you deliver it to a local station or hospital. You can drop it off with a note from your team.

BEING A GREAT ATHLETE ISN'T JUST ABOUT SCORING POINTS OR WINNING RACES — IT'S ALSO ABOUT BEING A PERSON OTHERS CAN COUNT ON. KINDNESS IS A LEGACY. AND REAL CHAMPIONS GIVE BACK.

My Day —

Date

What Time I Went To Bed Last Night?

What Time Did I Wake Up Today?

I had _____ hours of sleep

My focus for today is:
_____
_____
_____

Today's practice was...

3 things I want to accomplish today...

What I learned today?

What challenged me today?

Did I eat like a winner today?   YES   NO

Did I eat any C.R.A.P. today?   YES   NO

What color was my pee today?

Red   Orange   Dark Yellow   Yellow   Light Yellow   Clear

Did I poo today?   YES   NO

WHAT I ATE TODAY?

List two things I am grateful for today.

What's my mindset today?

Who and How did I serve or help somebody today?

TODAY'S MAGIC: The F.I.X.ed Athlete™ Program

The biggest problem you had in your day today, how did it make you feel? If you could say in one or two words...

Did I get rid of them?   YES   NO

Essential Oils I Used Today:

What I'm looking forward to tomorrow?

The SUPERSTAR In Training - Fitness Challenge

Tracking your baseline and progress over time helps you see just how far you've come—and where to focus your efforts next. It's not about being perfect; it's about getting stronger, faster, and more confident with every rep, jump, sprint, and skill. As a SUPERSTAR In Training, your goal is always to progress forward – both inside and out.

📅 TESTING DAY:

Time of Day: _____

Today's Body Weight (lbs): _____

💪 SELECT YOUR LEVEL

Pick the level based on your age group. Compete only with yourself—and go for that personal best!

LEVEL	AGE GROUP	INTENSITY
⭐ Level 1	Ages - & Under	Foundation Training (Fun Form & Focus)
⭐⭐ Level 2	Ages 10 – 12	Challenge Training (Speed & Strength)
⭐⭐⭐ Level 3	Ages 13 +	Elite Training (Power & Performance)

💪 THE SUPERSTAR FITNESS CHALLENGES 💪

In each of the following activities, record your **best of 3 attempts** for each test. You may decide to select any of the times, distances, or object you want in the Sprint, Jump Rope, and throw. Be honest. Be tough. Be proud.

TEST	Attempt #1	Attempt #2	Attempt #3	PERSONAL BEST
Push-Ups (Max reps)				
Sit-Ups (Max reps)				
Jump Rope (Reps in 1 – 2 - 5 minutes)				
Burpees (Reps in 1 minute)				
Plank Hold (Seconds)				
Wall Sit (Seconds)				
Sprint – 40 / 50 / 100 -yard dash (Seconds)				
Standing Throw (Ft/In) Baseball, Softball, Football				
High Jump Touch (Wall mark)				
Broad Jump (Ft/In)				
Leg Raise Hold – 6 in. (Seconds)				

My Day —

My focus for today is:
_____
_____
_____
_____

Date _____
What Time I Went To Bed Last Night? _____
What Time Did I Wake Up Today? _____
I had _____ hours of sleep

Today's practice was...

3 things I want to accomplish today...
1. _____
2. _____
3. _____

What I learned today?

What challenged me today?

Did I eat like a winner today? YES NO

Did I eat any C.R.A.P. today? YES NO

What color was my pee today?
Red Orange Dark Yellow Yellow Light Yellow Clear

Did I poo today? YES NO

WHAT I ATE TODAY?

List two things I am grateful for today.
_____
_____

What's my mindset today?

Who and How did I serve or help somebody today?

TODAY'S MAGIC: The F.I.X.ed Athlete™ Program
The biggest problem you had in your day today, how did it make you feel? If you could say in one or two words...

Did I get rid of them? YES NO

Essential Oils I Used Today:

What I'm looking forward to tomorrow?

SUPERFOODS WORDSEARCH

HEY SUPERSTAR

Eat like a Champion!   Feel like a Champion!   Perform like a Champion!

Your Challenge:
Find all of the SUPERFOODS in the puzzle below...

C	H	I	C	K	E	N	K	R	S	Q	I	F	K	T	O	Y	S
N	R	A	W	P	U	M	P	K	I	N	S	E	E	D	S	Q	K
R	C	H	W	C	Z	S	W	M	S	P	H	B	E	E	T	S	C
B	F	R	J	H	L	W	C	G	I	C	I	E	I	Z	K	X	I
L	K	B	P	I	M	E	G	E	A	V	R	R	W	F	A	E	D
U	R	A	H	A	M	E	A	U	A	V	R	Z	I	S	J	Q	D
E	A	T	L	S	H	T	B	N	Q	E	O	N	K	V	O	U	Z
B	N	A	S	E	H	P	V	D	B	R	O	C	C	O	L	I	Z
E	H	R	A	E	U	O	P	K	J	E	A	A	A	S	L	N	E
R	G	T	L	D	W	T	C	K	W	N	E	E	J	D	X	O	N
R	G	C	M	S	S	A	D	K	S	J	N	F	U	L	O	A	N
I	S	H	O	W	L	T	O	D	I	E	Z	H	U	Y	U	S	T
E	Z	E	N	B	Z	O	E	W	A	L	N	U	T	S	T	Z	K
S	T	R	A	W	B	E	R	R	I	E	S	N	X	T	T	B	Q
H	E	R	A	C	W	S	A	R	D	I	N	E	S	K	W	W	I
L	T	I	Z	A	H	Q	R	K	K	T	G	Z	A	Y	S	J	H
H	G	E	E	U	P	K	G	W	S	P	I	N	A	C	H	E	M
B	S	S	S	R	O	P	G	K	C	I	X	O	S	Z	S	U	Y

EGGS	BLUEBERRIES	PUMPKIN SEEDS	AVOCADOS
SALMON	BLACKBERRIES	CHIA SEEDS	BROCCOLI
CLEAN BEEF	STRAWBERRIES	SEAWEED SNACKS	BEETS
SARDINES	TART CHERRIES	KALE	SWEET POTATOES
CHICKEN	WALNUTS	SPINACH	QUINOA

Answers on page #306

MyDay —

My focus for today is:
_____
_____
_____

Date	What Time I Went To Bed Last Night?
	What Time Did I Wake Up Today?
I had _____ hours of sleep	

Today's practice was...

3 things I want to accomplish today...

What I learned today?

What challenged me today?

Did I eat like a winner today? YES NO

Did I eat any C.R.A.P. today? YES NO

What color was my pee today?

Red   Orange   Dark Yellow   Yellow   Light Yellow   Clear

Did I poo today? YES NO

WHAT I ATE TODAY?

List two things I am grateful for today.

What's my mindset today?

Who and How did I serve or help somebody today?

TODAY'S MAGIC: The F.I.X.ed Athlete™ Program
The biggest problem you had in your day today, how did it make you feel? If you could say in one or two words...

Did I get rid of them? YES NO

Essential Oils I Used Today:

What I'm looking forward to tomorrow?

Hey Superstar: Hydration & Urine Colors

Knowing your urine colors is important for athletes because it's one of the simplest and most accurate ways to monitor hydration levels, which are essential for peak performance, safety, and recovery. Color the urine samples below to best know how you are doing with staying hydrated...Coconut water, bone broth, & electrolyte drinks are great natural hydration boosters.

COLOR the urine samples then match them with their counterpart

#1 RED

A — OVERHYDRATED if too frequent

#2 ORANGE

B — DEHYDRATED

#3 DARK YELLOW

C — ALERT Parent & Coaches GET IMMEDIATE MEDICAL HELP!

#4 LIGHT YELLOW

D — SEVERELY DEHYDRATED Alert Parent & Coaches

#5 CLEAR

E — OPTIMAL HYDRATION

MyDay –

My focus for today is:
_____
_____
_____

Date _____

What Time I Went To Bed Last Night? _____

What Time Did I Wake Up Today? _____

I had _____ hours of sleep

Today's practice was...

3 things I want to accomplish today...
1. _____
2. _____
3. _____

What I learned today?

What challenged me today?

Did I eat like a winner today?   YES   NO

Did I eat any C.R.A.P. today?   YES   NO

What color was my pee today?
Red   Orange   Dark Yellow   Yellow   Light Yellow   Clear

Did I poo today?   YES   NO

WHAT I ATE TODAY?

List two things I am grateful for today.
1. _____
2. _____

What's my mindset today?

Who and How did I serve or help somebody today?

TODAY'S MAGIC: The F.I.X.ed Athlete™ Program
The biggest problem you had in your day today, how did it make you feel? If you could say in one or two words...

Did I get rid of them?   YES   NO

Essential Oils I Used Today:

What I'm looking forward to tomorrow?

SUPERSTAR VISUAL MEMORY ACTIVITY
Sports

How to play:
- Set your timer for allotted amount of time (15-60 seconds suggested).
- When ready, start the timer and study the images on the page. Try to remember as many as you can!
- When time's up, close the book or cover the page.
- Now set your timer for 1-2 minutes.
- Write down as many images as you can remember. Be specific! (For example, "running shoes" or "track spikes" is better than just "shoes")
- When time's up, stop writing.
- Open the book and check your list against the image page.
    - Score 1 point for each correct item.
    - Give yourself an extra point for very specific details.
- Challenge yourself to beat your score next time!

Play this game often to improve your visual memory.
Try it alone or compete with teammates!

TIP: Great athletes have strong visualization skills. This game can help you develop those skills for better performance in your sport. Can you remember the 35 items? How about some of the unique details?

Remember: You can practice this mental exercise anytime, anywhere - before practice, after training, or before bed. The more you practice, the stronger your mind, memory, and visual skills will becomes. ALSO: Start looking for clues on the playing field...

© 2025 Barb V   All Rights Reserved

My Day —

My focus for today is:
_____
_____
_____
_____

Date
I had _____ hours of sleep

What Time I Went To Bed Last Night?
What Time Did I Wake Up Today?

3 things I want to accomplish today...
1. _____
2. _____
3. _____

Today's practice was...

What I learned today?

What challenged me today?

Did I eat like a winner today?   YES   NO

Did I eat any C.R.A.P. today?   YES   NO

What color was my pee today?
Red   Orange   Dark Yellow   Yellow   Light Yellow   Clear

Did I poo today?   YES   NO

WHAT I ATE TODAY?

List two things I am grateful for today.

What's my mindset today?

Who and How did I serve or help somebody today?

TODAY'S MAGIC: The F.I.X.ed Athlete™ Program
The biggest problem you had in your day today, how did it make you feel? If you could say in one or two words...

Did I get rid of them?   YES   NO

Essential Oils I Used Today:

What I'm looking forward to tomorrow?

ETIQUETTE FOR ATHLETES

Etiquette is the Silent Language of Respect.

For young athletes, knowing and using proper etiquette - whether in practice, competition, or daily life - reflects discipline, maturity, sportsmanship, and emotional intelligence. Etiquette helps athletes build stronger relationships with coaches, teammates, opponents, officials, and fans.

BE THE CLASS - ACT ATHLETE

Objective: Practice proper athlete etiquette in real-life scenarios and reflect on your experiences.

Challenge for Young Athletes:

Choose 5 scenarios this week where you will intentionally practice elite etiquette. Here are some examples:

- Shake hands with a referee and say, "Thank you for your time today."
- Congratulate an opponent genuinely after a game, win or lose.
- Help clean up the team area after practice without being asked.
- Greet your coach, teammates, or teammate's parents with eye contact and a **"Good morning!", "Nice work today!",** or **"How is your day going today?"**
- Hold a door open or assist someone carrying sports equipment or a young child.

Journal your experiences. After each scenario, write down:

- What happened
- How you responded
- How the other person reacted
- How it made you feel

PLUS:

Interview a coach or adult about why etiquette matters in sports and life.

Ask:
- "What's the best example of good sportsmanship or etiquette you've seen?"
- "Why do you think it matters as much as skill or talent?"
- "What advice can you give me about etiquette that will change my future as an athlete?"

Wrap-Up Reflection:

Write a paragraph titled: **"I Am the Example"** where you reflect on:
- What you learned about yourself
- How you want to be remembered by others in sports
- One new etiquette habit you will use every week

PROPER ETIQUETTE...

- ☑ **On the field, - builds a positive team culture, promotes fair play, and earns respect.**
- ☑ **Off the field, it opens doors for leadership roles, scholarship opportunities, endorsements, and long-term success.**
- ☑ **In life, it reinforces habits of kindness, integrity, and self-awareness that transcend sports.**

My Day —

My focus for today is:

_____

_____

_____

Date	What Time I Went To Bed Last Night?
	What Time Did I Wake Up Today?
I had _____ hours of sleep	

Today's practice was...

3 things I want to accomplish today...

1. _____
2. _____
3. _____

What I learned today?

What challenged me today?

Did I eat like a winner today?   YES   NO

Did I eat any C.R.A.P. today?   YES   NO

What color was my pee today?

Red   Orange   Dark Yellow   Yellow   Light Yellow   Clear

Did I poo today?   YES   NO

WHAT I ATE TODAY?

List two things I am grateful for today.

What's my mindset today?

Who and How did I serve or help somebody today?

TODAY'S MAGIC: The F.I.X.ed Athlete™ Program

The biggest problem you had in your day today, how did it make you feel? If you could say in one or two words...

Did I get rid of them?   YES   NO

Essential Oils I Used Today:

What I'm looking forward to tomorrow?

MyDay—

My focus for today is:
_____
_____
_____
_____

Date

What Time I Went To Bed Last Night?

What Time Did I Wake Up Today?

I had _____ hours of sleep

Today's practice was...

3 things I want to accomplish today...

1. _____
2. _____
3. _____

What I learned today?

What challenged me today?

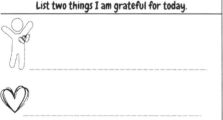

Did I eat like a winner today?   YES   NO

Did I eat any C.R.A.P. today?   YES   NO

What color was my pee today?

Red   Orange   Dark Yellow   Yellow   Light Yellow   Clear

Did I poo today?   YES   NO

WHAT I ATE TODAY?

List two things I am grateful for today.

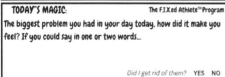

What's my mindset today?

Who and How did I serve or help somebody today?

TODAY'S MAGIC: The F.I.X.ed Athlete™ Program

The biggest problem you had in your day today, how did it make you feel? If you could say in one or two words...

Did I get rid of them?   YES   NO

Essential Oils I Used Today:

What I'm looking forward to tomorrow?

ETIQUETTE FOR ATHLETES
A WEEKLY CHALLENGE!

HEY SUPERSTAR

Developing Leadership & Respect
This week you are going to strengthen your social conduct and sportsmanship by practicing one key etiquette behavior each day for a full week — at practice, school, home, or in public.

Instructions:
1. Print or draw a 7-day challenge chart with space for each day's action and reflection.
2. Each day, the athlete chooses (or is assigned) one etiquette behavior from the list below.
3. The athlete must put that behavior into action during the day and reflect briefly on:
   - Who they interacted with
   - What happened
   - How it felt
   - What difference it made (for them or someone else)

Sample Etiquette Behaviors for Each Day:
Day 1: Give someone your full attention while they're speaking (eye contact, no interruptions).
Day 2: Say "thank you" or "I appreciate you" to at least 3 people — teammates, parents, coach, bus driver, etc.
Day 3: Shake hands (or fist bump) and compliment an opponent after a game or practice.
Day 4: Arrive early and prepared — show that you respect others' time.
Day 5: Pick up after yourself and someone else without being asked (locker room, field, classroom).
Day 6: Share credit publicly for a team achievement or success (even if you stood out).
Day 7: Write a short note of gratitude or encouragement to someone who supports your journey (coach, parent, teammate, trainer, teacher).

Reflection Prompts (Each Day):
1. What did I do today to show great etiquette?
2. Who did it impact, and how?
3. How did it feel to lead with respect?
4. Would I want someone to treat me this way?
5. Track your own question:
6. Track your own question:

	SUN	MON	TUE	WED	THR	FRI	SAT
#1							
#2							
#3							
#4							
#5							
#6							

My Day –

My focus for today is:
_____
_____
_____

Date	What Time I Went To Bed Last Night?
	What Time Did I Wake Up Today?
I had _____ hours of sleep	

3 things I want to accomplish today...

Today's practice was...

What I learned today?

What challenged me today?

Did I eat like a winner today?   YES   NO

Did I eat any C.R.A.P. today?   YES   NO

What color was my pee today?
Red   Orange   Dark Yellow   Yellow   Light Yellow   Clear

Did I poo today?   YES   NO

WHAT I ATE TODAY?

List two things I am grateful for today.

What's my mindset today?

Who and How did I serve or help somebody today?

TODAY'S MAGIC: The F.I.X.ed Athlete™ Program
The biggest problem you had in your day today, how did it make you feel? If you could say in one or two words...

Did I get rid of them?   YES   NO

Essential Oils I Used Today:

What I'm looking forward to tomorrow?

A SILENT SIDELINE CHALLENGE
A Powerful Exercise in Inner Confidence and Athletic Growth

This week, we're asking for a powerful pause.

During practices and games, all parents, coaches, teammates, and fans are invited to go completely silent:
- No cheering
- No clapping
- No coaching
- No signs, whistles, or gestures

Instead, we'll observe, support, and reflect—all in silence.

This Week's Challenge:

Before the Game or Practice: Post These Reminders

Place posters and signs at the field, gym, or arena entry points and around the area that read:

WELCOME TO SILENT SIDELINE WEEK

Today is about growth, focus, and independence.

Thank you for honoring this space and giving our athletes the chance to shine from within.

Why This Is Important

Silent Sideline Week teaches athletes to:
- Stay grounded and focused from within, not from external energy.
- Build decision-making skills, resilience, and ownership of their performance.
- Stay centered and play for their own reasons, not to please the crowd.
- Parents, guardians, and coaches will learn to:
- Reflect on their own energy and emotions during the athlete's performance.
- Understand the power of letting athletes figure things out on their own.
- See mistakes as essential growth steps—not moments to fix or control.

After the Game or Practice: Team & Family Debrief

Have each group reflect in these 3 categories:

1. **ATHLETES:**
- What did you notice when no one was shouting?
- Did you feel more or less focused? Why?
- How did you problem-solve or lead yourself?

2. **ADULTS:**
- How did it feel to remain silent?
- Did you notice your own tension, excitement, or desire to coach?
- What surprised you about your athlete's performance?

3. **COACHES:**
- Did players communicate more with each other?
- Did anyone step into leadership roles?
- Were athletes more thoughtful or responsive?

🏆 Make This a Season Tradition 🏆

Consider repeating Silent Sideline:
- Once every 4-6 weeks
- Start during pre-season
- During key scrimmages or learning-focused sessions
- For team bonding and culture reset moments

WHY?

Because ***giving athletes room to think, fall, grow, and lead*** — without the noise — ***is one of the greatest gifts we can give them.***

My Day -

My focus for today is:
_____
_____
_____

Date _____

What Time I Went To Bed Last Night? _____

What Time Did I Wake Up Today? _____

I had _____ hours of sleep

Today's practice was...

3 things I want to accomplish today...
1. _____
2. _____
3. _____

What I learned today?

What challenged me today?

Did I eat like a winner today?   YES   NO

Did I eat any C.R.A.P. today?   YES   NO

What color was my pee today?

Red   Orange   Dark Yellow   Yellow   Light Yellow   Clear

Did I poo today?   YES   NO

WHAT I ATE TODAY?

List two things I am grateful for today.
_____
_____

What's my mindset today?

Who and How did I serve or help somebody today?

TODAY'S MAGIC: The F.I.X.ed Athlete™ Program
The biggest problem you had in your day today, how did it make you feel? If you could say in one or two words...

Did I get rid of them?   YES   NO

Essential Oils I Used Today:

What I'm looking forward to tomorrow?

HEY SUPERSTAR UPBEAT WORDS WORDSEARCH

Eat like a Champion! Feel like a Champion! Perform like a Champion!

Your Challenge: FIND ALL 15 OF THE UPBEAT WORDS IN THE PUZZLE BELOW...

A	H	S	U	D	H	M	H	J	N	N	T	Q	X	X
Y	F	Y	B	C	V	Y	B	C	H	V	H	D	F	A
A	I	W	R	E	U	L	O	D	S	G	R	Y	C	L
A	X	B	H	U	A	C	R	G	I	A	O	V	F	T
Y	E	K	G	D	N	S	N	B	W	W	W	O	A	C
H	D	E	O	V	N	F	T	R	A	E	E	E	Q	I
W	L	Y	L	D	U	F	O	M	B	G	R	X	M	R
B	I	S	D	I	I	F	W	R	O	G	A	T	H	I
M	F	N	E	L	O	N	I	M	L	D	A	R	E	Z
N	E	O	N	G	S	P	N	G	U	I	E	E	F	T
J	U	M	P	E	R	E	X	X	F	U	F	M	N	C
B	A	L	L	E	R	F	I	X	C	O	D	E	A	D
Q	P	I	U	Y	M	R	J	Z	A	E	L	I	G	M
W	F	O	C	U	S	E	D	K	R	N	S	U	D	X
Z	C	Y	M	F	L	F	W	Q	I	I	Q	W	G	W

Answers on page #306

GREAT
FIXED LIFE
LIFT BIG
BORN TO WIN
GO FORWARD

BEAST MODE
FOCUSED
WINNER
RUN FOR LIFE
JUMPER

THROWER
FIX CODE
GOLDEN
EXTREME
BALLER

My Day –

My focus for today is:
_____
_____
_____

Date _____

What Time I Went To Bed Last Night? _____

What Time Did I Wake Up Today? _____

I had _____ hours of sleep

Today's practice was...

3 things I want to accomplish today...

1. _____
2. _____
3. _____

What I learned today?

What challenged me today?

Did I eat like a winner today? YES NO

Did I eat any C.R.A.P. today? YES NO

What color was my pee today?

Red   Orange   Dark Yellow   Yellow   Light Yellow   Clear

Did I poo today? YES NO

WHAT I ATE TODAY?

List two things I am grateful for today.

What's my mindset today?

Who and How did I serve or help somebody today?

TODAY'S MAGIC: The F.I.X.ed Athlete™ Program

The biggest problem you had in your day today, how did it make you feel? If you could say in one or two words...

Did I get rid of them? YES NO

Essential Oils I Used Today:

What I'm looking forward to tomorrow?

COMPLETE THE IMAGE

HEY SUPERSTAR

Imagine this:
The stadium was electric, but inside, everything was still.
As the anthem began to play, the Superstar stepped onto the tallest step of the podium. The golden sunlight poured down like a spotlight, catching the shimmer of the medal now hanging around their neck. Their hands—calloused from thousands of hours of practice—rose slowly to their heart.
Their eyes sparkled with tears—not just from victory, but from the memory of every early morning, every tough moment, every time they wanted to quit and chose to rise instead. Confetti danced in the air like tiny stars. The flag waved high behind them. The crowd erupted, but the Superstar just smiled, closed their eyes for a second, and whispered: "I did it."

🌀 Your Challenge 🌀

- Draw what you imagine this moment looks like.
- Use what you see in your mind:
- What is the Superstar wearing?
- What does their medal look like?
- Are there tears, sweat, or confetti on their face?
- What emotion is written in their body language?
- What colors do you see around the podium?
- What flag is waving behind them?
- Is there a crowd, or do you focus only on the SUPERSTAR Athlete?

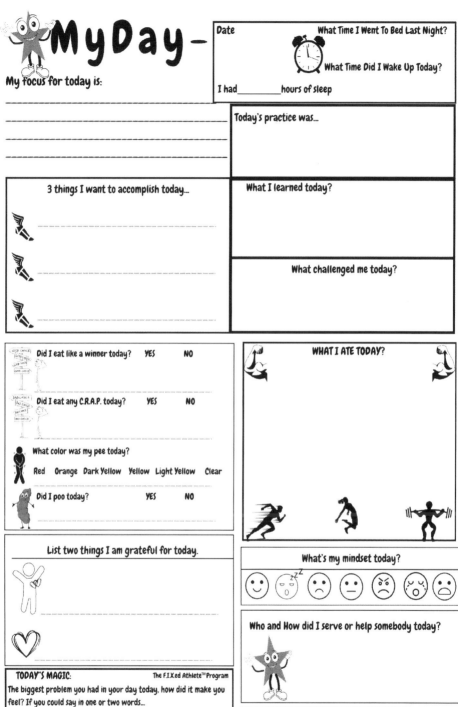

COMPETITION

Are you ready for some strategic thinking, decision-making, pattern recognition, anticipation, adaptability skills and some 1:1 competition? All skills that are necessary to have as they make you a better athlete and a more powerful **SUPERSTAR In Training**! Today you will play my Penalty Box game (directions on page 140) and some Tic-Tac-Toe games.

My Day –

My focus for today is:
_____
_____
_____

Date	What Time I Went To Bed Last Night?
	What Time Did I Wake Up Today?
I had _____ hours of sleep	

Today's practice was...

3 things I want to accomplish today...
- _____
- _____
- _____

What I learned today?

What challenged me today?

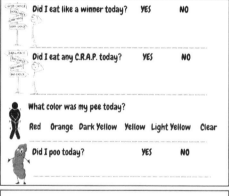

Did I eat like a winner today?   YES   NO

Did I eat any C.R.A.P. today?   YES   NO

What color was my pee today?

Red   Orange   Dark Yellow   Yellow   Light Yellow   Clear

Did I poo today?   YES   NO

WHAT I ATE TODAY?

List two things I am grateful for today.

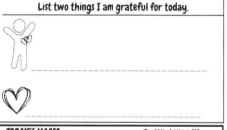

What's my mindset today?

Who and How did I serve or help somebody today?

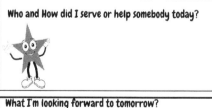

TODAY'S MAGIC: The F.I.X.ed Athlete™ Program
The biggest problem you had in your day today, how did it make you feel? If you could say in one or two words...

Did I get rid of them?   YES   NO

Essential Oils I Used Today:

What I'm looking forward to tomorrow?

NERVOUS SYSTEM TRAINING
BREATH REGULATES YOUR YOUR HEART RATE – FOCUS – REACTION TIMES

Breathing is one of the fastest ways to shift your state — from stress to calm or from fatigue to focus. Athletes who can control their breathing have a competitive edge.

KEY CONCEPTS:
- Focus & Attention sets the scene for the nervous system
- Breath regulates heart rate, focus, and reaction time.
- Short, shallow breaths = stress.
- Slow, controlled breaths = calm power.

NERVOUS SYSTEM TRAINING EXERCISES

1. The F.I.X. Code
Full-Body Energy Clearing & Reset

Focus: *Emotional regulation, energetic release, nervous system reset*

How It Works:
The F.I.X. Code helps athletes release stored negative emotions, stress, and nervous system overload. By clearing blocked energies in different body regions (gut, heart, muscles, brain), the body rebalances and resets into a calm, focused state.

Benefits:
- Improves performance clarity
- Enhances recovery from emotional triggers
- Builds emotional resilience and inner peace

2. 🫁 Box Breathing 🫁 (Tactical Breathing)
Calms the Fight-or-Flight Response

Focus: *Parasympathetic nervous system activation*

How It Works:
Breathe in a square rhythm — inhale, hold, exhale, hold — all for equal counts. This method sends a signal of safety to the nervous system, helping reduce anxiety and improve focus before or after competition.

Try This:
- Inhale for 4 counts
- Hold for 4 counts
- Exhale for 4 counts
- Hold for 4 counts
- Repeat for 2–3 minutes

Benefits:
- Lowers stress hormones
- Improves heart rate variability
- Enhances decision-making under pressure

3. Grounding Exercises (Body-Scanning & Barefoot Connection)
Re-syncs the Body with the Earth's Energy

Focus: *Recalibrating the vagus nerve and resetting sensory overwhelm*

How It Works:
Athletes walk or stand barefoot on grass or soil while doing a body scan—noticing tension, temperature, and feelings from feet to head. This reconnects the body with natural rhythms and helps regulate overstimulation from noise, screens, or intense training.

Benefits:
- Reduces inflammation
- Clears static nervous energy
- Boosts body awareness and mood

4. Dynamic Vision + Balance Training (Vestibular Reset)
Train the Inner Ear-Brain-Muscle Loop

Focus: *Resetting the vestibular (balance) system and improving coordination*

How It Works:
Use balance boards, spinning movements, or head-turn drills combined with visual targets (like ball tracking or eye saccades). This trains the vestibular system — a key piece of nervous system regulation tied to movement, posture, and calm alertness.

Try This Simple Version:
- Stand on one leg
- Slowly turn your head side to side while focusing on a spot
- Switch legs and repeat

Benefits:
- Improves balance, reflexes, and posture
- Trains the body to stay calm and stable during motion
- Reduces motion-triggered anxiety and disorientation

MyDay –

My focus for today is:

_____
_____
_____

Date	What Time I Went To Bed Last Night?
	What Time Did I Wake Up Today?
I had _____ hours of sleep	

Today's practice was...

3 things I want to accomplish today...

1. _____
2. _____
3. _____

What I learned today?

What challenged me today?

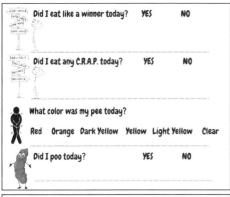

Did I eat like a winner today? YES NO

Did I eat any C.R.A.P. today? YES NO

What color was my pee today?

Red   Orange   Dark Yellow   Yellow   Light Yellow   Clear

Did I poo today? YES NO

WHAT I ATE TODAY?

List two things I am grateful for today.

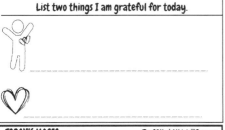

What's my mindset today?

Who and How did I serve or help somebody today?

TODAY'S MAGIC: The F.I.X.ed Athlete™ Program

The biggest problem you had in your day today, how did it make you feel? If you could say in one or two words...

Did I get rid of them? YES NO

Essential Oils I Used Today:

What I'm looking forward to tomorrow?

HEY SUPERSTAR — ESSENTIAL OILS CROSSWORD

DO YOU KNOW WHICH ESSENTIAL OIL TO RECH FOR DURING YOUR DAY?

Your Challenge:
Here's a 20-question crossword puzzle designed to help athletes learn more about essential oils, their effects on performance, and how to promote faster recovery times and potentially fewer injuries. This crossword puzzle is perfect for building your memory & recall, vocabulary development, learning and analytical thinking, pattern recognition, skill acquisition, and strategic thinking... while reinforcing lessons through play and cognitive engagement. ALL skills SUPERSTAR Athletes need to take their play to the next level...

Solutions on page #307

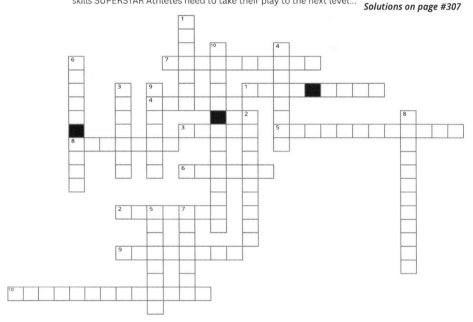

Across:

1. WHICH BLEND IS EXCELLENT FOR MUSCLE RECOVERY AFTER TRAINING?
2. WHICH RESPIRATORY BLEND PROMOTES BCLEAR BREATHING AND STAMINA?
3. WHICH EMOTIONAL SUPPORT BLEND HELPS WITH BRAVERY BEFORE GAMES, PRACTICES, OR SCHOOL TESTS?
4. WHICH CITRUS OIL BOOSTS ENERGY AND FOCUS?
5. WHAT IS THE METHOD CALLED WHEN YOU INHALE OILS THROUGH THE AIR?
6. WHICH CALMING OIL IS RECOMMENDED AT BEDTIME FOR RELAXATION OF YOUNG ATHLETES?
7. WHICH OIL HELPS RELAX MUSCLES AFTER WORKOUTS AND TRAINING SESSIONS AND IS EXCELLENT FOR TENDONS AND LIGAMENT ISSUES?
8. WHAT IS IT CALLED WHEN YOU APPLY ESSENTIAL OILS DIRECTLY TO THE SKIN?
9. WHICH IMMUNE-SUPPORTING OIL IS PART OF INJURY RECOVERY BLENDS?
10. ESSENTIAL OILS ARE A _____ TOOL, NOT A REPLACEMENT FOR MEDICAL CARE.

Down:

1. WHAT BRAND OF ESSENTIAL OILS DO WE RECOMMEND DUE TO THEIR PURITY AND TESTING?
2. WHICH ESSENTIAL OIL SUPPORTS BOTH ENERGY AND CLEAR BREATHING?
3. WHAT SHOULD YOU ALWAYS USE TO DILUTE ESSENTIAL OILS BEFORE APPLYING TO SENSITIVE SKIN?
4. WHICH OIL HELPS WITH BOTH SLEEP AND STRESS RELIEF?
5. ESSENTIAL OILS ARE CONCENTRATED PLANT _____.
6. WHAT SAFETY TEST SHOULD YOU TAKE BEFORE APPLYING OILS TO SKIN?
7. WHICH OIL HELPS YOUNG ATHLETES FOCUS DURING SCHOOL OR COMPETITIONS?
8. WHICH OIL SUPPORTS INJURY RECOVERY AND IS OFTEN USED WITH FIR AND TEA TREE OILS?
9. WHERE SHOULD YOU APPLE A SMALL AMOUNT OF OIL FIRST TO TEST SKIN REACTION?
10. WHO CAN BENEFIT MOST FROM THESE SPECIFIC OIL ROUTINES?

My Day

My focus for today is:
_____
_____
_____

Date

What Time I Went To Bed Last Night?

What Time Did I Wake Up Today?

I had _____ hours of sleep

Today's practice was...

3 things I want to accomplish today...

What I learned today?

What challenged me today?

Did I eat like a winner today?   YES   NO

Did I eat any C.R.A.P. today?   YES   NO

What color was my pee today?

Red   Orange   Dark Yellow   Yellow   Light Yellow   Clear

Did I poo today?   YES   NO

WHAT I ATE TODAY?

List two things I am grateful for today.

What's my mindset today?

Who and How did I serve or help somebody today?

TODAY'S MAGIC: The F.I.X.ed Athlete™ Program

The biggest problem you had in your day today, how did it make you feel? If you could say in one or two words...

Did I get rid of them?   YES   NO

Essential Oils I Used Today:

What I'm looking forward to tomorrow?

WHO ARE YOU – SUPERSTAR?
MENTAL RESILIENCE & SELF-WORTH

Many athletes struggle when their identity is only linked to sports, winning, or performing. This creates pressure, anxiety, or depression if injured or not "at the top." Your mental health and the strength of your mindset will determine your longevity in anything that you do.

IDENTITY BEYOND SPORT
You're more than your sport.
Athletes who have balanced identities are more confident and resilient.
Mental toughness is knowing your value, even when you're not performing to your peak.

ACTIVITY:

Write 5 things **you're proud of** that have nothing to do with sport. (e.g., kindness, effort, helping others, creativity, music, youth groups, church, choir, painting).

Write 2 things that you are **willing to teach someone else** (not sport related) and decide who you will teach; what and when to within the next month.

This will anchor and increase your self-worth in who you are — not just what you do.

MyDay -

My focus for today is:
_____
_____
_____

Date

What Time I Went To Bed Last Night?

What Time Did I Wake Up Today?

I had_____ hours of sleep

Today's practice was...

3 things I want to accomplish today...

- _____
- _____
- _____

What I learned today?

What challenged me today?

Did I eat like a winner today? YES NO

Did I eat any C.R.A.P. today? YES NO

What color was my pee today?

Red   Orange   Dark Yellow   Yellow   Light Yellow   Clear

Did I poo today? YES NO

WHAT I ATE TODAY?

List two things I am grateful for today.

What's my mindset today?

Who and How did I serve or help somebody today?

TODAY'S MAGIC: The F.I.X.ed Athlete™ Program

The biggest problem you had in your day today, how did it make you feel? If you could say in one or two words...

Did I get rid of them? YES NO

Essential Oils I Used Today:

What I'm looking forward to tomorrow?

EYE HEALTH & VISUAL TRAINING
MENTAL RESILIENCE & SELF-WORTH

Vision isn't just about seeing clearly — it's about how well your brain processes what you see. This affects reaction speed, depth perception, and tracking moving objects — all of the crucial elements in sports.

CROSS TRAINING:
Many elite athletes do visual training drills to improve performance.
Screen time fatigue can weaken eye-tracking and focus under pressure. This is why all of our activity books focus on reducing screen times. *(Pun intended!)*

EYE-TRAINING EXERCISES
Train Your Eyes to See Like a Champion

1. Pencil Push-Ups (Near-Far Focusing)
Purpose:
  Strengthens focus, eye convergence, and tracking skills.
What You Need:
A pencil or pen with writing or a small sticker on it.
Instructions:
1. Hold the pencil straight out in front of you at arm's length.
2. Focus on a letter or mark on the pencil.
3. Slowly bring the pencil toward your nose, keeping your eyes focused on that mark.
4. Stop as soon as the pencil looks blurry or you see double.
5. Hold it there for 5 seconds, then move it slowly back to arm's length.
6. Repeat 10 times.

Tips:
Keep your head still — let your eyes do the work. Breathe slow and stay relaxed.

2. Saccades (Quick Eye-Jumps)
Purpose:
  Improves rapid eye movement, attention, and visual processing speed.
What You Need:
Two sticky notes or paper targets with letters or numbers on them.
Instructions:
1. Place the two targets on a wall, spaced about 12–18 inches apart at eye level.
2. Stand 2–3 feet away.
3. Look at the letter or number on the left.
4. Snap your eyes quickly to the one on the right.
5. Go back and forth as fast as you can — but stay accurate.
6. Do this for 30 seconds, then rest.
7. Repeat 2–3 rounds.

Tips:
Keep your head still.   Don't move your body — just your eyes!

3. Outdoor "Focus Walks"
Purpose:
  Trains depth perception, distance focus, and calm visual awareness in motion.
What You Need:
Your surroundings! A backyard, sidewalk, or park.
Instructions:
1. Walk slowly and calmly outside.
2. First, focus on something far away (like a tree or building).
3. Then shift your focus to something nearby (like your hand, a flower, or rock).
4. Keep alternating: far → near → far → near.
5. Try this pattern for 5 minutes.

Bonus Challenge:
- Spot 3 things of each color (green, red, blue).
- Or count how many moving things you can notice.

WHY THIS MATTERS: Your eyes guide your body — in every sport.
- Training your vision helps with:
- Faster reactions
- Better coordination
- Sharper focus under pressure
- Less visual fatigue

My Day –

My focus for today is:
_____
_____
_____

Date _____

What Time I Went To Bed Last Night? _____

What Time Did I Wake Up Today? _____

I had _____ hours of sleep

Today's practice was...

3 things I want to accomplish today...

1. _____
2. _____
3. _____

What I learned today?

What challenged me today?

Did I eat like a winner today?   YES   NO

Did I eat any C.R.A.P. today?   YES   NO

What color was my pee today?
Red   Orange   Dark Yellow   Yellow   Light Yellow   Clear

Did I poo today?   YES   NO

WHAT I ATE TODAY?

List two things I am grateful for today.

What's my mindset today?

Who and How did I serve or help somebody today?

TODAY'S MAGIC: The F.I.X.ed Athlete™ Program

The biggest problem you had in your day today, how did it make you feel? If you could say in one or two words...

Did I get rid of them?   YES   NO

What I'm looking forward to tomorrow?

Essential Oils I Used Today:

THE POWER OF PLAYING IN THE ZONE

F.I.X.ed Athletes

Don't Stay Stuck in Negative Feelings. (F.I.X.ed = Focus Increases eXcellence) They quickly recognize unhealthy, unhelpful emotions; eliminate them with their professional **F.I.X. Code Coach** and shift into a powerful, performance-enhancing state. These feelings may be fleeting or deeply rooted, but every one of them pulls attention away from the present moment, where elite performance happens. Teaching athletes to recognize, name, and eliminate these feelings is a vital part of mastering focus, flow, and mental excellence.

Here are the top 50 negative feelings we've helped athletes get rid of just this month…
Circle the **negative feelings** that keep you from performing at your best, in sports, school, and everything you do…

Unprepared, Impatient, Frustrated, Betrayed, Distracted, Nervous, Self-conscious, Ashamed, Disrespected, Overwhelmed, Powerless, Misunderstood, Angry, Insecure, Rejected, Blamed, Limited, Fearful, Ignored, Jealous, Hopeless, Depressed, Lonely, Unworthy, Confused, Criticized, Anxious, Dismissed, Judged, Hesitant, Doubtful, Belittled, Stuck, Defeated, Inferior, Discouraged, Trapped, Regretful, Afraid of failure, Cheated, Pressured, Defensive, Taken for Granted, Tense, Embarrassed, Disconnected, Envious, Isolated, Guilty, Sad

Coaching / Parenting Tip:

F.I.X.ed Athletes train their minds like they train their bodies. They don't deny emotions — they recognize them, get rid of them, and refocus fast. Every moment is a chance to upgrade your mindset. When you're ready to have your athlete(s) playing their best, set up a **FREE 15-minute session** with Barb V, your uniquely trained F.I.X. Code for Athletes & Coaches specialist. Let your athlete experience it for themselves, and you can too! Book now at: https://calendly.com/barbv

My Day —

My focus for today is:
_____
_____
_____

Date	What Time I Went To Bed Last Night?
	What Time Did I Wake Up Today?
I had _____ hours of sleep	

Today's practice was...

3 things I want to accomplish today...
1. _____
2. _____
3. _____

What I learned today?

What challenged me today?

Did I eat like a winner today?   YES   NO

Did I eat any C.R.A.P. today?   YES   NO

What color was my pee today?
Red   Orange   Dark Yellow   Yellow   Light Yellow   Clear

Did I poo today?   YES   NO

WHAT I ATE TODAY?

List two things I am grateful for today.

What's my mindset today?

Who and How did I serve or help somebody today?

TODAY'S MAGIC: The F.I.X.ed Athlete™ Program
The biggest problem you had in your day today, how did it make you feel? If you could say in one or two words...

Did I get rid of them?   YES   NO

Essential Oils I Used Today:

What I'm looking forward to tomorrow?

TELL US A STORY

HEY SUPERSTAR

Use Your Imagination: Tell us the story of this **SUPERSTAR**...

Your Challenge:
Using your creative thinking, visualization, imagination, emotional regulation and the power of words... write a story that tells all about this SUPERSTAR!

　　Think it.　　Write it.　　Make it unforgettable

MyDay–

My focus for today is:
_____
_____
_____

Date	What Time I Went To Bed Last Night?
	What Time Did I Wake Up Today?
I had _____ hours of sleep	

Today's practice was...

3 things I want to accomplish today...
1. _____
2. _____
3. _____

What I learned today?

What challenged me today?

Did I eat like a winner today?   YES   NO

Did I eat any C.R.A.P. today?   YES   NO

What color was my pee today?
Red   Orange   Dark Yellow   Yellow   Light Yellow   Clear

Did I poo today?   YES   NO

WHAT I ATE TODAY?

List two things I am grateful for today.

What's my mindset today?

Who and How did I serve or help somebody today?

TODAY'S MAGIC: The F.I.X.ed Athlete™ Program
The biggest problem you had in your day today, how did it make you feel? If you could say in one or two words...

Did I get rid of them?   YES   NO

Essential Oils I Used Today:

What I'm looking forward to tomorrow?

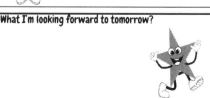

HEY SUPERSTAR POSITIVE FEELINGS WORDSEARCH
WHEN F.I.X.ed ATHLETES ARE PLAYING IN THE ZONE

Your Challenge:
Find all 20 of the positive feelings that a F.I.X.ed Athlete feels when they get rid of the negative feelings that keep them from playing their best...

```
L D A I X E U B S F W T R F C B
D C Y C N G R O U N D E D D E R
S T A F C S R N P I K K C E N A
H L N L O O P B P V C D C R T V
Y G I B M C U I O G S G O N E E
B X R C P X U N R Z A E N P R I
Z I D V T R U S T I N G N A E W
R X R E A D Y N E A E W E T D A
C A P A B L E K D D B D C I D E
C L E A R D U Y Z W A L T E S K
J I N I I W R E S I L I E N T P
X V P F K H V I D A X O D T M J
W N N I Y V N W O I T I V J X R
W O R T H Y B Y P P P W C E F T
C N Q G B X I M Q X B C X H D G
A C O U R A G E O U S G Y N G I
```

CALM	SUPPORTED	INSPIRIED	VALUED
CONFIDENT	CLEAR	PATIENT	FOCUSED
READY	COURAGEOUS	TRUSTING	CONNECTED
CENTERED	BRAVE	WORTHY	GROUNDED
LOVED	RESILIENT	CAPABLE	ACCOUNTABLE

Solutions on page #307

My Day -

Date _____

What Time I Went To Bed Last Night? _____

What Time Did I Wake Up Today? _____

I had _____ hours of sleep

My focus for today is:
_____
_____
_____
_____

Today's practice was...

3 things I want to accomplish today...
- _____
- _____
- _____

What I learned today?

What challenged me today?

Did I eat like a winner today?   YES   NO

Did I eat any C.R.A.P. today?   YES   NO

What color was my pee today?

Red   Orange   Dark Yellow   Yellow   Light Yellow   Clear

Did I poo today?   YES   NO

WHAT I ATE TODAY?

List two things I am grateful for today.

What's my mindset today?

Who and How did I serve or help somebody today?

TODAY'S MAGIC: The F.I.X.ed Athlete™ Program

The biggest problem you had in your day today, how did it make you feel? If you could say in one or two words...

Did I get rid of them?   YES   NO

Essential Oils I Used Today:

What I'm looking forward to tomorrow?

WRITE YOUR ACCEPTANCE SPEECH FOR YOUR LIFETIME ACHIEVEMENT AWARD

Instructions: WHAT HAVE YOU ACCOMPLISHED OVER YOUR LIFETIME... Now it's your turn to **write your acceptance speech** for receiving a lifetime achievement award in your sport. What will you say are the most powerful memories that you have accomplished over your athletic career? **BUT WAIT!** ...**BEFORE** you write that speech - you must first write the **INTRODUCTION** segment of the speech that the person introducing you reads about just some of the **Highlights** of your career...

- To get started, watch some of the YouTube speeches the GOATS have given over the years...
- Include your major accomplishments...
- What were the biggest awards that you earned?
- What did you do that most others never even got close to doing?
- Include accomplishments that got you started on your path through your most recent one.
- Make sure to include your SUPERSTAR accomplishments in both sports as well as in life.
- **REMEMBER:** this is being read by somebody else about you - before you give your acceptance speech.
- **ACTUALLY, TOMORROW - YOU WILL WRITE YOUR ACCEPTANCE SPEECH...**

My Day -

My focus for today is:

_____
_____
_____

Date _____

What Time I Went To Bed Last Night? _____

What Time Did I Wake Up Today? _____

I had _____ hours of sleep

Today's practice was...

3 things I want to accomplish today...

- _____
- _____
- _____

What I learned today?

What challenged me today?

Did I eat like a winner today?   YES   NO

Did I eat any C.R.A.P. today?   YES   NO

What color was my pee today?

Red   Orange   Dark Yellow   Yellow   Light Yellow   Clear

Did I poo today?   YES   NO

WHAT I ATE TODAY?

List two things I am grateful for today.

What's my mindset today?

Who and How did I serve or help somebody today?

TODAY'S MAGIC: The F.I.X.ed Athlete™ Program

The biggest problem you had in your day today, how did it make you feel? If you could say in one or two words...

Did I get rid of them?   YES   NO

Essential Oils I Used Today:

What I'm looking forward to tomorrow?

WRITE YOUR ACCEPTANCE SPEECH FOR YOUR LIFETIME ACHIEVEMENT AWARD

Instructions: WHAT HAVE YOU ACCOMPLISHED OVER YOUR LIFETIME...
Now it's your turn to **write your acceptance speech** for receiving a lifetime achievement award in your sport. What will you say are the most powerful memories that you have accomplished over your athletic career?
Okay - NOW you can write your **Lifetime Achievement Award Acceptance Speech...**

- **To get started...** watch some YouTube videos of your favorite heroes acceptance speeches...
- Make sure to thank all of the people that you want and what they did for you and why THEY were so important in your career.
- Highlight 3 major moments that influenced you the most or created the biggest impact on your career.
- Tell 2 stories that were important to you that most people may have never even known about your journey.
- This is your opportunity to share what you really want to **Be Remembered For...**
- End with a list of 3-5 key elements that future athletes, coaches, and fans can use in their lives today that will inspire them or set them on a strong and solid path to becoming a **SUPERSTAR** in their own lives.

My Day –

My focus for today is:

_____
_____
_____

Date	What Time I Went To Bed Last Night?
	What Time Did I Wake Up Today?

I had _____ hours of sleep

Today's practice was...

3 things I want to accomplish today...

1. _____
2. _____
3. _____

What I learned today?

What challenged me today?

Did I eat like a winner today?   YES   NO

Did I eat any C.R.A.P. today?   YES   NO

What color was my pee today?

Red   Orange   Dark Yellow   Yellow   Light Yellow   Clear

Did I poo today?   YES   NO

WHAT I ATE TODAY?

List two things I am grateful for today.

What's my mindset today?

Who and How did I serve or help somebody today?

TODAY'S MAGIC: The F.I.X.ed Athlete™ Program

The biggest problem you had in your day today, how did it make you feel? If you could say in one or two words...

Did I get rid of them?   YES   NO

Essential Oils I Used Today:

What I'm looking forward to tomorrow?

THE POWER OF KIND WORDS
Etiquette For Athletes

Instructions:
Today's challenge is all about the power of positive words and personal development.
Write a Letter to Someone from Another Team
Write your letter on paper, decorate it if you'd like, and make sure you send it! You never know how much a positive message can mean to someone.

Who: A referee, a coach from another team, or a player you competed against.

Why: This isn't just about saying "good game." It's about building strong communication, showing respect, and becoming a leader — even after the final whistle.

Skills You're Building:
- Communication
- Etiquette & Sportsmanship
- Creative Thinking
- Emotional Regulation
- Handwriting Skills
- Focus & Concentration
- Spatial Awareness (where things go on a page!)

Instructions:
1. Choose someone from another team or sport who left a positive impression on you.
2. Write them a short, kind letter — it could be about how they played, something you noticed, or how they treated others.
3. Use your best handwriting and follow letter format (Dear ___, Sincerely, ___).
4. Be specific, be kind, be thoughtful.
5. Ask your coach or adult how you can deliver or mail it.

What to Include in Your Letter:
- A greeting with their name or role (if known)
- One or two things you admired about them
- How it made you feel
- A thank-you or encouraging message
- Your first name, team, and age (optional)

Why This Matters:
Kindness and sportsmanship go beyond the scoreboard. Writing a letter like this develops the heart of a champion and shows you're thinking bigger than just winning. You're becoming the kind of athlete that others remember — for all the right reasons.

PRACTICE Writing Your Letter here...
before doing it in a card or on letter paper...

My Day

My focus for today is:
_____
_____
_____

Date _____
What Time I Went To Bed Last Night? _____
What Time Did I Wake Up Today? _____
I had _____ hours of sleep

Today's practice was...

3 things I want to accomplish today...

What I learned today?

What challenged me today?

Did I eat like a winner today? YES NO

Did I eat any C.R.A.P. today? YES NO

What color was my pee today?
Red Orange Dark Yellow Yellow Light Yellow Clear

Did I poo today? YES NO

WHAT I ATE TODAY?

List two things I am grateful for today.

What's my mindset today?

Who and How did I serve or help somebody today?

TODAY'S MAGIC: The F.I.X.ed Athlete™ Program
The biggest problem you had in your day today, how did it make you feel? If you could say in one or two words...

Did I get rid of them? YES NO

Essential Oils I Used Today:

What I'm looking forward to tomorrow?

JUGGLING INCREASES ATHLETE FOCUS!
Different Sizes – Different Weights – Different Shapes

Hey Superstar

Now that you have been juggling for about 8 weeks, let's add some different difficulties to your juggling routine. Have you noticed an improved difference in your hand-eye coordination in your sport? How about in your ability to focus or concentrate on multiple things happening around you? If you are playing with any type of juggling every day, you will be noticing these improvements soon.

New Challenge:
Add movement to your body as you juggle. Add different shapes, sizes, object weights.

1. CREATE A JUGGLING CIRCUIT CHALLENGE

Turn juggling into a fitness-style circuit. Set up stations like:
- Station 1: 3-ball endurance – juggle as long as possible.
- Station 2: Movement juggling – walk or jog slowly while juggling.
- Station 3: Juggle and squat – do a squat between each throw.
- Station 4: Reverse cascade – learn or attempt reverse juggling pattern.
- Station 5: One-up – juggle 2 balls in one hand, and toss the third higher every few throws.

2. JUGGLING TRICK-OFF (LIKE A DANCE BATTLE)
- One athlete does a juggling trick (behind the back, under the leg, high throws, etc.).
- The other must copy it or one-up it with something flashier.
- Encourage creativity: "Who can make the judges laugh or cheer the most?"

3. MEMORY PATTERN GAME
- Call out or flash a pattern or trick name they must execute immediately (e.g., "under-the-leg", "claw catch").
- Increase the sequence over time, like "Simon Says with juggling."

4. FREESTYLE SHOWCASE
- Set it to music if you want.
- Let them perform solo or in small groups.
- Add "style points" for theme, teamwork, and creativity—not just skill.

5. PARTNER JUGGLING
WORK ON PASSING OR TANDEM JUGGLING:
- 2-person, 6-ball pass (each with 3).
- 3-person juggling triangle – each person throws and catches to another in a sequence.
- "Drop & Replace" relay – juggle until you drop, then a teammate tags in.

6. CREATE A JUGGLING SHOW TO TEACH & SHOWCASE YOUR SKILLS
- Team up with friends and teammates to coach younger athletes what you can do & teach them to start juggling.
- Add new elements to your juggling - like juggling with ping pong balls as you bounce them off a ping pong paddle instead of using your hands to juggle. Hold a ping pong paddle in each of your hands and juggle 3 or more ping pong balls at once
- Rotate the ping pong paddle in your hand every time a ball hits one side

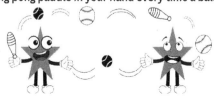

MyDay-

My focus for today is:

_____
_____
_____

Date

What Time I Went To Bed Last Night?

What Time Did I Wake Up Today?

I had _____ hours of sleep

Today's practice was...

3 things I want to accomplish today...

What I learned today?

What challenged me today?

Did I eat like a winner today? YES NO

Did I eat any C.R.A.P. today? YES NO

What color was my pee today?

Red   Orange   Dark Yellow   Yellow   Light Yellow   Clear

Did I poo today? YES NO

WHAT I ATE TODAY?

List two things I am grateful for today.

What's my mindset today?

Who and How did I serve or help somebody today?

TODAY'S MAGIC: The F.I.X.ed Athlete™ Program

The biggest problem you had in your day today, how did it make you feel? If you could say in one or two words...

Did I get rid of them? YES NO

Essential Oils I Used Today:

What I'm looking forward to tomorrow?

SUPERSTAR VISUAL MEMORY ACTIVITY
Performance Foods VS. C.R.A.P.

How to play:
- Set your timer for allotted amount of time (15-60 seconds suggested).
- When ready, start the timer and study the images on the page. Try to remember as many as you can!
- When time's up, close the book or cover the page.
- Now set your timer for 1-2 minutes.
- Write down as many images as you can remember. Be specific! (For example, "running shoes" or "track spikes" is better than just "shoes")
- When time's up, stop writing.
- Open the book and check your list against the image page.
   - Score 1 point for each correct item.
   - Give yourself an extra point for very specific details.
- Challenge yourself to beat your score next time!

This activity builds memory/recall, pattern recognition, attention to detail, situational awareness, visualization and imagery skills. Try it alone or compete with teammates!

TIP: Great athletes have strong visualization skills. This game can help you develop those skills for better performance in your sport. Can you spot the 25 C.R.A.P. items and the 30 PERFOMANCE foods? How about some of the unique details?

Remember: You can practice this mental exercise anytime, anywhere - before practice, after training, or before bed. The more you practice, the stronger your mind, memory, and visual skills will becomes. ALSO: Start looking for clues on the playing field...

© 2025 Barb V   All Rights Reserved

MyDay-

My focus for today is:

_____
_____
_____

Date	What Time I Went To Bed Last Night?
	What Time Did I Wake Up Today?
I had _____ hours of sleep	

Today's practice was...

3 things I want to accomplish today...

What I learned today?

What challenged me today?

WHAT I ATE TODAY?

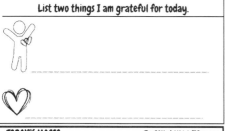

List two things I am grateful for today.

What's my mindset today?

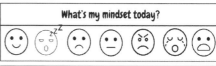

Who and How did I serve or help somebody today?

TODAY'S MAGIC: The F.I.X.ed Athlete™ Program

The biggest problem you had in your day today, how did it make you feel? If you could say in one or two words...

Did I get rid of them? YES NO

Essential Oils I Used Today:

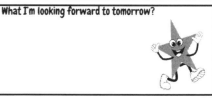

What I'm looking forward to tomorrow?

CREATE A BANNER
Your Energy. Your Message.

HEY SUPERSTAR

A Team Banner is a visual reminder of who you are, what you and your team stand for, and where you're headed. It's a symbol of unity and power that your team can rally behind. Plus, it's a great way to show that YOU own the energy of the game — and your energy echoes!

Your Challenge:
Create a banner that represents your team's spirit and energy. This banner will inspire you and your teammates and will be visible during games or practices.

Instructions:
1. Team Message – Think about one thing your team believes in or something that fires you up. It could be a motivational phrase like:
   - "We Rise Together"
   - "Stronger Every Play"
   - "Own Your Energy – It Echoes!"
   - "Believe. Achieve. Dominate!"
2. Design Your Banner
   - Pick a theme: What colors, symbols, and images represent your team?
   - Make it bold: Use large letters and shapes that stand out.
   - Get creative: Draw or use printouts of logos, mascots, or anything that represents your team's energy.
   - Add your personal touch: Is there a specific play, memory, or motto that fuels your team? Include it!
3. Work Together
   - If you're doing this as a team, work together to add your ideas. Everyone can contribute a word, image, or part of the design!
4. Hang It Up
   - Once your banner is complete, make sure to hang it where the whole team can see it every day — during practices, in the locker room, or at the game!

When you see your banner, remember:
The energy you put in will echo with your team and fans...

Let it remind you that
YOU'RE STRONGER WHEN YOU OWN YOUR ENERGY & MAKE IT CONTAGIOUS!

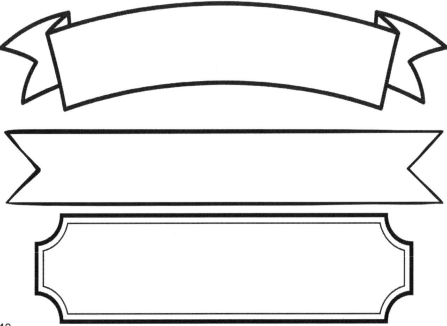

MyDay -

My focus for today is:

_____
_____
_____

Date _____

What Time I Went To Bed Last Night?

What Time Did I Wake Up Today?

I had _____ hours of sleep

Today's practice was...

3 things I want to accomplish today...

What I learned today?

What challenged me today?

Did I eat like a winner today?   YES   NO

Did I eat any C.R.A.P. today?   YES   NO

What color was my pee today?

Red   Orange   Dark Yellow   Yellow   Light Yellow   Clear

Did I poo today?   YES   NO

WHAT I ATE TODAY?

List two things I am grateful for today.

What's my mindset today?

Who and How did I serve or help somebody today?

TODAY'S MAGIC: The F.I.X.ed Athlete™ Program

The biggest problem you had in your day today, how did it make you feel? If you could say in one or two words...

Did I get rid of them?   YES   NO

Essential Oils I Used Today:

What I'm looking forward to tomorrow?

HEY SUPERSTAR ETIQUETTE FOR ATHLETES CROSSWORD
WHAT WILL YOU DO IN THIS SITUATION?

TEST YOUR KNOWLEDGE:
- Proper etiquette shows character, not just talent.
- Athletes with strong etiquette are often seen as leaders, even without a title.
- Respecting others creates an environment where everyone can grow and perform better.
- In moments of stress or conflict, etiquette helps athletes regulate their emotions and respond wisely.

Solutions on page #308

Across:

1. Being on time to events shows this trait
2. Before posting online, young athletes, coaches, parents, and fans should always do this - _____
3. Young fans view athletes as this
4. Your clothes should be suitabe for the situation; this is called dressing _____
5. Use your platform to uplift - not divide - others. This is called using your patform _____
6. Instead of yelling or lashing out when angry, athletes must control their _____
7. Spreading false information can hurt your image and trust. Always _____ facts first
8. You represent not just yourself but also your _____ and community
9. Avoid public arguments. Settle disputes in _____
10. Show admiration to competitors when they succeed - this is true _____

Down:

1. How you should respond to online criticism to protect your character
2. Athletes should avoid using this type of language in any setting
3. This action shows that you value and honor others' contributions to your success
4. When interacting with diverse culures, athletes shoud show this _____
5. Avoid blaming others and instead take full _____ when you mess up
6. Social media never forgets. Every post becomes part of your digital _____
7. Engage with community events not for photos but to make a real _____
8. When listening to others, focus and show you care - this is called _____ listening
9. Good _____ builds respect and understanding
10. Your words, behavior, and presence leave lasting _____ on others.

My Day —

My focus for today is:
_____
_____
_____
_____

Date	What Time I Went To Bed Last Night?
	What Time Did I Wake Up Today?
I had _____ hours of sleep	

Today's practice was...

3 things I want to accomplish today...

1. _____
2. _____
3. _____

What I learned today?

What challenged me today?

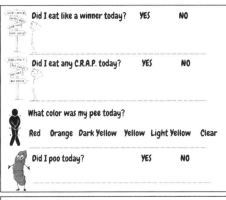

Did I eat like a winner today?   YES   NO

Did I eat any C.R.A.P. today?   YES   NO

What color was my pee today?
Red   Orange   Dark Yellow   Yellow   Light Yellow   Clear

Did I poo today?   YES   NO

WHAT I ATE TODAY?

List two things I am grateful for today.

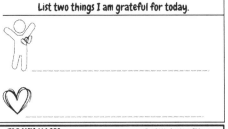

What's my mindset today?

Who and How did I serve or help somebody today?

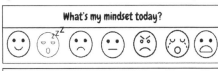

TODAY'S MAGIC: The F.I.Xed Athlete™ Program

The biggest problem you had in your day today, how did it make you feel? If you could say in one or two words...

Did I get rid of them?   YES   NO

Essential Oils I Used Today:

What I'm looking forward to tomorrow?

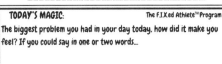

HEY SUPERSTAR PICK YOUR OWN CONSEQUENCE
Take Personal Responsibility!

This is the week where **You Take Responsible** for something you did that deserves some type of consequence that your parent(s), teacher, or coach would typically prescribe. **THIS WEEK, YOU assign your own**, appropriate consequence. It may be a natural consequence where the adults in your life, won't step in, but rather allow you to take responsibility for whatever you did to deserve a consequence.

Responsibility   Integrity   &   Emotional Growth

Being a strong athlete isn't just about strength, speed, or skill—it's about character. One of the most powerful things an athlete can do is to own up to their actions. Real leaders step up even when it's uncomfortable. By practicing responsibility **now, you build:**

- ✓ SELF-DISCIPLINE
- ✓ EMOTIONAL MATURITY
- ✓ RESPECT FROM OTHERS
- ✓ BETTER DECISION-MAKING
- ✓ A STRONGER MINDSET FOR FUTURE SUCCESS

Remember: When you take responsibility, you're showing others you can be trusted—even when things don't go perfectly.

Instructions:

Reflect: Think about a recent situation where you made a poor choice—maybe you were disrespectful, broke a rule, didn't give full effort, or acted out emotionally.

Describe It:
- What happened?
- Why do you think it was wrong?
- How did it affect others (and yourself)?

Choose a Consequence:
What would be a fair, meaningful, and growth-focused consequence for your actions?

Be honest:
What will help you learn, grow, and not repeat this choice?

Write Your Commitment:
- Describe the consequence you've chosen.
- When and how will you complete it?
- What will you do differently next time?

Ask for Feedback:
If you're brave enough, share your decision with a trusted adult (parent, coach, teacher) and ask if they agree it's a strong choice.

Example:
Action: I rolled my eyes at my coach when she gave me feedback.

Why it was wrong: That was disrespectful, and I let frustration take over.

Chosen consequence: I will write her a note of apology and stay after practice to help clean up equipment for 3 days.

Lesson: I want to be coachable, even when I don't like what I hear.

Every day this week, track your behavior and check in with yourself...
- **Did I act with integrity today?**
- **Did I own my mistakes?**
- **Did I step up instead of hiding from responsibility?**

My Day –

My focus for today is:
_____
_____
_____

Date _____
What Time I Went To Bed Last Night? _____
What Time Did I Wake Up Today? _____
I had _____ hours of sleep

Today's practice was...

3 things I want to accomplish today...
1. _____
2. _____
3. _____

What I learned today?

What challenged me today?

Did I eat like a winner today?   YES   NO

Did I eat any C.R.A.P. today?   YES   NO

What color was my pee today?
Red   Orange   Dark Yellow   Yellow   Light Yellow   Clear

Did I poo today?   YES   NO

WHAT I ATE TODAY?

List two things I am grateful for today.

What's my mindset today?

Who and How did I serve or help somebody today?

TODAY'S MAGIC: The F.I.X.ed Athlete™ Program
The biggest problem you had in your day today, how did it make you feel? If you could say in one or two words...

Did I get rid of them?   YES   NO

Essential Oils I Used Today:

What I'm looking forward to tomorrow?

CREATE YOUR OWN PUZZLE
TAKE YOUR GAME TO THE NEXT LEVEL!

Using the crossword puzzle frame below, create your own sports crossword puzzle. You come up with the questions that properly complete - fill in - the empty boxes of the crossword puzzle. This may sound easy, but after all of the crossword puzzles you have done so far in this book, now it's your turn to make up your own. I have provided you space for 22 answers to the across and down questions you will write to complete the puzzle. HAVE FUN!

Across:
1.
2.
3.
4.
5.
6.
7.
8.
9.
10.
11.

Down:
1.
2.
3.
4.
5.
6.
7.
8.
9.
10.
11.

MyDay—

My focus for today is:
_____
_____
_____

Date	What Time I Went To Bed Last Night?
	What Time Did I Wake Up Today?
I had _____ hours of sleep	

Today's practice was...

3 things I want to accomplish today...

What I learned today?

What challenged me today?

Did I eat like a winner today? YES NO

Did I eat any C.R.A.P. today? YES NO

What color was my pee today?
Red Orange Dark Yellow Yellow Light Yellow Clear

Did I poo today? YES NO

WHAT I ATE TODAY?

List two things I am grateful for today.

What's my mindset today?

Who and How did I serve or help somebody today?

TODAY'S MAGIC: The F.I.X.ed Athlete™ Program
The biggest problem you had in your day today, how did it make you feel? If you could say in one or two words...

Did I get rid of them? YES NO

Essential Oils I Used Today:

What I'm looking forward to tomorrow?

MyDay -

My focus for today is:

_____
_____
_____

Date	What Time I Went To Bed Last Night?
	What Time Did I Wake Up Today?
I had _____ hours of sleep	

Today's practice was...

3 things I want to accomplish today...

1. _____
2. _____
3. _____

What I learned today?

What challenged me today?

Did I eat like a winner today?   YES   NO

Did I eat any C.R.A.P. today?   YES   NO

What color was my pee today?

Red   Orange   Dark Yellow   Yellow   Light Yellow   Clear

Did I poo today?   YES   NO

WHAT I ATE TODAY?

List two things I am grateful for today.

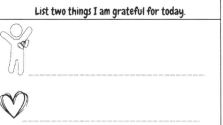

What's my mindset today?

Who and How did I serve or help somebody today?

TODAY'S MAGIC: The F.I.X.ed Athlete™ Program

The biggest problem you had in your day today, how did it make you feel? If you could say in one or two words...

Did I get rid of them?   YES   NO

Essential Oils I Used Today:

What I'm looking forward to tomorrow?

HEY SUPERSTAR

GET FASTER
INCREASE YOUR REFLEX - REACTION TIME

Review page #166 for details...

Note: You can skip circling or crossing out the word so you can do this more than once...

CIRCLE then DO the ACTION Words
CROSS OUT the NON-ACTION Words

JUMP	SPIN	SKIP	SQUAT	THROW	Duck	Punch	RUN	HOP	COACH
THROW	Punch	Duck	HOP	COURT	SQUAT	JUMP	CALL	POINT	SPIN
Duck	JUMP	HOP	RUN	BENCH	Punch	HOP	FLOOR	TIME	RUN
REF	RUN	FUN	JUMP	TIME OUT	SQUAT	SPIN	Punch	Duck	FIELD
SQUAT	Punch	SPIN	Duck	HOP	FAN	RUN	JUMP	WIN	THROW
THROW	Duck	HOP	BALL	FUN	Punch	TRACK	POOL	RUN	RED
HOP	Punch	SPIN	RUN	LOSE	THROW	HYPE	Duck	HOP	JUMP
JUMP	THROW	RUN	GLOVE	Duck	BAR	Punch	PHONE	RUN	BALL
STRIKE	Punch	SQUAT	JUMP	HOP	SPIN	HOP	BEAM	Duck	SAFE
Duck	SPIN	TOOL	HOP	UMP	Punch	JUMP	THROW	SQUAT	SPIN
HOP	Punch	JUMP	YARD	RUN	HOP	Duck	GREEN	HOP	STOP

DESIGN YOUR OWN

DESIGN YOUR OWN

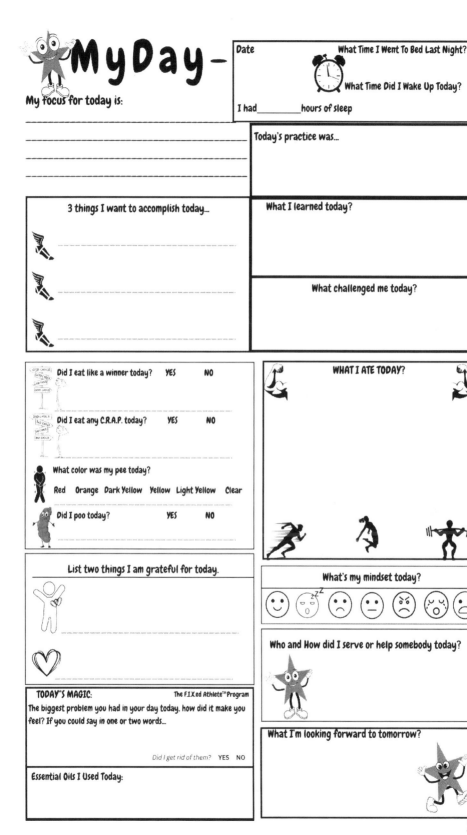

EMOTIONAL REGULATION

Athletes need to know how to recognize, manage, and reframe their emotions during competition, training, or daily life—just like most elite athletes do. Naming emotions activates the prefrontal cortex, reducing the emotional intensity in the brain's amygdala. Reframing builds resilience, confidence, and composure. Practicing in a safe space makes it easier to do under pressure in real competition. F.I.X.ed Athletes take it even further by eliminating how the emotion runs their subconscious and attacks their nervous system. Thus, allowing them to play in the flow state (the zone) without negative emotions.

Name It!   **F.I.X. It!**   **Play On...**

Read the following scenarios - *Name It!* (your emotion that you would feel in that situation,) then either *F.I.X. It!* (with your *F.I.X. Code Coach*) or *Tame It!* with a skill that you've learned... then play on...

1. You dropped the ball during the final play.
2. A referee made a call you think was unfair.
3. Your teammate yelled at you for making a mistake.
4. You missed a shot or goal you normally make.
5. You were benched after starting the game.
6. The crowd was cheering for the other team.
7. Your coach gave you tough feedback in front of everyone; players, parents, and fans.
8. You forgot a key play or position during a game.
9. Your team lost a close match.
10. You got hurt and had to sit out.
11. A teammate got the spotlight even though you played well too.
12. You made a mistake that cost your team points.
13. Your family couldn't come to watch the game.
14. You were nervous before a big competition.
15. You scored but didn't get acknowledged for it.

NAME IT!

1. _____
2. _____
3. _____
4. _____
5. _____
6. _____
7. _____
8. _____
9. _____
10. _____
11. _____
12. _____
13. _____
14. _____
15. _____

How will you Tame It?

1. _____   9. _____
2. _____   10. _____
3. _____   11. _____
4. _____   12. _____
5. _____   13. _____
6. _____   14. _____
7. _____   15. _____
8. _____

My Day —

My focus for today is:
_____
_____
_____
_____

Date	What Time I Went To Bed Last Night?
	What Time Did I Wake Up Today?
I had _____ hours of sleep	

Today's practice was...

3 things I want to accomplish today...

1. _____
2. _____
3. _____

What I learned today?

What challenged me today?

Did I eat like a winner today?   YES   NO

Did I eat any C.R.A.P. today?   YES   NO

What color was my pee today?

Red   Orange   Dark Yellow   Yellow   Light Yellow   Clear

Did I poo today?   YES   NO

WHAT I ATE TODAY?

List two things I am grateful for today.

What's my mindset today?

Who and How did I serve or help somebody today?

TODAY'S MAGIC: The F.I.X.ed Athlete™ Program

The biggest problem you had in your day today, how did it make you feel? If you could say in one or two words...

Did I get rid of them?   YES   NO

Essential Oils I Used Today:

What I'm looking forward to tomorrow?

MyDay –

My focus for today is:
_____
_____
_____

Date	What Time I Went To Bed Last Night?
	What Time Did I Wake Up Today?
I had _____ hours of sleep	

Today's practice was...

3 things I want to accomplish today...
1. _____
2. _____
3. _____

What I learned today?

What challenged me today?

Did I eat like a winner today?   YES   NO
_____

Did I eat any C.R.A.P. today?   YES   NO
_____

What color was my pee today?

Red   Orange   Dark Yellow   Yellow   Light Yellow   Clear

Did I poo today?   YES   NO
_____

WHAT I ATE TODAY?

List two things I am grateful for today.
_____
_____

What's my mindset today?

Who and How did I serve or help somebody today?

TODAY'S MAGIC: The F.I.X.ed Athlete™ Program

The biggest problem you had in your day today, how did it make you feel? If you could say in one or two words...

Did I get rid of them?   YES   NO

Essential Oils I Used Today:

What I'm looking forward to tomorrow?

MIRROR DRAWINGS

HEY SUPERSTAR

Athletes need the skills that mirror drawings provide. Focus, Concentration, Visual-Spatial Awareness, Hand-Eye Coordination, Analytical Thinking, Visual Tracking, Creative Thinking, Visualization, Pattern Recognition, Memory Recall, Attention To Detail, Mindfulness... **HAVE FUN!**   ANSWERS on Page #308

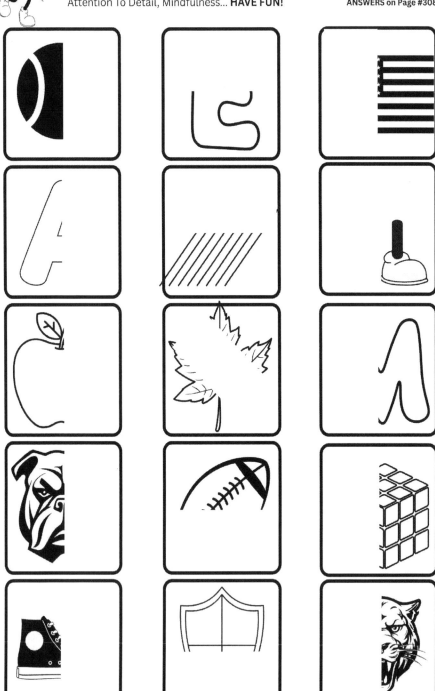

MyDay -

My focus for today is:
_____
_____
_____

Date	What Time I Went To Bed Last Night?
	What Time Did I Wake Up Today?
I had _____ hours of sleep	

Today's practice was...

3 things I want to accomplish today...

What I learned today?

What challenged me today?

Did I eat like a winner today?   YES   NO

Did I eat any C.R.A.P. today?   YES   NO

What color was my pee today?

Red   Orange   Dark Yellow   Yellow   Light Yellow   Clear

Did I poo today?   YES   NO

WHAT I ATE TODAY?

List two things I am grateful for today.

What's my mindset today?

Who and How did I serve or help somebody today?

TODAY'S MAGIC: The F.I.X.ed Athlete™ Program

The biggest problem you had in your day today, how did it make you feel? If you could say in one or two words...

Did I get rid of them?   YES   NO

Essential Oils I Used Today:

What I'm looking forward to tomorrow?

NO REMINDERS WEEK
100% Personal Responsibility!

HEY SUPERSTAR

This is the week where **You Become 100% Responsible** for your schedule, gear, mindset, attitude, and preparation—without any reminders from parents, coaches, or teachers. No one wakes you up. No one reminds you about practice, your jersey, your schoolwork, or your water bottle. You are in charge!

This Week's Challenge:

YOUR MISSION:
- Be your own coach, motivator, time manager, and team captain this week.
- Set alarms, checklists, and personal reminders if needed—but don't rely on others to do it for you.
- Prove to yourself (and those around you) that you can own your own success.

WHY THIS MATTERS:
Learning to manage your own schedule and responsibilities:
- Builds confidence and independence
- Helps you develop elite habits
- Strengthens focus and discipline
- Reduces stress for those around you (coaches, parents)
- Prepares you for higher levels of sport and life

CHALLENGE RULES:
1. No reminders allowed. Ask your family not to prompt you this week.
2. Prepare the night before. Lay out your clothes, pack your bag, and plan your meals.
3. Set alarms or use a planner to track your commitments.
4. Check in with yourself daily. Did you remember everything? What could you do better tomorrow?
5. Keep a quick log of your success each day.

REFLECTION QUESTIONS:
- What went well this week without reminders?
- What was the hardest part?
- How did it feel to be in full control of your day?
- Did anything surprise you?
- What will you continue doing after this challenge?

BONUS TASK:

Write a thank-you card or note to someone who usually reminds you or helps you stay on track — Let them know now that you know how much they do!

MyDay-

My focus for today is:

_____
_____
_____

Date	What Time I Went To Bed Last Night?
	What Time Did I Wake Up Today?
I had _____ hours of sleep	

Today's practice was...

3 things I want to accomplish today...

_____

_____

_____

What I learned today?

What challenged me today?

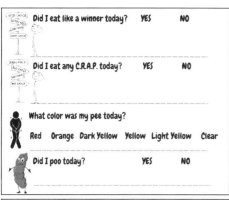

WHAT I ATE TODAY?

List two things I am grateful for today.

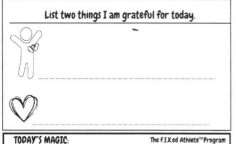

What's my mindset today?

Who and How did I serve or help somebody today?

TODAY'S MAGIC: The F.I.X.ed Athlete™ Program

The biggest problem you had in your day today, how did it make you feel? If you could say in one or two words...

Did I get rid of them?   YES   NO

Essential Oils I Used Today:

What I'm looking forward to tomorrow?

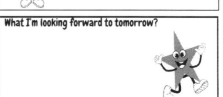

PERSONAL DEVELOPMENT

WHAT WILL YOU DO?

Read each short scenario (A - J) carefully. Then, match it to the best personal development response/outcome (1 - 10) listed below. Each response should only be used once.

A. You missed a game-winning shot and feel like quitting.

B. Your teammate made a mistake during a big play, and you're feeling upset.

C. You were nervous before a competition, so you used breathing techniques.

D. You noticed you're feeling tired every day, so you decide to improve your sleep habits.

E. You were tempted to skip practice, but you went anyway.

F. You tried a new skill, failed at first, but kept practicing until you improved.

G. You didn't get the position you wanted on the team, but you congratulated the person who did.

H. You caught yourself spending too much time on your phone, so you created screen-free time blocks.

I. You wrote a letter to thank your coach for believing in you.

J. You were feeling discouraged, so you read your favorite motivational quote to reset your mindset.

1. Practicing gratitude builds stronger relationships and shows emotional maturity.

2. Using calm breathing is a powerful tool for emotional regulation and focus.

3. Learning from failure helps develop mental toughness and confidence.

4. Recognizing screen-time habits and making changes improves focus and balance.

5. Encouraging others builds team unity and shows leadership.

6. Choosing discipline over comfort shows you're committed to your long-term goals.

7. Managing emotions toward others promotes empathy and strong teamwork.

8. Using quotes and positive self-talk helps shift your mindset and build resilience.

9. Building healthy sleep habits improves athletic performance and mental clarity.

10. Accepting disappointment with grace helps build character and sportsmanship.

ANSWER KEY: A-3 / B-7 / C-2 / D-9 / E-6 / F-3 / G-10 / H-4 / I-1 / J-8

My Day –

My focus for today is:

_____
_____
_____

Date	What Time I Went To Bed Last Night?
	What Time Did I Wake Up Today?
I had _____ hours of sleep	

Today's practice was...

3 things I want to accomplish today...

1. _____
2. _____
3. _____

What I learned today?

What challenged me today?

Did I eat like a winner today?   YES   NO

Did I eat any C.R.A.P. today?   YES   NO

What color was my pee today?

Red   Orange   Dark Yellow   Yellow   Light Yellow   Clear

Did I poo today?   YES   NO

WHAT I ATE TODAY?

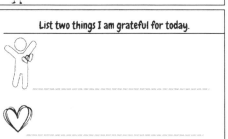

List two things I am grateful for today.

What's my mindset today?

Who and How did I serve or help somebody today?

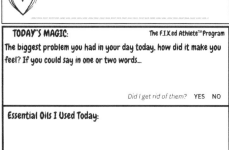

TODAY'S MAGIC: The F.I.X.ed Athlete™ Program

The biggest problem you had in your day today, how did it make you feel? If you could say in one or two words...

Did I get rid of them?   YES   NO

Essential Oils I Used Today:

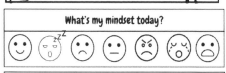

What I'm looking forward to tomorrow?

SECRET GRATITUDE MISSION

HEY SUPERSTAR

ACTIVITY:
Do Something Kind for Someone You Know - that doesn't live in your home.

PURPOSE:
As a young athlete, you work hard to build a strong body — but true strength also comes from having a strong heart. This week's mission is to show appreciation to some of the quiet heroes in your community: First Responders, including Police Officers. Choose someone you know who doesn't live with you, and find a meaningful way to give back or show your gratitude.

WHY THIS MATTERS:

✓ **Gratitude in Action**
Showing other somebody cares is important — showing gratitude is powerful. It builds character and makes the world better.

✓ **Many People Help Athletes Like You Every Day**
The key this week is to show anonymous gratitude. The secret of showing someone cares is almost as powerful as showing them that they matter. Your appreciation may one day come full circle.

✓ **Teamwork Is Bigger Than Sports**
You're part of a larger team — the human team. Just like teammates lift each other up, we lift up our community too. Show them that someone notices them and care enough to show it.

YOUR CHALLENGE:

- **PICK SOMEONE NEAR YOU:**
  - A TREACHER
  - ANOTHER PARENT
  - SOMEONE WHO OFTEN WORKS HARD WITH LITTLE GRATITUDE

- **CREATE AND DELIVER A SMALL ACT OF KINDNESS:**

  Here are some great options:

  ☑ **HEALTHY SNACK PACKS:**
  Include items like trail mix, fruit cups, water bottles, or granola bars. Add a note of encouragement or thanks - but do not tell them who it came from.

  ☑ **HANDWRITTEN CARDS OR POSTERS**
  Write a message like:
  > "Thank you for helping those in your community."
  > "You're an MVP In On My Team."
  > "We notice what you do — and we're grateful."

  ☑ **CARE BASKET FROM THE TEAM**
  Gather small items (snacks, coffee, thank-you notes, mini gift cards) and decorate a box or bag with your team colors - but not individual names.

- **MAKE THE DELIVERY:**
  Ask someone to deliver it to them - without letting them know who sent it.

BEING A GREAT ATHLETE ISN'T JUST ABOUT SCORING POINTS OR WINNING RACES —

IT'S ALSO ABOUT BEING A PERSON OTHERS CAN COUNT ON.

KINDNESS IS A LEGACY. AND REAL CHAMPIONS GIVE BACK.

My Day –

My focus for today is:
_____
_____
_____

Date	What Time I Went To Bed Last Night?
	What Time Did I Wake Up Today?
I had _____ hours of sleep	

Today's practice was...

3 things I want to accomplish today...

1. _____
2. _____
3. _____

What I learned today?

What challenged me today?

Did I eat like a winner today?	YES	NO
Did I eat any C.R.A.P. today?	YES	NO

What color was my pee today?

Red   Orange   Dark Yellow   Yellow   Light Yellow   Clear

Did I poo today?	YES	NO

WHAT I ATE TODAY?

List two things I am grateful for today.

What's my mindset today?

Who and How did I serve or help somebody today?

TODAY'S MAGIC: The F.I.X.ed Athlete™ Program

The biggest problem you had in your day today, how did it make you feel? If you could say in one or two words...

Did I get rid of them? YES   NO

Essential Oils I Used Today:

What I'm looking forward to tomorrow?

CREATE A THROWER'S OBSTACLE COURSE
Well sort-of, kind of... keep reading

Back on page #180, you created your own obstacle course. Today, you are going to **design your own Mini-Thrower's Obstacle Course** using whatever you have around you—your home, room, backyard. But this isn't just about throwing sporting equipment, it's about fine-motor skills, visual discrimination, reflex reaction, mental adjustments, and pattern recognition... Today you're looking for objects like the lid of a 16oz. soda bottle. Squeezing that lid between your thumb and index finger, just right will send it spinning and flying across the room.

START small Indoors

Step 1: Physical Abilities
Challenge: Using your creativity, select small objects to manipulate with your fingers, hands, breath, wind that you create by waving something else, etc.
Examples: Pinching a bottle cap to shoot it across the room through the air. Kicking a paper-football with your index finger on your non-dominant hand. Blowing a ping pong ball across the table.

Step 2: Create Targets
These train your focus, build your pattern recognition, engage your problem solving skills, and test your calmness under pressure.
Examples: Set up targets around the room while standing in a single space. Create a mini-golf like course across your backyard using the bottle cap, paper-football, or paper airplane. Add points.

For Coaches...
If your athletes are required to throw balls or objects, one of our favorite practices involved creating a "golf course" on our discus, javelin, baseball & softball, and lacrosse fields using old car tires... When accuracy matters: **TRAIN IT!** It's also a great indoor activity too. We also switched our standard equipment with racquet balls, ping pong balls, etc... you get the picture.

Step 3: Set Obstacles Between You & Your Targets
This engages all physical and cognitive skills.
Examples: Indoors or outdoors, build on Steps 1 & 2, making each obstacle more difficult. Outdoors - consider playing through a water sprinkler or muddy field. When you train for real-life obstacles, they no longer are seen as obstacles.

GO BIG OUTDOORS

My Day —

My focus for today is:

_____
_____
_____
_____

Date	What Time I Went To Bed Last Night?
	What Time Did I Wake Up Today?
I had _____ hours of sleep	

3 things I want to accomplish today...

1. _____
2. _____
3. _____

Today's practice was...

What I learned today?

What challenged me today?

Did I eat like a winner today?   YES   NO

Did I eat any C.R.A.P. today?   YES   NO

What color was my pee today?

Red   Orange   Dark Yellow   Yellow   Light Yellow   Clear

Did I poo today?   YES   NO

WHAT I ATE TODAY?

List two things I am grateful for today.

What's my mindset today?

Who and How did I serve or help somebody today?

TODAY'S MAGIC: The F.I.X.ed Athlete™ Program

The biggest problem you had in your day today, how did it make you feel? If you could say in one or two words...

Did I get rid of them?   YES   NO

Essential Oils I Used Today:

What I'm looking forward to tomorrow?

Schulte Tables for Athletes
SPORTS

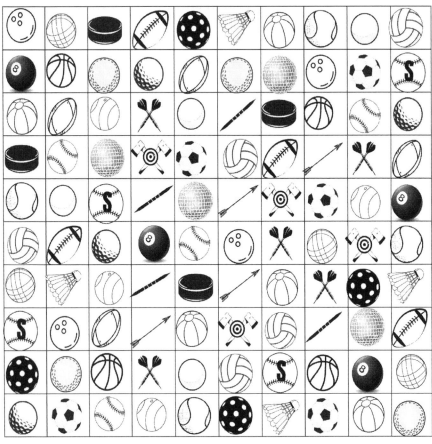

My Time: _____   Date: __/__   My Time: _____   Date: __/__

My Time: _____   Date: __/__   My Time: _____   Date: __/__

My Time: _____   Date: __/__   My Time: _____   Date: __/__

My Time: _____   Date: __/__   My Time: _____   Date: __/__

My Time: _____   Date: __/__   My Time: _____   Date: __/__

My Time: _____   Date: __/__   My Time: _____   Date: __/__

My Time: _____   Date: __/__   My Time: _____   Date: __/__

My Time: _____   Date: __/__   My Time: _____   Date: __/__

My Time: _____   Date: __/__   My Time: _____   Date: __/__

MyDay —

My focus for today is:
_____
_____
_____
_____

Date _____

What Time I Went To Bed Last Night? _____

What Time Did I Wake Up Today? _____

I had _____ hours of sleep

3 things I want to accomplish today...
1. _____
2. _____
3. _____

Today's practice was...

What I learned today?

What challenged me today?

Did I eat like a winner today?   YES   NO

Did I eat any C.R.A.P. today?   YES   NO

What color was my pee today?
Red   Orange   Dark Yellow   Yellow   Light Yellow   Clear

Did I poo today?   YES   NO

WHAT I ATE TODAY?

List two things I am grateful for today.

What's my mindset today?

Who and How did I serve or help somebody today?

TODAY'S MAGIC: The F.I.X.ed Athlete™ Program
The biggest problem you had in your day today, how did it make you feel? If you could say in one or two words...

Did I get rid of them?   YES   NO

Essential Oils I Used Today:

What I'm looking forward to tomorrow?

🌟 NO REMINDERS WEEK! 🌟
Pack Your Own Sports Bag Like a Champion!

This week, you're leveling up! No reminders. No "Did you pack your socks?" from grown-ups. You're the captain now — and champions come prepared!

Whether you're going to practice or a competition, your job today is to pack your own bag and double-check it like a pro. The best athletes in the world don't just train their muscles — they train their minds and their habits. The hardest part about this activity is the NATURAL CONSEQUENCES that you will experience. If you do this well - you may only have to learn this lesson ONCE!

✅ Step 1: Check the Weather & Know Where You're Going
✓ Is it indoors or outdoors?
✓ Hot, cold, or rainy?
✓ Is there a locker room or not?

🌑 Step 2: Think Through Your Whole Day
✓ Do you go straight from school?
✓ Do you need snacks?
✓ Are you leaving straight from home?

👟 My All-Star Sports Bag Checklist
Check off what you need. Add your own gear at the bottom!

✓ITEMS - NOTES
☐ Uniform or practice clothes, shirt, shorts/pants, team gear
☐ Sport-specific shoes, cleats, court shoes, sneakers
☐ Socks (extra pair!) Just in case they get wet or dirty
☐ Water bottle Filled and cold!
☐ Healthy snack or light fuel, fruit, bar, sandwich
☐ Gear or equipment: Ball, glove, racket, goggles, etc.
☐ Towel for sweat or showers
☐ Deodorant / wipes -Stay fresh!
☐ Essential oils: _____ _____ _____ _____
☐ Hair ties/headbands If you need them
☐ Notebook / journal / playbook **Superstar In Training PLAYbook**? 🌑
☐ Phone & charger (if allowed) Keep it in a safe pocket
☐ Cash or card (optional) For emergencies or snacks
☐ Change of clothes Post-practice comfort or clean dry gear
☐ First Aid item Band-aids, blister pads, Allergy-inhaler, etc.
☐ Any medication If you need it, double-check it!

📗 My Extras ✓

☐ _____ ☐ _____ ☐ _____

☐ _____ ☐ _____ ☐ _____

💭 My Pre-Check Pep Talk to Myself:
"I'm in charge. I come prepared. My success starts before I even arrive. No excuses, just excellence."

🌟 Next time I'll make sure to pack:_____

My Day —

My focus for today is:
_____
_____
_____

Date _____

What Time I Went To Bed Last Night? _____

What Time Did I Wake Up Today? _____

I had _____ hours of sleep

Today's practice was...

3 things I want to accomplish today...
1. _____
2. _____
3. _____

What I learned today?

What challenged me today?

Did I eat like a winner today?   YES   NO

Did I eat any C.R.A.P. today?   YES   NO

What color was my pee today?
Red   Orange   Dark Yellow   Yellow   Light Yellow   Clear

Did I poo today?   YES   NO

WHAT I ATE TODAY?

List two things I am grateful for today.

What's my mindset today?

Who and How did I serve or help somebody today?

TODAY'S MAGIC: The F.I.X.ed Athlete™ Program
The biggest problem you had in your day today, how did it make you feel? If you could say in one or two words...

Did I get rid of them?   YES   NO

Essential Oils I Used Today:

What I'm looking forward to tomorrow?

FOLLOW A PATH

Are you ready to work your focus, concentration, spatial awareness, perpetual speed, flow-state control, kinesthetic awareness, mindfulness and some hand-eye coordination? All of these skills are used by athletes and using your finger to trace the lines of these race track-like objects will strengthen all of these skills...

How fast can you trace the tracks without going out of the lines?

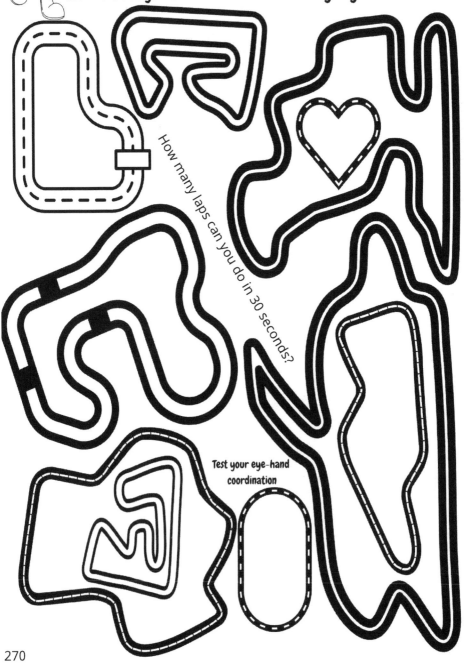

How many laps can you do in 30 seconds?

Test your eye-hand coordination

My Day

My focus for today is:
_____
_____
_____

Date	What Time I Went To Bed Last Night?
	What Time Did I Wake Up Today?
I had _____ hours of sleep	

Today's practice was...

3 things I want to accomplish today...
1. _____
2. _____
3. _____

What I learned today?

What challenged me today?

Did I eat like a winner today?   YES   NO

Did I eat any C.R.A.P. today?   YES   NO

What color was my pee today?

Red   Orange   Dark Yellow   Yellow   Light Yellow   Clear

Did I poo today?   YES   NO

WHAT I ATE TODAY?

List two things I am grateful for today.

What's my mindset today?

Who and How did I serve or help somebody today?

TODAY'S MAGIC: The F.I.X.ed Athlete™ Program
The biggest problem you had in your day today, how did it make you feel? If you could say in one or two words...

Did I get rid of them?   YES   NO

Essential Oils I Used Today:

What I'm looking forward to tomorrow?

Hey SUPERSTAR

FIND YOUR GENIUS

You might not think a physicist like Albert Einstein has much to do with sports, but his story has something powerful to teach every athlete. Einstein wasn't always seen as a genius. He struggled in school, didn't fit the mold, and thought deeply about things others overlooked. But what made him a genius wasn't just intelligence—it was curiosity, imagination, and a relentless drive to understand the universe, no matter how strange or difficult the questions got.

That's something any great athlete can relate to. To excel in sports, you need more than talent. You need vision, discipline, creativity, and the courage to keep going when things don't make sense or don't go your way.

Einstein once said, 'It's not that I'm so smart. It's just that I stay with problems longer.' That's the mindset of champions. Greatness in anything—science, sports, or life—comes from pushing your limits and believing in your own unique way of seeing the world.

Einstein said, **"If you judge a fish by its ability to climb a tree, it'll live its whole life believing that it is stupid, thinking it's a failure."** The same goes for athletes. Your greatness might not look like someone else's—but that doesn't make it less. Own your style, your strengths, your path. That's where real genius—and real success—lives.

Today's Activity: Think about what both of these quotes mean to you and list our your strengths, your vision, your creativity, your skills, and everything that makes you a **SUPERSTAR GENIUS in your own way.**

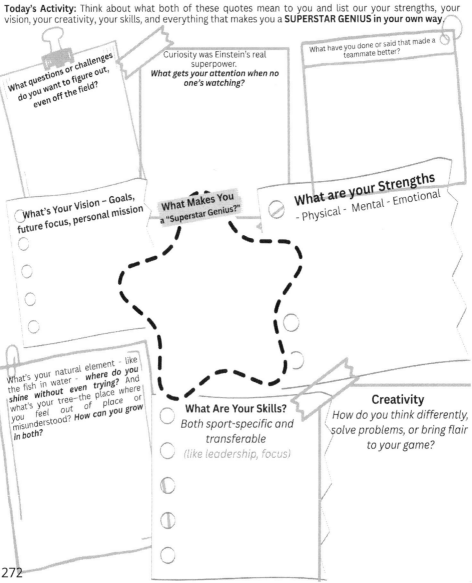

My Day —

My focus for today is:
_____
_____
_____

Date

What Time I Went To Bed Last Night?

What Time Did I Wake Up Today?

I had _____ hours of sleep

3 things I want to accomplish today...

1. _____
2. _____
3. _____

Today's practice was...

What I learned today?

What challenged me today?

Did I eat like a winner today?   YES   NO

Did I eat any C.R.A.P. today?   YES   NO

What color was my pee today?
Red   Orange   Dark Yellow   Yellow   Light Yellow   Clear

Did I poo today?   YES   NO

WHAT I ATE TODAY?

List two things I am grateful for today.

What's my mindset today?

Who and How did I serve or help somebody today?

TODAY'S MAGIC: The F.I.X.ed Athlete™ Program
The biggest problem you had in your day today, how did it make you feel? If you could say in one or two words...

Did I get rid of them?   YES   NO

Essential Oils I Used Today:

What I'm looking forward to tomorrow?

HABITS & GOALS CROSSWORD PUZZLE
BRAIN POWER MEETS: MINDSET – HABITS & GOALS

Using what you have learned, answer these 22 **Superstar In Training** questions. This is your last crossword puzzle of this journey... Answers can be found on page #309.

Across:

1. THE PART OF YOUR BRAIN THAT GROWS FROM PRACTICING JUGGLING AND FOCUS.
2. THE PERSON YOU'RE TRYING TO BECOME IN 10 YEARS.
3. WHAT POWERS YOUR GAME AND BODY - CHOOSE THE HEALTHY KIND.
4. A PLANT-BASED TOOL USED TO BOOST ENERGY, FOCUS, AND RECOVERY.
5. THE SECRET PERFORMANCE FORMULA: FOCUS, INCREASES, _____ (FROM THE F.I.X.ED ATHLETE'S PROGRAM
6. A SPECIFIE, MEASURABLE DREAM YOU'RE WORKING TOWARDS WITH A DEADLINE.
7. A WRITTEN PLAN FOR WHAT AND WHEN YOU EAT FOR PERFORMANCE.
8. AN INNER VOICE THAT SAYS, "YOU'VE GOT THIS!"
9. THE POWER OF BELIEVING IN IMPROVEMENT EVERY DAY.
10. THE "F" IN F.I.X.ED ATHLETE STANDS FOR _____ - "KEEPING YOUR EYE ON THE PRIZE."
11. A CALMING ESSENTIAL OIL USED BEFORE BED OR PRACTICE

Down:

1. WHAT WE WRITE TO OUR FUTURE SELF TO TRACK GROWTH AND DREAMS.
2. THE ABILITY TO RECOVER FROM MISTAKES AND KEEP GOING.
3. THE TYPE OF ROOM WHERE EVERYTHING HAS A SPOT.
4. A WORD THAT MEANS MAKING SMALL SMART DECISIONS OVER TIME.
5. A SKILL YOU PRACTICE WITH WRITING LETTERS, ASKING QUESTIONS, AND INTERVIEWING OTHERS.
6. A METHOS TO UNPLUG AND PROTECT YOUR FOCUS AND SLEEP.
7. THE NAME OF THE FULL MENTAL AND PHYSICAL PERFORMANCE PROGRAM FOR ATHLETES DESIGNED BY BARB V
8. AN ACTIVITY THAT TEACHES YOU FOCUS, COORDINATION, AND MEMORY.
9. WHAT YOU SHOULD SHARE WITH OTHERS AND YOURSELF TO BUILD CONNECTION AND KINDNESS.
10. WORKING WITH OTHERS, LISTENING, AND DOING YOUR ROLE WELL BUILDS _____
11. WHAT WE DO WHEN WE PUT DOWN DEVICES AND PLAY, THINK, OR CREATE

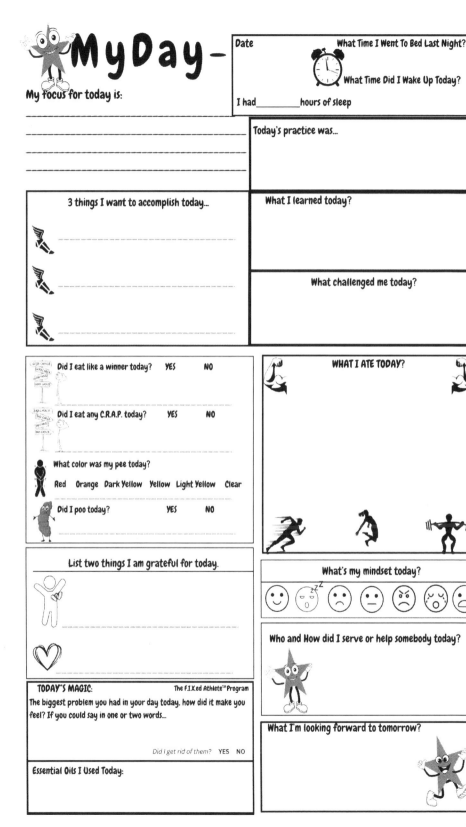

WRITE A LETTER TO THE AUTHOR
Tell Me What You Liked BEST About This Book...

Instructions:
Today's activity is you opportunity to write to me directly and tell me what you have liked the BEST about this book.

Write a Letter to Barb V, the author of this book...
Write your letter on paper, decorate it if you'd like, and make sure you send it! You never know how your words may impact me and the next book like this that I write... who knows, I will probably give you a "SHOUT OUT" in my next book.

Who: Barb V

Why: Yes — me! I want to hear from YOU, the amazing young athlete holding this book.

Skills You're Building:
- Skills You're Building:
- Self-Expression
- Reflection
- Communication
- Confidence
- Focus
- Writing Skills

Instructions:
1. Write a letter to me — the author of this book — and tell me a little about you and your athletic journey.

You can include:
- What sport(s) you play
- What page or activity helped you the most
- Your biggest win, toughest loss, or something you learned from this book
- A question you'd like to ask me
- What you're working on to be your best

How To Write Your Letter:
- Use your best handwriting and follow letter format:
- Dear Author,
- Sincerely, [Your Name]

Optional Writing Prompts to Get You Started:
- "One thing I've learned from your book is..."
- "This is how I bounce back after I lose..."
- "A goal I have this season is..."
- "If we met, I'd want to tell you..."
- "Thank you for helping me believe..."

Mail it to:
Barb V
Author of SUPERSTAR In Training
The Kid Factor Publishing
140 W. 29th Street Suite #325
Pueblo, Colorado 81008

PRACTICE Writing Your Letter here...
before doing it in a card or on letter paper...

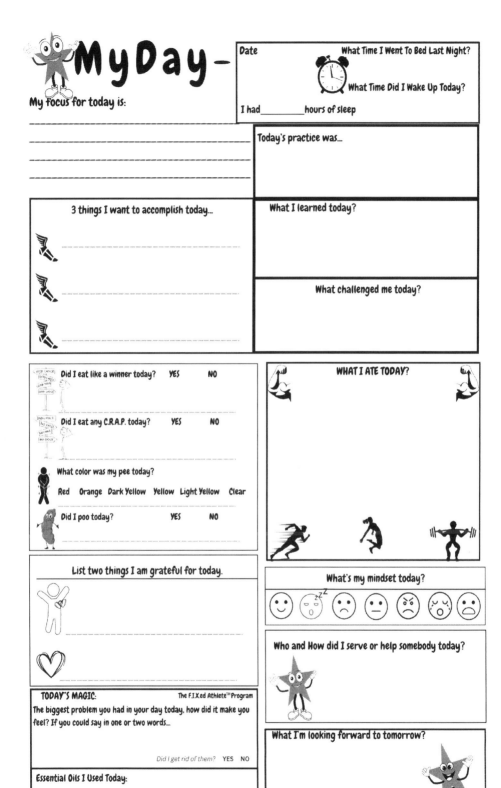

MyDay —

My focus for today is:
_____
_____
_____

Date	What Time I Went To Bed Last Night?
	What Time Did I Wake Up Today?
I had _____ hours of sleep	

Today's practice was...

3 things I want to accomplish today...

1. _____
2. _____
3. _____

What I learned today?

What challenged me today?

Did I eat like a winner today?   YES   NO

Did I eat any C.R.A.P. today?   YES   NO

What color was my pee today?
Red   Orange   Dark Yellow   Yellow   Light Yellow   Clear

Did I poo today?   YES   NO

WHAT I ATE TODAY?

List two things I am grateful for today.

What's my mindset today?

Who and How did I serve or help somebody today?

TODAY'S MAGIC: The F.I.X.ed Athlete™ Program
The biggest problem you had in your day today, how did it make you feel? If you could say in one or two words...

Did I get rid of them?   YES   NO

Essential Oils I Used Today:

What I'm looking forward to tomorrow?

SUPERSTAR'S CONTROL WORKSHEET

Place a checkmark ( ) in the box of the items under "What I CAN Control" that you believe you have a good handle on and circle the boxes that you are currently working on or that you need to focus more on. When you complete them and feel like you have them under control, then put a checkmark in its box. Don't erase the circles when you earn the checkmark so you can monitor how far you have come and where you have made progress. Eventually, you want to earn a checkmark in each of the boxes under "What I CAN Control".

What I CAN Control	What I CANNOT Control
☐ My Effort Level During Practice	Coach's Decisions About Playing Time
☐ My Sleep Schedule And Habits	Other Players' Performance
☐ My Nutrition And Hydration	Officials' Calls During Games
☐ My Attitude At Practice And Games	Weather Conditions
☐ My Response To Mistakes	Facility/Equipment Quality
☐ My Preparation Before Games	Opponents' Strategies
☐ My Focus During Competition	Crowd Behavior
☐ My Communication With Teammates	Team Roster Decisions
☐ My Time Management	Illness Or Unexpected Injuries
☐ How I Speak To Myself	Family Conflicts Or Personal Issues
☐ The Goals I Set For Myself	Genetic Physical Limitations
☐ How I Respond To Feedback	Team Win-Loss Record
☐ My Body Language	Teammates' Effort Levels
☐ My Training Outside Of Team Practice	Social Media Comments About You
☐ My Knowledge Of The Sport And Rules	Age/Experience Of Opponents
☐ How I Treat My Body (Recovery/Rest)	Play Calls Or Game Strategy
☐ My Punctuality	Transportation Issues
☐ How I Handle Pressure	Last-Minute Schedule Changes
☐ My Coachability	Parents' Behavior At Games
☐ How I Support My Teammates	College Recruiters' Opinions
☐ My Mental Preparation	Past Performances/Mistakes
☐ My Equipment Maintenance	Others' Expectations Of You
☐ How I Study Film/Game Situations	Team Selection Criteria
☐ The Questions I Ask To Improve	Political Factors In Sports
☐ How I Use Failures As Learning Opportunities	Others' Recognition Of Your Effort
☐ What I Study In & Out Of My Sport	Social Media & The News

©2025 Barb V All Rights Reserved   The F.I.X.ed Athlete™ Program   The Kid Factor, LLC

My Day –

My focus for today is:
_____
_____
_____

Date _____
What Time I Went To Bed Last Night? _____
What Time Did I Wake Up Today? _____
I had _____ hours of sleep

Today's practice was...

3 things I want to accomplish today...
- _____
- _____
- _____

What I learned today?

What challenged me today?

Did I eat like a winner today?   YES   NO

Did I eat any C.R.A.P. today?   YES   NO

What color was my pee today?
Red   Orange   Dark Yellow   Yellow   Light Yellow   Clear

Did I poo today?   YES   NO

WHAT I ATE TODAY?

What's my mindset today?

Who and How did I serve or help somebody today?

List two things I am grateful for today.

TODAY'S MAGIC: The F.I.X.ed Athlete™ Program
The biggest problem you had in your day today, how did it make you feel? If you could say in one or two words...

Did I get rid of them?   YES   NO

Essential Oils I Used Today:

What I'm looking forward to tomorrow?

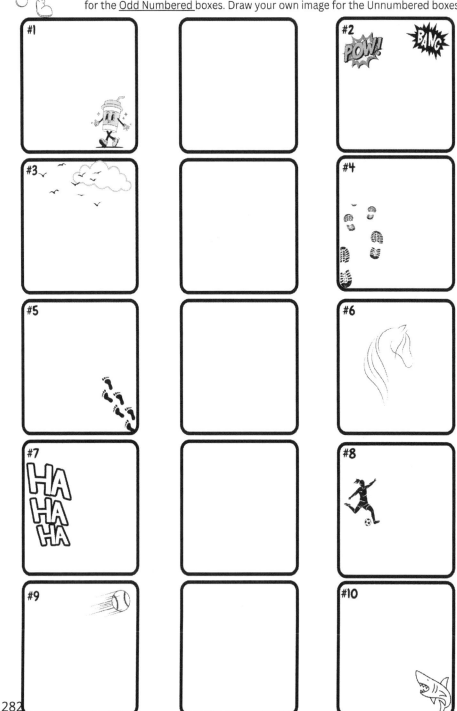

MyDay —

My focus for today is:
_____
_____
_____

Date _____

What Time I Went To Bed Last Night?

What Time Did I Wake Up Today?

I had _____ hours of sleep

Today's practice was...

3 things I want to accomplish today...
1. _____
2. _____
3. _____

What I learned today?

What challenged me today?

Did I eat like a winner today?   YES   NO

Did I eat any C.R.A.P. today?   YES   NO

What color was my pee today?

Red   Orange   Dark Yellow   Yellow   Light Yellow   Clear

Did I poo today?   YES   NO

WHAT I ATE TODAY?

List two things I am grateful for today.

What's my mindset today?

Who and How did I serve or help somebody today?

TODAY'S MAGIC: The F.I.X.ed Athlete™ Program

The biggest problem you had in your day today, how did it make you feel? If you could say in one or two words...

Did I get rid of them?   YES   NO

Essential Oils I Used Today:

What I'm looking forward to tomorrow?

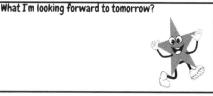

SUPERSTAR IN TRAINING ACTIVITY ★

Team Pep Talk: Own Your Energy – It Echoes!

Your words can fire up a team, shift the mood, and turn doubt into drive.

Today, YOU are the voice that leads.

Write a pep talk to inspire your team before a big game or challenge.

- ☑ Be honest
- ☑ Be bold
- ☑ Be YOU

Message to include: ☀ Own Your Energy – It Echoes! ☀

Start your pep talk below. Write from the heart. You're the spark.

_____

_____

_____

_____

_____

_____

_____

_____

_____

_____

_____

_____

_____

_____

_____

_____

_____

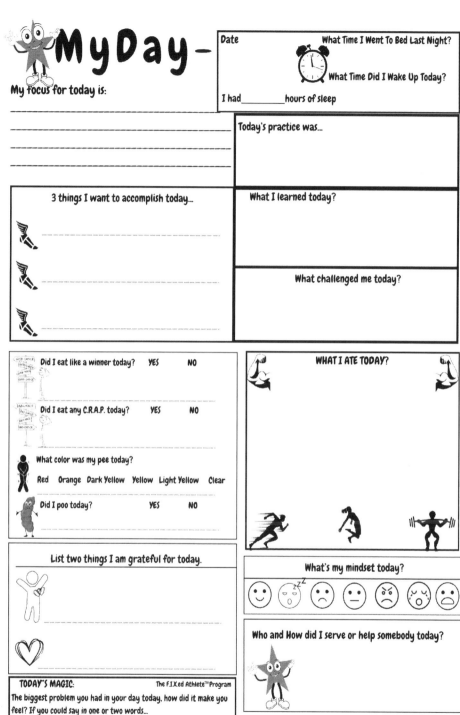

MY "Dear Future Me" LETTER
The power of Future Perfect Planning

Instructions: A **DEAR FUTURE ME** letter...
Use this page to write your Dear Future Me letter. On page #106 of this book, you are asked to write this powerful personal development letter to your future self.

Dear Me,

Sincerely,

Date:

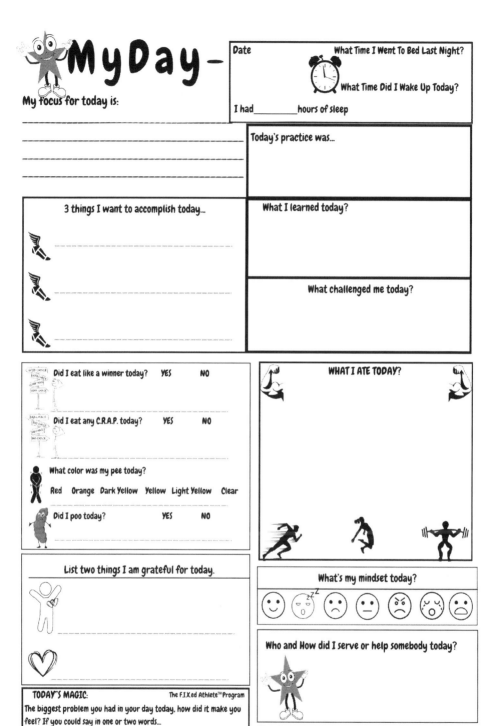

Trivia Time: Are you ready to test your knowledge, learn new things, engage your analytical thinking, memory, and recall? All skills that will make you a better athlete and a powerful **SUPERSTAR In Training**! These athletes were once where you are today... Today's Topic:

ELITE ATHLETES IN THEIR SPORT

1) TONY HAWK
2) Multiple Ballon d'Or Winner World Cup Champion with Argentina
3) 7-Time Super Bowl Champion
4) MICHAEL JORDAN
5) MICHALE PHELPS
6) Most Decorated Female Track & Field Olympian in U.S. History
7) SIMONE BILES
8) USAIN BOLT
9) RONDA ROUSEY
10) JENNIE FINCH
11) SERENA WILLIAMS Advocate for Women's Equality in Sports
12) TIGER WOODS
13) Trailblazer in Winter Sports. Youngest Woman to Win Olympic Gold in Halfpipe
14) ROGER FEDERER
15) KATIE LEDECKY

A. ALLYSON FELIX
B. Most Decorated Gymnast Ever Known for Pushing the Limits
C. CHLOE KIM
D. World's Fastest Man. 8-Time Olympic Gold Medalist
E. 2004 Olympic Gold Medalist in Softball. Her 71 mph Softball Pitches are Equivalent to 95 mph in MLB
F. First Female Fighter in UFC, Olympic Medalist in Judo
G. 15 Major Championships - Helped to Popularize Golf
H. TOM BRADY
I. 23 Grand Slam Singles Titles
J. 20 Grand Slam Titles. Known for Sportsmanship & Grace
K. Olympic Swimmer Known for Dominating Long-Distance Freestyle. Multiple Olympic Gold
L. LIONEL MESSI
M. 6-Time NBA Champion. Got Cut From His High School Basketball Team
N. Pioneer of Modern Skateboarding 1st to Land a 900
O. Most Decorated Olympian Ever 23 Gold Medals

Answer Key: 1-N / 2-L / 3-H / 4-M / 5-O / 6-A / 7-B / 8-D / 9-F / 10-E / 11-I / 12-G / 13-C / 14-J / 15-K

MyDay –

My focus for today is:

_____
_____
_____

Date	What Time I Went To Bed Last Night?
	What Time Did I Wake Up Today?
I had _____ hours of sleep	

Today's practice was...

3 things I want to accomplish today...

1. _____
2. _____
3. _____

What I learned today?

What challenged me today?

- Did I eat like a winner today?   YES   NO
- Did I eat any C.R.A.P. today?   YES   NO
- What color was my pee today?
  Red   Orange   Dark Yellow   Yellow   Light Yellow   Clear
- Did I poo today?   YES   NO

WHAT I ATE TODAY?

List two things I am grateful for today.

What's my mindset today?

Who and How did I serve or help somebody today?

TODAY'S MAGIC: The F.I.X.ed Athlete™ Program

The biggest problem you had in your day today, how did it make you feel? If you could say in one or two words...

Did I get rid of them?   YES   NO

Essential Oils I Used Today:

What I'm looking forward to tomorrow?

My Day -

My focus for today is:
_____
_____
_____

Date
What Time I Went To Bed Last Night?
What Time Did I Wake Up Today?
I had _____ hours of sleep

Today's practice was...

3 things I want to accomplish today...

What I learned today?

What challenged me today?

Did I eat like a winner today?   YES   NO

Did I eat any C.R.A.P. today?   YES   NO

What color was my pee today?

Red   Orange   Dark Yellow   Yellow   Light Yellow   Clear

Did I poo today?   YES   NO

WHAT I ATE TODAY?

List two things I am grateful for today.

What's my mindset today?

Who and How did I serve or help somebody today?

TODAY'S MAGIC: The F.I.X.ed Athlete™ Program
The biggest problem you had in your day today, how did it make you feel? If you could say in one or two words...

Did I get rid of them?   YES   NO

Essential Oils I Used Today:

What I'm looking forward to tomorrow?

The SUPERSTAR In Training - Fitness Challenge

Tracking your baseline and progress over time helps you see just how far you've come—and where to focus your efforts next. It's not about being perfect; it's about getting stronger, faster, and more confident with every rep, jump, sprint, and skill. As a SUPERSTAR In Training, your goal is always to progress forward – both inside and out.

📅 TESTING DAY:

Time of Day: _____

Today's Body Weight (lbs): _____

🎯 SELECT YOUR LEVEL

Pick the level based on your age group. Compete only with yourself—and go for that personal best!

LEVEL	AGE GROUP	INTENSITY
⭐ Level 1	Ages - & Under	Foundation Training (Fun Form & Focus)
⭐⭐ Level 2	Ages 10 – 12	Challenge Training (Speed & Strength)
⭐⭐⭐ Level 3	Ages 13 +	Elite Training (Power & Performance)

💪 THE SUPERSTAR FITNESS CHALLENGES 💪

In each of the following activities, record your **best of 3 attempts** for each test. You may decide to select any of the times, distances, or object you want in the Sprint, Jump Rope, and throw. Be honest. Be tough. Be proud.

TEST	Attempt #1	Attempt #2	Attempt #3	PERSONAL BEST
Push-Ups (Max reps)				
Sit-Ups (Max reps)				
Jump Rope (Reps in 1 – 2 - 5 minutes)				
Burpees (Reps in 1 minute)				
Plank Hold (Seconds)				
Wall Sit (Seconds)				
Sprint – 40 / 50 / 100 -yard dash (Seconds)				
Standing Throw (Ft/In) Baseball, Softball, Football				
High Jump Touch (Wall mark)				
Broad Jump (Ft/In)				
Leg Raise Hold – 6 in. (Seconds)				

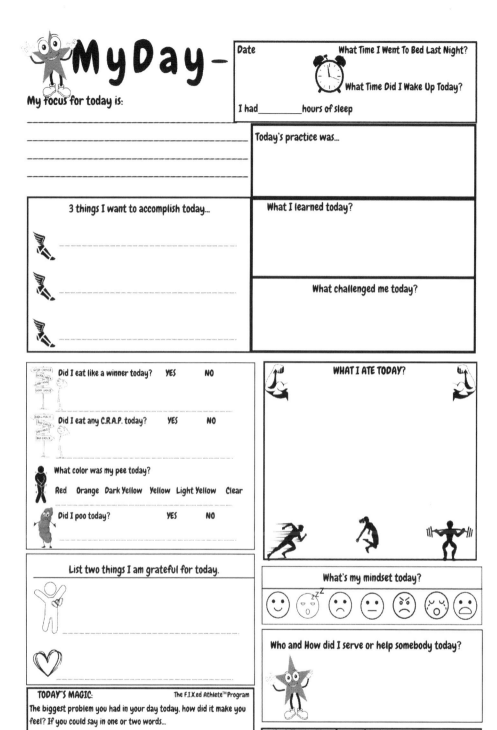

Trivia Time: Are you ready to test your knowledge, learn new things, engage your analytical thinking, memory, and recall? All skills that will make you a better athlete and a powerful **SUPERSTAR In Training**!

Today's subject:

Pro sports with their city, or mascot...

1) HOUSTON, TX

2) KANSAS CITY, MO

3) COZMO

4) LEO the LION

5) FLAMES & HARVEY the HOUND

6) BLAZE

7) DINGER

8) ELLIE the ELEPHANT

9) TORO

10) BOLTMAN

11) AL the OCTOPUS

12) BOSTON, MA

13) G-WIZ

14) STUFF the MAGIC DRAGON

15) BOSTON RED SOX

A. WALLY the GREEN MONSTER

B. LUCKY the LEPRECHAUN

C. REAL SALT LAKE

D. DETROIT RED WINGS

E. CONNECTICUT SUN

F. NEW YORK LIBERTY

G. L A GALAXY

H. HOUSTON TEXANS

I. WASHINTON, D.C.

J. ORLANDO, FL

K. CURRENT

L. COLORADO ROCKIES

M. CALGARY, AB

N. LOS ANGELAS CHARGERS

O. HOUSTON DASH

Answer Key: 1-O / 2-K / 3-G / 4-C / 5-M / 6-E / 7-L / 8-F / 9-H / 10-N / 11-D / 12-B / 13-I / 14-J / 15-A

MyDay-

My focus for today is:

_____
_____
_____

Date

What Time I Went To Bed Last Night?

What Time Did I Wake Up Today?

I had _____ hours of sleep

Today's practice was...

3 things I want to accomplish today...

What I learned today?

What challenged me today?

Did I eat like a winner today?   YES   NO

Did I eat any C.R.A.P. today?   YES   NO

What color was my pee today?

Red   Orange   Dark Yellow   Yellow   Light Yellow   Clear

Did I poo today?   YES   NO

WHAT I ATE TODAY?

List two things I am grateful for today.

What's my mindset today?

Who and How did I serve or help somebody today?

TODAY'S MAGIC: The F.I.X.ed Athlete™ Program

The biggest problem you had in your day today, how did it make you feel? If you could say in one or two words...

Did I get rid of them?   YES   NO

Essential Oils I Used Today:

What I'm looking forward to tomorrow?

MyDay-

My focus for today is:
_____
_____
_____

Date	What Time I Went To Bed Last Night?
	What Time Did I Wake Up Today?
I had _____ hours of sleep	

Today's practice was...

3 things I want to accomplish today...
1. _____
2. _____
3. _____

What I learned today?

What challenged me today?

Did I eat like a winner today?   YES   NO

Did I eat any C.R.A.P. today?   YES   NO

What color was my pee today?

Red   Orange   Dark Yellow   Yellow   Light Yellow   Clear

Did I poo today?   YES   NO

WHAT I ATE TODAY?

List two things I am grateful for today.

What's my mindset today?

Who and How did I serve or help somebody today?

TODAY'S MAGIC: The F.I.X.ed Athlete™ Program
The biggest problem you had in your day today, how did it make you feel? If you could say in one or two words...

Did I get rid of them?   YES   NO

Essential Oils I Used Today:

What I'm looking forward to tomorrow?

SUPERSTAR VISUAL MEMORY ACTIVITY
POSITIVE WORDS FOR ATHLETES

How to play:
- Set your timer for allotted amount of time (15-60 seconds suggested).
- When ready, start the timer and study the positive words & phrases on the page. Try to remember as many as you can! IGNORE the Negative words and phrases.
- When time's up, close the book or cover the page.
- Now set your timer for 1-2 minutes.
- Write down as many of the positive words & phrases as you can remember. Be specific! (For example, "I'm A Winner" or "I AM A WINNER" is better than just "Winner")
- When time's up, stop writing.
- Open the book and check your list against this page.
  - Score 1 point for each correct item.
  - Give yourself an extra point for very specific details.
- Challenge yourself to beat your score next time!

Play this game often to improve your visual memory. Try it alone or compete with teammates!

TIP: Great athletes have strong visualization skills. This game can help you develop those skills for better performance in your sport. Can you remember the 15 different POSITIVE words and phrases? How about some of the unique details? Were you able to ignore the 7 negative words and phrases?

Remember: You can practice this mental exercise anytime, anywhere – before practice, after training, or before bed. The more you practice, the stronger your mind, memory, and visual skills will becomes. ALSO: Start looking for clues on the playing field...

© 2025 Barb V   All Rights Reserved

My Day –

My focus for today is:
_____
_____
_____
_____

Date _____
What Time I Went To Bed Last Night? _____
What Time Did I Wake Up Today? _____
I had _____ hours of sleep

Today's practice was...

3 things I want to accomplish today...
1. _____
2. _____
3. _____

What I learned today?

What challenged me today?

Did I eat like a winner today?   YES   NO

Did I eat any C.R.A.P. today?   YES   NO

What color was my pee today?
Red   Orange   Dark Yellow   Yellow   Light Yellow   Clear

Did I poo today?   YES   NO

WHAT I ATE TODAY?

List two things I am grateful for today.

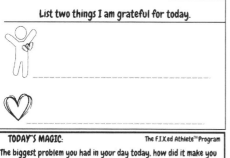

What's my mindset today?

Who and How did I serve or help somebody today?

TODAY'S MAGIC: The F.I.X.ed Athlete™ Program
The biggest problem you had in your day today, how did it make you feel? If you could say in one or two words...

Did I get rid of them?   YES   NO

Essential Oils I Used Today:

What I'm looking forward to tomorrow?

Section # 4
ANSWER KEYS

Solution page 112

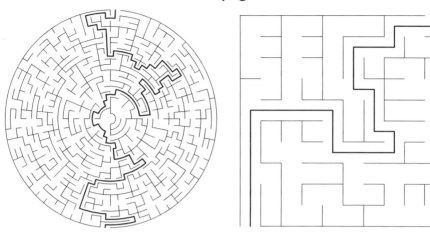

Answers from page #120

Across:
1. This popular treat is high in added sugar.
2. Too much sugar can affect your _____ health long term.
3. Sugar may make you feel tired or _____
4. Sugar can also be called this on a label _____
5. A common sugary drink.
6. Sugar hudes in snacks under this word that starts with "M."
7. Instead of sugar, athltese should fuel with whole _____
8. Athletes should stop eating these four categories of poor performance foods.

Down:
1. Natural sugar fround in fruit.
2. Sugar gives you a quick _____ but then a crash.
3. Athletes need this type of energy, not sugar spikes.
4. A natural sweetener made by bees.
5. This form of syrup is used in many processed foods.
6. Sugar messes with you _____ function and focus.
7. This is the best drink for hydration.

Solution from page #162

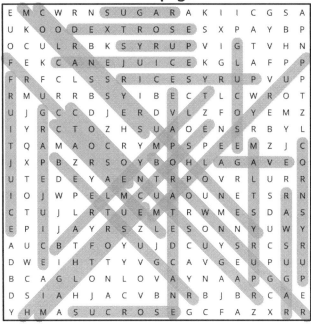

Solution from page #130
SUGAR WORD SCRAMBLE

1) **ASPERTAME**
2) **SUCRALOSE**
3) **SACCHARIN**
4) **ACESULFAME**
5) **NEOTAME**
6) **ADVATAME**
7) **ALITAME**
8) **XYLITOL**
9) **SORBITOL**
10) **MALTITOL**
11) **MANNITOL**
12) **ISOMALT**
13) **LACTITOL**
14) **DEXTRAN**
15) **DEXTRIN**
16) **CARAMEL**
17) **FRUCTOSE**
18) **MALT**
19) **TURBINADO**
20) **CYCLAMATE**

Answers from page #154

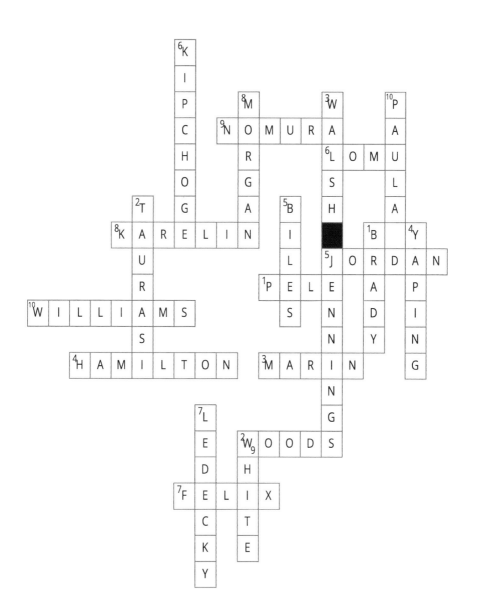

303

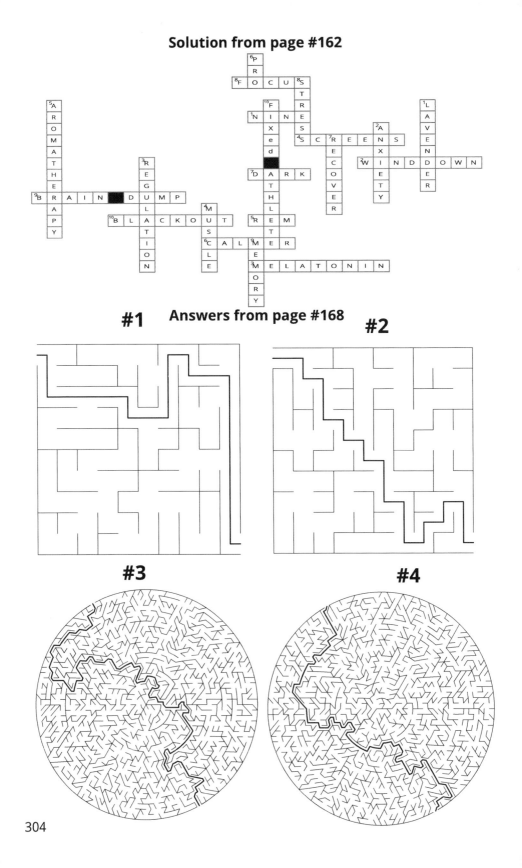

Answers on page #305

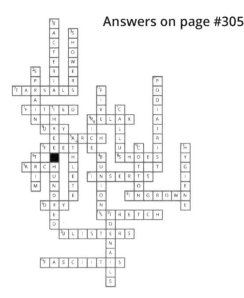

Across:
1. Footwear should be properly _____ to avoid blisters
2. These occur when soes rub the wrong way
3. When your toenail grows into the skin
4. Soaking your feet in warm water helps this
5. Stretch this part of the foot to help prevent plantar fasciitis
6. Important to do after washing feet
7. These foot bones give your foot structure and movement
8. Worn-out _____ can cause foot and ankle injuries
9. Skin between toes should be kept _____ to avoid fungus
10. A foot injury that causes sharp heel pain
11. These can be used in shoes to support arches
12. What athletes shoud check daily for cuts, swelling, or blisters
13. Before and after worksouts, always do this with your feet
14. Raised part of your foot that needs support

Down:
1. Thick skin that forms from friction
2. Common injury from not warming up properly
3. Never walk barefoot in these public places
4. Wearing shoes that are too small cause this foot condition
5. Type of fungus that causes itching and cracking between toes
6. Alsays do this to your toenails to avoid snagging
7. Running shoes should be replaced every _____ miles
8. Acronym for treating minor injuries (Rest, Ice, Compression, Elevation)
9. Should be cut straight across to prevent ingrown nails
10. Choose socks made from this material to avoid sweat buildup
11. The type of doctor who specializes in foot care
12. The number of toes on each foot
13. A bad smell can be caused by this build-up in shoes
14. Practice good _____ to avoid infections

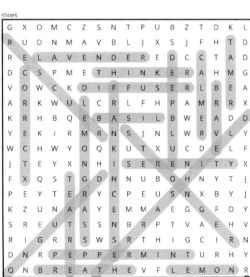

Solutions from page #186

305

SUPERFOOD WORD SEARCH page #196

C	H	I	C	K	E	N	K	R	S	Q	I	F	K	T	O	Y	S
N	R	A	W	P	U	M	P	K	I	N	S	E	E	D	S	Q	K
R	C	H	W	C	Z	S	W	M	S	P	H	B	E	E	T	S	C
B	F	R	J	H	L	W	C	G	I	C	I	E	I	Z	K	X	I
L	K	B	P	I	M	E	G	E	A	V	R	R	W	F	A	E	D
U	R	A	H	A	M	E	A	U	A	V	R	Z	I	S	J	Q	D
E	A	T	L	S	H	T	B	N	Q	E	O	N	K	V	O	U	Z
B	N	A	S	E	H	P	V	D	B	R	O	C	C	O	L	I	Z
E	H	R	A	E	U	O	P	K	J	E	A	A	A	S	L	N	E
R	G	T	L	D	W	T	C	K	W	N	E	E	J	D	X	O	N
R	G	C	M	S	S	A	D	K	S	J	N	F	U	L	O	A	N
I	S	H	O	W	L	T	O	D	I	E	Z	H	U	Y	U	S	T
E	Z	E	N	B	Z	O	E	W	A	L	N	U	T	S	T	Z	K
S	T	R	A	W	B	E	R	R	I	E	S	N	X	T	T	B	Q
H	E	R	A	C	W	S	A	R	D	I	N	E	S	K	W	W	I
L	T	I	Z	A	H	Q	R	K	K	T	G	Z	A	Y	S	J	H
H	G	E	E	U	P	K	G	W	S	P	I	N	A	C	H	E	M
B	S	S	S	R	O	P	G	K	C	I	X	O	S	Z	S	U	Y

UPBEAT WORD WORDSEARCH page #210

A	H	S	U	D	H	M	H	J	N	N	T	Q	X	X
Y	F	Y	B	C	V	Y	B	C	H	V	H	D	F	A
A	I	W	R	E	U	L	O	D	S	G	R	Y	C	L
A	X	B	H	U	A	C	R	G	I	A	O	V	F	T
Y	E	K	G	D	N	S	N	B	W	W	W	O	A	C
H	D	E	O	V	N	F	T	R	A	E	E	E	Q	I
W	L	Y	L	D	U	F	O	M	B	G	R	X	M	R
B	I	S	D	I	I	F	W	R	O	G	A	T	H	I
M	F	N	E	L	O	N	I	M	L	D	A	R	E	Z
N	E	O	N	G	S	P	N	G	U	I	E	E	F	T
J	U	M	P	E	R	E	X	X	F	U	F	M	N	C
B	A	L	L	E	R	F	I	X	C	O	D	E	A	D
Q	P	I	U	Y	M	R	J	Z	A	E	L	I	G	M
W	F	O	C	U	S	E	D	K	R	N	S	U	D	X
Z	C	Y	M	F	L	F	W	Q	I	I	Q	W	G	W

Essential Oils page #218

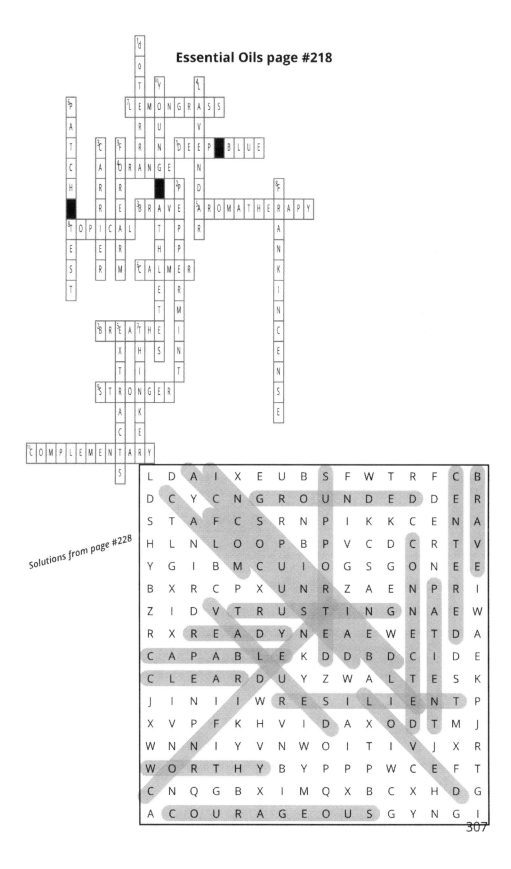

Solutions from page #228

Solutions for page #242

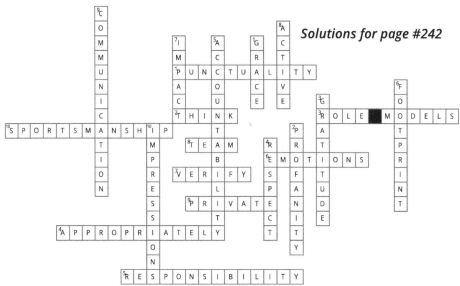

Solutions for page #256 **MIRROR DRAWINGS**

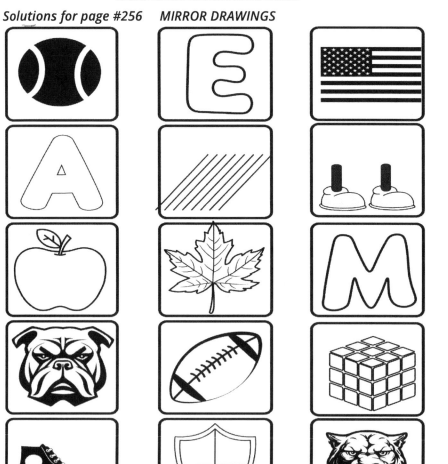

Solutions for page #274

Section # 5
BRAIN DUMPS

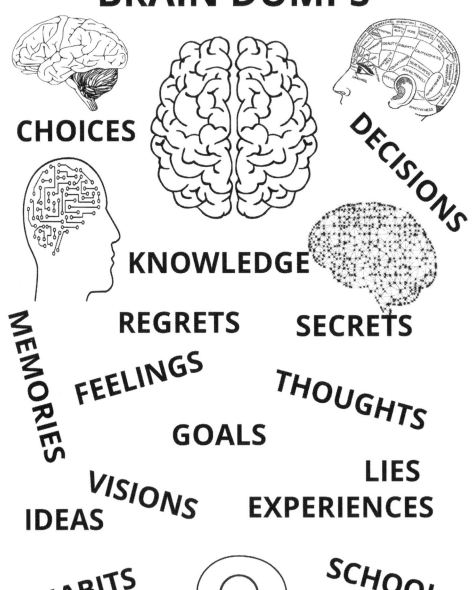

date

to do list

brain dump time...

random thoughts

think and make decision about

date

to do list

brain dump time...

random thoughts

think and make decision about

date

brain dump time...

to do list

random thoughts

think and make decision about

date

brain dump time...

to do list

random thoughts

think and make decision about

Section # 6
MY COMPETITIONS

My Competitions

Date	DESCRIPTION	MY PERFOMANCE	THOUGHTS

Date	DESCRIPTION	MY PERFOMANCE	THOUGHTS

Date	DESCRIPTION	MY PERFOMANCE	THOUGHTS

Date	DESCRIPTION	MY PERFOMANCE	THOUGHTS

Date	DESCRIPTION	MY PERFOMANCE	THOUGHTS

Date	DESCRIPTION	MY PERFOMANCE	THOUGHTS

Date	DESCRIPTION	MY PERFOMANCE	THOUGHTS

My Competitions

Date	DESCRIPTION	MY PERFOMANCE	THOUGHTS

Date	DESCRIPTION	MY PERFOMANCE	THOUGHTS

Date	DESCRIPTION	MY PERFOMANCE	THOUGHTS

Date	DESCRIPTION	MY PERFOMANCE	THOUGHTS

Date	DESCRIPTION	MY PERFOMANCE	THOUGHTS

Date	DESCRIPTION	MY PERFOMANCE	THOUGHTS

Date	DESCRIPTION	MY PERFOMANCE	THOUGHTS

My Competitions

Date	DESCRIPTION	MY PERFOMANCE	THOUGHTS

Date	DESCRIPTION	MY PERFOMANCE	THOUGHTS

Date	DESCRIPTION	MY PERFOMANCE	THOUGHTS

Date	DESCRIPTION	MY PERFOMANCE	THOUGHTS

Date	DESCRIPTION	MY PERFOMANCE	THOUGHTS

Date	DESCRIPTION	MY PERFOMANCE	THOUGHTS

Date	DESCRIPTION	MY PERFOMANCE	THOUGHTS

Section # 7
RESOURCES

CONTACT US

Hey Superstars –
Parents, Coaches, & Teachers...

Trusted – Needed – Life-Changing!!!

Meet our friends at ParenT(w)een Connection...

Raising a champion isn't just about training hard and competing harder. It's about building strong minds, open hearts, and rock-solid relationships — especially between young athletes and their biggest cheerleaders: their parents!

ParenTweenConnection.com

That's why we're proud partner with, endorse and celebrate **ParenT(w)een Connection** — the go-to hub for parents navigating the rollercoaster tween and teen years. Whether you're a parent, coach, or athlete, this is the resource you didn't know you were missing.

ParenT(w)een Connection bridges the communication gap between parents and their pre-teens/teens — because **being understood matters**. From empowering tools to expert-backed strategies and real-life conversations that actually help, *this is the community where families win together.*

👬 We LOVE ParenT(w)een Connection because:

✓ They believe parenting isn't meant to be done alone

✓ They make hard talks easier and more meaningful

✓ They help turn conflict into connection

✓ They understand how sports, growth, and emotions all collide

✓ They're champions of both kids and parents!

So if you've ever thought, **"I just want to understand my athlete better..."** — or **"I want to help my parents see what I'm going through..."** — then this is for YOU!

Check out Parent Tween Connection today. Tell Clarissa that you heard about the **ParenT(w)een Connection** from **Superstar In Training** as ask her about the specials we've arrange for you!

BECAUSE STRONG FAMILIES BUILD STRONG ATHLETES — FROM THE INSIDE OUT.

PERFORMANCE BREAKTHROUGHS BEGIN ON THE INSIDE!

Hey Superstars - Parents, Coaches, & Teachers...

We believe every athlete deserves to compete with a clear mind, full heart, and fully functioning body. That's why we're so excited to introduce the program that's changing the game from the inside out
— The F.I.X.ed Athlete™ Program —
a revolutionary nervous system reset and energy-clearing experience designed specifically for athletes who want to win without what's weighing them down.

BarbV.Fun

Developed by a world-class athlete, educator, and mindset mentor (yes — that's ME!), this breakthrough method gives young athletes the tools to:

- ☑ RELEASE NEGATIVE EMOTIONS AND MENTAL CLUTTER
- ☑ LET GO OF STRESS, SHAME, FEAR, AND SELF-DOUBT
- ☑ CALM THE NERVOUS SYSTEM BEFORE BIG MOMENTS
- ☑ BUILD INNER STRENGTH, CLARITY, AND CONFIDENCE
- ☑ BOUNCE BACK FASTER FROM SETBACKS AND MISTAKES
- ☑ EXPERIENCE THE HANDS-ON COGNITIVE ACTIVITIES IN A CLINIC

Whether it's pressure before the big game, frustration after a tough practice, or emotional overload from school and life
— The F.I.X.ed Athlete™ - teaches you how to pause, reset, and power up.

This isn't just mindset training - it's mind-body mastery. From pre-competition focus to post-game recovery, our program helps athletes clear out the junk, so they can show up as their strongest, sharpest, and most resilient selves.

Train your brain. Clean your energy.
Elevate your performance. Own your greatness.
Get F.I.X.ed - and become UNSTOPPABLE!

For those ready to take your performances to the NEXT LEVEL, reach out and take advantage of our 20-minute offer to try

Bring Barb V to your team for a ½ Day or Full-Day F.I.X.ed Athlete Clinic

The F.I.X. Code for FREE!

A ½ Day or Full-Day F.I.X.ed Athlete Program Will change the Trajectory of Your Athletic Journey - Guaranteed!

Hey Superstars – Parents, Coaches, & Teachers...

Powerful – Pure – Proven!!!

When it comes to helping young athletes play, sleep, recover, and focus at their best — what goes on and in their bodies matters. That's why we're proud to endorse doTERRA Essential Oils, the gold standard in natural wellness and performance support.

my.doterra.com/buildabox

Whether it's a deep breath before competition, quicker recovery after a hard practice, better sleep the night before a game, or balancing emotions after a tough day — doTERRA delivers real, plant-powered results.

From locker rooms to bedtime routines, doTERRA is the trusted tool in our athlete wellness toolbox — and it should be in yours too!

Here's why doTERRA makes the cut for our Young Athlete Tribe:

✓ **Certified Pure Tested Grade®**
   – No toxins, no fillers, just nature's best
✓ **Athlete Essentials**
   – Focus blends, muscle soothers, energy boosters, and calming oils
✓ **Sleep Support** – Oils that help the body and mind rest & restore
✓ **Emotional Balance**
   – Manage mood, stress, and performance anxiety naturally
✓ **Customizable wellness kits**
   – Build your own box to match your sport and goals!

I Look forward to Seeing You Soon

For those serious about incorporating these powerful natural tools into your athletic program, I offer an exclusive **Essential Oils for Athletes Masterclass** twice a month on zoom, designed specifically for coaches and parents.

Grab your copy of my new book: Essential Oils for ATHLETES!

Let me help you "BUILDaBOX" of the Top 25 Essential Oils for Athletes!

Made in the USA
Columbia, SC
15 June 2025

fc92ff2b-65c5-42fc-86d0-ea2ba6c02b3dR02